RETHINKING
MULTICULTURAL
EDUCATION

RETHINKING MULTICULTURAL EDUCATION

Case Studies in Cultural Transition

Edited by Carol Korn and Alberto Bursztyn

Foreword by Joe Kincheloe
Nina Neimark, Imprint Adviser

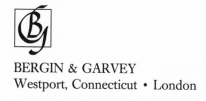

BERGIN & GARVEY
Westport, Connecticut • London

Library of Congress Cataloging-in-Publication Data

Rethinking multicultural education : case studies in cultural transition / edited by Carol Korn and Alberto Bursztyn ; foreword by Joe Kincheloe.
 p. cm.
 Includes bibliographical references and index.
 ISBN 0–89789–544–4 (alk. paper)—ISBN 0–89789–871–0 (pbk. : alk. paper)
 1. Multicultural education—United States. 2. Minorities—Education—United States.
I. Korn, Carol, 1953– II. Bursztyn, Alberto, 1952–
LC1099.3.R49 2002
370.117'0973—dc21   2001043011

British Library Cataloguing in Publication Data is available.

Library of Congress Catalog Card Number: 2001043011
ISBN: 0–89789–544–4
  0–89789–871–0

First published in 2002

Bergin & Garvey, 88 Post Road West, Westport, CT 06881
An imprint of Greenwood Publishing Group, Inc.
www.greenwood.com

Printed in the United States of America

The paper used in this book complies with the Permanent Paper Standard issued by the National Information Standards Organization (Z39.48–1984).

10 9 8 7 6 5 4 3 2 1

In memory of our mothers, Celia Milstein Korn and Jenny Reznik Bursztyn, and for our fathers, Harry Korn and Valentin Bursztyn, whose transitions across geographic, cultural, and class divides shaped our earliest experiences and motivated a life-long interest in how people negotiate passages in their lives. We also dedicate this book to our children, Dan and Josh, whose own transitions, both physical and metaphoric, remind us of the universality of human experience.

Contents

Foreword: Exploring a Transformative Multiculturalism— Justice in a Zeitgeist of Despair

Joe Kincheloe

Rethinking Multicultural Education: Case Studies in Cultural Transition can best be understood as a work that takes shape in a particular social, cultural, political, and educational context. Over the last thirty years we have witnessed a well-planned, persistent, and successful effort to re-educate Americans around issues of race, class, gender, sexuality, and their relation to social justice (Apple, 1996; McLaren, 2000). Education as an institution has been dramatically affected by this reactionary project. Reacting to perceived social, political, cultural, and educational changes of the 1960s, protectors of dominant power relations sensed an opportunity to advocate a return to "traditional values," neoclassical economic policy, long-standing racial and gender relations, and a fragmented and fact-based accountability-friendly school curriculum.

In this context the guardians of tradition promoted a new cultural narrative that played well to white male audiences frustrated with the changes they saw taking place in the world. Via the power of the new narrative, the guardians of tradition engaged these white men and their allies in what might be labeled the recovery of white supremacy and patriarchy perceived to have been lost in the civil rights movement and the women's movement. The reeducation process was directly connected to this notion of recovery of what had been lost. Throughout *Rethinking Multicultural Education*, especially in the particular case studies of student and teacher interactions in the everyday life of the classroom, we see reflections of this larger sociocultural dynamic.

In the multicultural domain of race Aaron Gresson (1995, 2001) argues that this new white story of the need for recovery inverts a traditional black narrative. Because of the dominant culture's portrayal of the economic success of Blacks and other minority groups—a portrait much less accurate than represented—many Whites believe that non-Whites in the last three decades of the twentieth and the first decade of the twenty-first century have greater power and opportunity than Whites. This preposterous position posits that this new African American, Latino, and Native American *privilege* has been gained at the expense of more deserving white Americans—especially upper-middle-class white males. The story is promoted in a variety of spheres, including education, and in a number of ways, but always with the same effect: the production of *white anger* directed at non-Whites and women in particular. Such anger works, of course, to divide poor and working-class people of all races and genders, to support the interests of privileged power wielders, and to shape the nature of what occurs in schools.

Such a dominant sociopolitical and pedagogical story induces many Whites to see themselves as a people under threat. Sociologists have long maintained that individuals and groups who perceive themselves under threat often react with an attempt to reassess their power and regain their former social position—the phenomenon of status anxiety. This reassertion, of course, takes many forms and has many degrees. Manifestations may include modest efforts to reassert one's self-worth by way of private expression of racial disdain—"The parents in the community don't care enough about their children to be concerned with their education,"—or racial superiority—"So many of the teachers who work in our school don't make a good impression with their loud 'street talk' and everything."

Other examples of this reeducation of America may operate more at the level of group recovery, with the passage of "English only" legislation in heavily Latino areas such as Florida and Arizona, anti-bilingual education and anti-affirmative action measures in California, or battles over multicultural curricula as evidenced throughout the nation (Frankenberg, 1993; Kincheloe, Steinberg, Rodriguez & Chennault, 1998; Rodriguez & Villaverde, 2000). More extreme expressions involve the recent dramatic growth of white supremacist organizations and the terrorist activity associated with some of them—for example, the April 1995 bombing of the Oklahoma City federal building and the shootings at the Jewish day care center in Los Angeles in 1999. Most Americans, of course, are dismayed by this level of angry white reassertion, yet the perception of Whites as *"the real victims"* of U.S. racism becomes more and more deeply embedded into the white collective consciousness.

Within the conceptual context of racial recovery and the narrative of white victimization we can make much more sense of the everyday life of the contemporary classroom and formulate concrete ways of addressing the injustices that take place there daily. In this framework a concurrent and connected educational story began to take shape in the late

1970s and 1980s. In this era the guardians of tradition captured the public's educational imagination with its assertion that multiculturalism and white victimization were the causes of a national decline in general and a decline in education in particular. Education, the new narrative maintained, should have nothing to do with issues of social equality and should return to a "true American" view of schooling as a path to individual fortune. The guardian's educational narrative told a story of a multicultural dissolution of standards that precipitated a breakdown of authority, discipline, and quality in American schools. The widespread acceptance of this account indicates the success of the reeducation project.

TEACHING A TRANSFORMATIVE MULTICULTURALISM IN AN AGE OF RECOVERY

Those of us who promote a transformative multiculturalism have our work cut out for us in a "reeducated" and a racially and patriarchically "recovered" era. The sense of despair one senses in Deborah Nelson's and Margaret Rogers' words in Chapter 1 are sobering:

Sadly, Corey's teachers and I never reconciled our differences. Life at the school progressed as it always had. I found myself becoming skeptical that things would ever change, that others would ever question why things were the way they were. Would we ever have an opportunity as a school to experience ourselves as the empowered culture and social structure that Banks described? Time has put some distance between this incident and the present, but it continues to live with me, taunting me, challenging me. Where did I, we, go wrong? How could we have made it right?

One can easily understand the way such disappointment can mutate into a form of alienation and depression. In such circumstances many will be unable to continue the work of a transformative multiculturalism because of the psychic toll of daily frustration.

The same disappointment emerges in Alberto Bursztyn's analysis of special education in Chapter 8. After all the academic work of the last three decades documenting the way social context helps shape student performance in school, Bursztyn notes the ease with which educators frame disability as a pathology residing solely within the student. Social and cultural context be damned, the student has a "disorder" that shapes his or her ability as a scholar. A reductionistic assumption of an abstract individual floating freely outside of any formative context tacitly constructs the way we view the world of schooling and the students who inhabit it.

Time and again in the various chapters of this work the authors contend that in the *zeitgeist* of contemporary education efforts to address cultural intolerance, racism, or issues of diversity seem oddly out of place, even antiquated. Again Nelson and Rogers make the point:

When I asked specifically about topics dealing with cultural intolerance or issues of diversity and related some of the incidents that had occurred at my school, the facilitator empathized and explained that they had never had a formal request to address these concerns. A call to the Office of Staff Development provided little more information. The office's director explained, "We used to do that kind of stuff in the 1970s, but we haven't gotten any requests for it lately."

What use would we have for such programs in an era where the victims of race are white, many might ask. In an "era of personal responsibility" antiracist education would only hurt those it set out to help; it could give them an excuse for not trying. Such arguments are made every day. As Cheryl Holcomb-McCoy points out in Chapter 3, a racial and class code of silence has emerged in contemporary schools. If transformative multicultural educators are to make a difference, we must name this code and break it.

Only when such a code is broken can transformative multicultural educators address the racial harm a teacher or administrator might cause a child or a group of children. Helen Johnson's case study of Camille in Chapter 5 documents the ways racial recovery plays out in the actions of specific teachers and their students. While Camille had encountered a pluralistic form of multiculturalism in her teacher education with its books on different ethnic and racial experiences and ethnic "food days," her personal notions of cultural superiority shaped another more powerful curriculum. Middle- and upper-middle-class whiteness was Camille's norm, as she derided non-white experience and turned her classroom into a culturally hostile place. Her inability to understand her own actions is better understood in light of the cultural backdrop of racial recovery. Few experiences in Camille's everyday cultural transactions at the beginning of the twenty-first century would highlight the specific racial assumptions she was making about herself and the world around her.

In such a cultural context the attempt to deal with a Camille and countless others like her is rendered exceedingly difficult. Comfortable in their racial assumptions and often reinforced by interactions with peer group, media, and political leaders, the Camilles of the world are not likely to respond positively to the interventions of transformative multicultural educators. As I was recently attempting to address the assumptions of a teacher education student angry at the prospect of having to teach the children of "white trash welfare loafers," I was frustrated by the assurance of her position. As I explained that many individuals would take offense at her use of the term "white trash" and that there was a set of disturbing assumptions about poor students embedded in the characterization, she repeatedly told me, "But that's what they are. I can't help it." She was secure in her own class superiority and could draw upon a range of cultural supports to validate her values. How do marginalized students fare, I would ask in the spirit of Nelson and Rogers in Chapter 1, in the classrooms of teachers who possess such a distorted understanding of such students' experiences?

TRANSFORMATIVE MULTICULTURALISM, RECOVERY, REEDUCATION, AND THE STANDARDS MOVEMENT: MAKING CONNECTIONS

Both Carol Korn, in her Introduction, and Alberto Bursztyn, in Chapter 8 and his conclusion, contend that multicultural education is easily pushed aside in an era of standards movements and the fragmented, test-driven curricula that accompany them. As Bursztyn writes as he introduces Chapter 8:

In spite of demographic changes in school populations and teacher ranks, multicultural initiatives are in fact losing the spotlight to highly politicized arguments about school choice and centralized regulation of curriculum through implementation of state-mandated learning standards. Multicultural education, disparaged in conservative circles, stands in danger of becoming one of the many issues advocated in the noisy arena of school politics, fighting for attention and resources claimed by new teaching and testing programs, instructional technologies, and other perennial interests, such as creationism and school prayer.

As Korn and Bursztyn well understand, standards-driven school reform is often positioned directly in opposition to multicultural concerns. Indeed, I have argued that the contemporary standards movement cannot be understood outside the politics of recovery and the reeducation project referenced here. The progressive efforts of the last forty years to racially integrate and to address the needs of African American, Latino, Asian American, and economically poor students of all ethnicities and backgrounds has been framed as an attempt to destroy quality and standards in American schools. Rhetorical analysis of the speeches and policy documents of many political and educational leaders from the 1970s onward reveal patterns of calls for a return to the "quality education" of "the past"—the past used to signify a time before all of these egalitarian movements damaged our standards. Multicultural education has come to represent the contemporary expression of progressive attempts to undermine school quality.

Guardians of European, patriarchal privilege over the last few decades have successfully connected their reeducation project and its rhetoric of recovery to the visceral, affective, everyday concerns of many Americans. In many educational research projects in which I've been involved over the last couple of decades, I have heard numerous white parents of public school students complain about "all the effort schools are giving to help the black students or the Native American students. They take all the school's time and money." Upon examination of the schools referenced by these parents, I found time and again that an overwhelming majority of time and resources were relegated to the most economically privileged white students.

Such parents had internalized the guardians' reeducation program's concern with the threats to whiteness—signified as "us." Just like Helen Johnson's Camille, these parents saw diversity as a problem, an impediment not as a resource and a source of strength. What the parents I observed perceived had little relation to the "lived world." Indeed, from the early 1980s to the early twenty-first century, the gap between white and nonwhite economic status widened and opportunities for non-white professional mobility closed. The picture of the world framed by the conservative reeducators provided a very different understanding of the world (Kincheloe, 1999).

The case studies of Korn, Bursztyn, and their contributors make more sense when we understand them in the context of reeducation and recovery. It is in this context that we view the great anger directed at progressives and multiculturalists who are perceived to be wasting time and money trying to teach those groups that many reeducators designate as unteachable (see Herrnstein & Murray, 1994; Kincheloe, Steinberg, and Gresson, 1996). If African Americans, Latinos, and the poor simply cannot learn, reeducators and advocates of recovery maintain, then there is no reason to study issues such as social context, youth culture, school culture, identity formation, privilege and marginalization, or democratic schooling, to devise developmental education programs, or to concern ourselves with multicultural education.

In the eyes of the reeducators these activities are misdirected. Alberto Bursztyn's observation that students who are poor or non-white are disproportionately placed in special education programs and once placed rarely ever return to regular education or graduate from high school should not concern us. We must get on with our pursuit of high-quality education, the reeducators demand. Using classic reductionistic logic, they tell us to simply teach the great facts of Western culture, emphasize the achievements of the scientific method, and devise multiple-choice tests to *confirm* the "superiority" of the culturally and economically privileged. Decontextualized school standards that are easy to statistically manipulate for good public relations deftly fit the political needs of the reeducators.

The reeducation has successfully rewritten history and re-created public memory in a manner that justifies educational, social, and political policies that perpetuate and extend inequality in American society. Such policies are grounded on an effort to protect an uninhibited free market economics that is designed to raise the salaries of corporate leaders while dismissing the needs of the non-white and the poor in the name of economic efficiency. Many Americans have accepted the reeducators' contention that any form of government aid to the poor is harmful to the social and economic health of the larger society and that any aid to students from marginalized backgrounds having trouble in school is harmful to the quality of the educational system in general. The reeducation has involved the acceptance of the superiority of the privatized market economy, the absurdity of egalitarian programs, and the un-Americanness of multiculturally sensitive school curricula.

In this reductionistic, decontextualized manner the reeducators and advocates of recovery have renewed traditional social and educational efforts to adjust the poor and non-white to an unjust society. Education in this reactionary conception has little to do with civic responsibility and social justice, and those who challenge unequal opportunity are labeled whiners and complainers in the context constructed by the rhetoric of recovery. As a group that speaks of its fear that pluralism and a diversity of curricular sources are divisive, are tearing apart the American social fabric, it is ironic that the reeducators employ the binary "we" and "they" so often. "We," they argue, are the Americans who want standards in our schools; "they" are the multiculturalists who want to teach anti-American material and perpetuate an "anything goes" curriculum. "They" want to pamper the shiftless and lazy members of society who once may have been victims of discrimination but now in this post-racist, post-sexist era want something for nothing (Allison, 1995; Weil, 1998).

The role of the multiculturally sensitive teacher as scholar, researcher, contextual analyst, and educational expert does not resonate with the plans of reeducation. Many leaders of the standards movement are not comfortable with teachers with too much academic freedom, because they want to control the politics and ideology of what is taught. Such leaders often play important roles in the reeducation movement, as they promote a view of teacher as technician who passes along information, belief structures, and ways of approaching diversity provided by guardians of tradition and their standards test makers. Under the banner of teaching as the "transmission of the best of our cultural heritage"—meaning excluding as dangerous social, cultural, political, economic, and religious understandings from other cultures—reeducators de-skill and deprofessionalize teachers.

It is hard for me to imagine the fact—although I do acknowledge its existence—that in the twenty-first century in New York City and elsewhere educators are afraid to allow diverse cultural perspectives into classrooms and are uncomfortable with studying the ways race, class, and gender shape different students' relationships with the school. What an interesting commentary on the state of the American psyche. Advocates of a transformative multiculturalism cannot allow these hurtful and degrading ways of seeing to prevail in twenty-first century education. We must confront them, first, in the name of fairness and egalitarian democracy because they allow racist and class biased policies to shape our classrooms and, second, in the name of good scholarship because they undermine our effort to understand the complex ways schools work.

STUDYING THE COLLISION OF CONTEXTS

The notion of multicultural educators as scholars is an important theme that emerges in several chapters in the book. In multicultural teaching, the study of contexts that shape students, teachers, educational goals, and particular schools becomes an important teacher activity. Contextual analysis is necessary in making an observation in that a fuller meaning of what we see is impossible without it. The literal meaning of context involves "that which is braided together." Awareness of this braiding induces teacher-scholars to examine the ecology (as Helen Johnson reiterates in Chapter 5) of educational matters, as they realize that knowledge derives meaning only in the context created by other information. For instance, only in recent years has the medical profession begun to examine the context of disease; some physicians have come to argue that we should study the milieu of an illness and not simply the symptoms.

In the same manner many transformative multiculturalists have begun to acknowledge that the contextualization of what we understand is as important as the content. In response to standards promoters who argue for the exclusive importance of content and the need to "master" the basics as an initial step to learning, I would maintain in the name of a rigorous education that without contextualization and the establishment of a fabric of relevance, content learning is somewhat meaningless (Ferguson, 1980; Kincheloe, Steinberg, & Hinchey, 1999). This is exactly why standards in their technical format and top-down imposition do little to improve the quality of teaching, learning, and thinking. In the standards-driven context meaning making becomes somewhat irrelevant.

An example of the way meaning is dependent on context might involve a listener who lacks adequate context to understand the "order" of a musical form. In many cases such a listener will judge an avant-garde composition as meaningless. Europeans, upon hearing African music in their first intercultural encounters, for example, attempted to assess it in the terms of another musical form. Unable to appreciate the context that gave meaning to the African music, the Europeans did not hear the intentions of the composers and performers with their subtle rhythms and haunting melodies. They heard "primitive" noise (Bohm & Peat, 1987).

What Alberto Bursztyn refers to in Chapter 8 as "positivistic and rationalistic thinking" fails to convey a valuable perspective on teaching and learning as it fails in its reductionism to account for context. In modern empirical research, so-called scientific controls contribute to a more perfect isolation of the context being investigated. As in the special education context described by Bursztyn, attention to circumstances surrounding the object of inquiry must be temporarily suspended. This suspension of attention is based on the assumption that these extraneous circumstances will remain static enough to allow the study to be validated. In the rationalistic thinking of the special educators who researched (evaluated) Bursztyn's Javier, the boy was suspended in his isolated psychological state. Evaluators could only see him in terms of their construction of a "neuro-psychological condition" because other contextual aspects of Javier's life were irrelevant in their approach to producing knowledge about students.

Thus, the dismissal of contextual understanding in Javier's case was not some arcane epistemological issue that was germane only in the rarefied air of the seminar room. On the contrary, it was a lived dynamic that resulted, as Bursztyn tells us, in the student being given an abnormal label involving his inability to learn. Javier's cultural background and his emotional needs were irrelevant in the eyes of the professional evaluators. In settings like these, student and teacher behavior cannot be understood without careful attention to the setting and the individuals' relationships to the traditions, norms, roles, and values that are inseparable from the lived worlds of the cultures that intersect within them.

The inability of many traditional educational analysts to say very much that is meaningful about school life is due in part to their dismissal of context—the often invisible but foundational aspect of organizational life (Eisner, 1984; Wilson, 1977; Denzin & Lincoln, 2000; Hinchey, 1998). John Dewey (1916) long ago argued that many thinkers regard knowledge as self-contained, as complete in itself. Knowledge, Dewey contended, could never be viewed outside the context of its relationship to other information. We only have to call to mind, he wrote, what passes in our schools as acquisition of knowledge to understand how it is decontextualized and lacks any meaningful connection to the experience of students. Anticipating Bursztyn's and my concern with context, Dewey concluded that an individual is a sophisticated thinker to the degree that he or she sees an event not as something isolated but in its connection with the larger experiences of human beings.

Understanding these contextual/epistemological dynamics, the editors and contributors to this book work to examine the larger sociocultural and the specific classroom contexts in which multicultural concerns operate. In this sophisticated manner they model the professional behaviors and cognitive abilities that scholar-teachers bring to the multicultural complexities that construct the contemporary act of teaching. For example, Helen Johnson in Chapter 5 proposes a contextual research model for teachers. As a part of their everyday practice teachers learn about the contexts that shape their students' lives, as they visit students' families in an attempt to better understand the knowledge and skills students encounter outside of school. In the process of such inquiry, teachers meet with other teachers and researchers to reflect on what they are learning and to analyze its implications for teaching. In this manner scholar-teachers gain contextual insights that help them overcome the blinders of conventional school practices that punish marginalized students and reward the privileged.

TRANSFORMATIVE MULTICULTURALISM EXAMINES THE CONSTRUCTION OF CONSCIOUSNESS

Liberal and pluralist forms of multiculturalism as well as, of course, monoculturalism do not explore the ways that human consciousness is constructed around issues of race, class, gender, and sexuality. The ability of dominant power blocs to shape the ways individuals assume their racial, class, and gender identities and the ways they make sense of individuals with identities different than their own is a generally unexplored domain in American education. For example, a male school administrator's patriarchal actions toward women teachers draws upon a patriarchal power bloc with its long tradition of male social domination. Upper-middle-class students' control of the social life of the school (e.g., cheerleading, dictation of style, student government, proms, and homecoming activities, etc.) rests on a tradition of class domination and its accompanying class elite power bloc. The important point in both examples is that power is validated by its connection to larger social structures. Power's connection to everyday life depends on its relationship to its ability to shape individual consciousness.

In this context power's ability to shape consciousness helps to produce particular systems of instruction, methods of evaluation, definitions of teacher and student success, and classification systems that sort students into advanced, college-bound, general, vocational, or special educational tracks. Such divisions provide the knowledge, social practices, cultural capital, and skills required by the class-driven hierarchy of labor in the society's workplaces. The way that power interacts with consciousness and personal behavior in this case involves school leaders' inducement of students to believe that such class-based divisions of students and workers are natural and necessary. Transformative multicultural educators understand that students from outside the mainstream, the non-white and the poor, are convinced that they do not possess the ability to accomplish the academic skills necessary for mobility.

Here is where power's construction of individual consciousness precipitates such a tragedy for our students who face race, class, and gender obstacles. They are captured in the entanglements of power-produced myths of their cultural and academic inferiority. Many African American students, for example, who are often very successful in college, report that by the time they were middle school/junior high students the culture of the school had convinced them that higher education was not an option for them. Thus, students and their teachers have their consciousness constructed in a manner in which they come to accept the inferiority of African American, Latino, and poor people's intellectual ability.

The editors and contributors here—especially Peter Taubman in Chapter 6—are aware of the importance of consciousness construction in a transformative multiculturalism. As Deborah Nelson and Margaret Rogers ask in Chapter 1: "Don't educators have a professional responsibility to examine their own assumptions, values, and beliefs about racial identity, gender, religion, and sexual orientation?" I would agree with Peter Taubman's assertion that the contradictions of the contemporary American "racial matrix" have literally "driven us all crazy." The personal narratives and individual case studies used by all the contributors to this book direct the reader's attention toward this important domain of the race, class, gender, religious, and sexual dimensions of consciousness construction.

Carol Korn clearly recognizes this dynamic in her Introduction as she references the ways autobiographical analysis moves us to revisit our subjective understandings. Returning to this issue in Chapter 4, she writes of the necessity of exploring the seams of our life experiences and the ways we stitch them together—a metaphor for analyzing the ways our interactions with the world have shaped our identities, subjectivities, and consciousness. Such a process pushes us to the next frontier of multiculturalism, a presently occluded domain where racial, class, gender, religious, and sexual dynamics exert their most profound influences.

TRANSFORMATIVE MULTICULTURALISM AND THE OPPOSITIONAL IDENTITY OF THE MARGINALIZED

Another important conceptual theme that emerges in this work involves the ways that marginalized students develop an oppositional identity that resists the imposition of a dominant-cultural-inscribed curriculum and educational process in general. The question arises in Chapter 2 as Vernita Zubia and Beth Doll explore the ways cultural groups employ their ethnic identities to resist dominant culture. In Chapter 3 as Cheryl Holcomb-McCoy provides profound insight into her own identity formation as a middle-class black woman and black educator during her first year as a kindergarten teacher, we gain new awarenesses of the way oppositional identities are formed and the ways they shape one's relationship to the institution of schooling. A question that haunts these chapters involves the ways transformative multiculturalists might understand and appreciate these oppositional identities and draw upon them for emancipatory and scholarly outcomes.

The oppositional identity of a marginalized student, while taking on many different forms within and among different types of marginalization, is often characterized by a sense of mistrust or suspicion. Many marginalized young people spend their entire lives in communities where they must compete for scarce resources. In such situations trust cannot be taken for granted but must be studied and carefully, if not strategically, calculated. Given this adoption of mistrust as a survival skill within a student's community, it is not likely that such wariness will be reduced outside the home community. When the new context (school, for example) is one dominated by individuals from mainstream upper-middle-class Anglo culture, suspicion will only increase.

Students from racially or class marginalized backgrounds often enter our classrooms with not only this oppositional mistrust but with a cultivated sense of self-reliance—or at least a struggle for self-reliance. Because there are so few resources in the families and communities of such marginalized students, they learn early in their lives to depend on their own resources to procure the things they need. This characteristic points to a view of poor people and racially marginalized people that is significantly different from the ones painted by the guardians of tradition who advocate the end to public efforts to help such individuals overcome the obstacles they face. Many students, for example, who grow up in families that have had several generations of welfare recipients are not passive, unmotivated young people.

Although they often may be unmotivated by present academic learning possibilities, this does not mean that such students are not moved by the effort to improve their existential, material, and scholarly well-being—even if it takes superhuman and danger-filled efforts. Their absence of academic motivation does not have as much to do with laziness as with school's ability to convince them of its intrinsic worth, its relation to their lives, and its capacity to lift them out of their uncomfortable life circumstances. Transformative multiculturalists become students of these students and the cultures they bring to the classroom. As teachers come to understand the reasons for the oppositional identities, they can begin to depersonalize the intimidating defiance they sometimes encounter in the classroom and work to connect the passions and desires of their marginalized students with alternative knowledge and rationalities. This is one area where a transformative multiculturalism may bring about dramatic changes in the role that education plays in students' lives.

TRANSFORMATIVE MULTICULTURALISM AND THE ENCOUNTER WITH WHITENESS

Where we stand in the social web of reality, as illustrated previously, exerts a dramatic impact on how we understand the world, ourselves, and the role of education in both the culture at large and in our personal lives. With this understanding, teachers and students can begin to engage in both individually, socially, and pedagogically transformative activity. Indeed, this understanding is a foundational pillar of a transformative multiculturalism. Appreciating the socially constructed nature of individuals' ways of seeing, transformative multiculturalists devote much attention to the ways individuals construct knowledge and make meaning. In conservative, liberal, and pluralist forms of multiculturalism, studies of whiteness as an ethnicity have not been addressed. Transformative multiculturalists maintain that a study of the ways various forces construct white identity and subjectivity are shaped in contemporary American life should be a central feature of multicultural education.

Hollyce Giles in Chapter 7 picks up on these themes, arguing that white people in the U.S. are socialized to protect the privileges and entitlements of whiteness. In this context, she writes, white young people learn ways of seeing the world and themselves and modes of processing information that maintain these privileges. An important aspect of these meaning-making processes, Giles continues, involves the denial of the importance of race as a force in contemporary lives and an erasure of the presence of racism. This is accomplished, she maintains, by the use of the comfortable deficit model that positions non-white failure as a manifestation of individual incompetence.

Giles' points are central to the development of a transformative multiculturalism and what I have elsewhere described as a pedagogy of whiteness (Kincheloe, Steinberg, Rodriguez, and Chennault, 1998). In such a whiteness education, individuals begin to grasp the multiple ways that an ideology of white supremacy infiltrates the American consciousness, the ways the invisible power of whiteness shapes the norms by which everyone is measured. Thus, many of the contributors to *Rethinking Multicultural Education* "denormalize" whiteness, calling into question white ways of being as universal standards. A pedagogy of whiteness calls for a cultural reassessment and an educational commitment to rethinking the basis of a multicultural society.

Cheryl Holcomb-McCoy in Chapter 3 operates in this mode as she describes the way she viewed schooling as a first-year teacher. The power of whiteness insidiously shaped her understanding of school as "the social and educational equalizer" for all those who enter it. Holcomb-McCoy's encounters with racism became her own personal pedagogy of whiteness as she began to see the ways schools operate in less than egalitarian and racially neutral modes. Her understanding of these dynamics provided her with profound insights into white power and the ideology of white supremacy and the process by which they shape the lives of students from all racial and ethnic backgrounds.

Understanding Giles' and Holcomb-McCoy's socio-educational insights, white individuals work to get over their discomfort about discussing both the power of whiteness in general and how they appear to non-Whites in particular. Such white individuals learn to listen to the perceptions of African Americans, Latinos, and indigenous peoples, who often see them as people not to be trusted. In this context they begin to rethink their lives and worldviews in relation to such new understandings. Thus, white students and teachers begin to take seriously the transformative multiculturalist imperative to analyze their social, political, and educational positions vis-à-vis their whiteness. In the process white people start to appreciate that what they "objectively" see may not be as neutral as they originally thought. In this context a deeper level of self-knowledge and multicultural awareness is obtained—insights that lead to a lifetime of antiracist activity.

TRANSFORMATIVE MULTICULTURALISM AND THE POWER OF DIFFERENCE

A transformative multiculturalism values the power of difference. While the position rejects leftist, essentialist multiculturalism's view of racial, ethnic, or class groups as possessing a specific set of romanticized, fixed, essential characteristics, the transformative position works to make difference visible. In Chapter 4 Carol Korn provides a compelling description of her pedagogy at Brooklyn College. In her teacher education classes Korn induces her students to leave their familiar places, ways of making meaning, and ways of being in an exploration of new places that are characterized by difference. She writes that the new locales of difference offer risks and challenges that set up the possibility for transformative learning, indeed, such places are central to a transformative multiculturalism.

Korn's insight into the power of difference is illustrated by her analysis of the cultural "in-between space" that becomes a locale of "negotiated meanings." As students cross invisible borders, she contends, meanings they bring with them intersect with meanings from other cultural venues.

In this interaction the unexamined assumptions that permeate these meanings are exposed in the light of difference. The heart and soul of a transformative multiculturalism is directly related to this dynamic. This heart and soul involves the power of difference to expand each student's interpretive horizon, social understanding, and intellectual ability. As such a powerful force, difference must not simply be tolerated but cultivated as a spark to the development of a "transformative ontology"—a new way of being human.

A transformative multicultural description of a scholarly rigorous form of democratic thinking involves an understanding of difference that nurtures a sense of empathy. Cornel West (1993) argues that empathy vis-à-vis difference involves the ability to appreciate the anxieties and frustrations of others and never to lose sight of the humanity of the marginalized no matter how wretched their condition. The point emerging here involves the ethical and cognitive benefits derived from the confrontation with diversity and the different vantage points it provides us for viewing the lived world.

Taking a cue from liberation theologians in Latin America, transformative multiculturalists often begin their analysis of an institution by listening to those who have suffered most as a result of its existence. This moral imperative changes the way schooling and educational phenomena are approached by educational researchers, teachers, and students. These "different" ways of seeing allow transformative multiculturalists to tap into the cognitive power of empathy—a productive power that allows us access to deep patterns of racism, class bias, and sexism and the way they structure oppression in everyday life.

CONCLUSION: STAYING AFLOAT IN THE ZEITGEIST OF DESPAIR

In the reeducated, recovered American society of the early twentieth-first century, educators committed to justice grapple with the problems and possibilities delineated here. As I studied the various essays in this book, I was reminded of the cultural curriculum of whiteness that all of us, especially our students, encounter hourly in the information-saturated "hyperreality" of contemporary electronic culture. In the racially recovered social landscape, whiteness carefully masks its social location, using silences, euphemisms, and avoidances. As Holcomb-McCoy describes this process in Chapter 3:

Because I thought race and class were sources of tension among our staff, I often attempted to discuss these issues with other teachers. I remember trying to initiate a conversation with a white colleague on the topic. She commented that "there is too much talk about race and racism in the schools." Her view was that "personality differences" instead of race were the source of tension. White teachers often used such coded language to speak of sensitive racial and class situations. For instance, phrases such as "the community parents," "the apartment people," and "those people who don't speak English" were often used to describe minority parents. It was perceived as inappropriate or dangerous to use the word "race" or "racism" in faculty discussions.

This is how racial recovery works in its everyday, lived world articulation; this is how dominant power works to maintain an unjust status quo. Its effectiveness in this process exacerbates my/our despair.

When one understands these dynamics, it makes sense that Whites can use concepts such as equal opportunity while assuming that these terms in no way challenge white supremacy. In this context Whites can speak publicly—read, in racially mixed groups—about granting everyone a fair chance at success. In a recovered society, such talk continues to coexist with a pervasive, visceral belief that Whites will always be better qualified than non-Whites. This tacit dynamic of whiteness works because at some corporeal/emotional level many white people have learned to accept the minority deficit model. A majority of Whites believe that African Americans, for example, are less intelligent and not as hard working as white people. In this articulation of white power the reason for white racism toward non-Whites is the behavior of non-Whites. And this behavior in the reeducation is distorted, misrepresented, reprocessed, and distributed for mass consumption on a daily basis.

I discerned the effects of this racial misrepresentation, as I studied Nelson and Rogers' description of Corey. Corey had learned the recovery curriculum all too well: he was stupid, he thought, because he was black. I saw it again as I read Hollyce Giles' descriptions of the way parents of color were viewed by teachers as "incompetent, neglectful others" who were unconcerned with the education of their children. I see it in many of my teacher education students in New York City who speak of the poor as "white trash" and devise a variety of euphemisms and code words for non-Whites and their multitude of deficits including "unteachability." It is easy for proponents of a transformative multiculturalism to lose hope in such circumstances, to fall into a pit of cynicism and despair. I am heartened by the editors and contributors to *Rethinking Multicultural Education*'s ability to confront the pain of the contemporary zeitgeist and to keep hope alive.

REFERENCES

Allison, C. (1995). *Present and past: Essays for teachers in the history of education.* New York: Peter Lang.

Apple, M. (1996). Dominance and dependency: Situating *The Bell Curve* within the conservative restoration. In J. Kincheloe, S. Steinberg, & A. Gresson (Eds.), *Measured lies: The Bell Curve examined*. New York: St. Martin's Press.

Banks, J. A. (1995). *Multicultural education: Theory and practice* (3rd ed.). Boston: Allyn & Bacon.

Bohm, D., & Peat, F. (1987). *Science, order, and creativity*. New York: Bantam Books.

Denzin, N., & Lincoln, Y. (2000). *Handbook of qualitative research* (2nd ed.). Thousand Oaks, CA: Sage.

Dewey, J. (1916). *Democracy and education*. New York: Free Press.

Eisner, E. (1984). Can educational research inform educational practice? *Phi Delta Kappan, 65* (7), 447–452.

Ferguson, M. (1980). *The Aquarian conspiracy: Personal and social transformation in our time*. Los Angeles: J. P. Tarcher.

Frankenberg, R. (1993). *The social construction of whiteness: White women, race matters*. Minneapolis: University of Minnesota Press.

Gresson, A. (2001). *America's atonement*. New York: Peter Lang.

———. (1995). *The recovery of race in America*. Minneapolis: University of Minnesota Press.

Herrnstein, R. J., & Murray, C. A. (1994). *The bell curve: Intelligence and class structure in American life*. New York: Free Press.

Hinchey, P. (1998). *Finding freedom in the classroom: A practical introduction to critical theory*. New York: Peter Lang.

Kincheloe, J. (1999). *How do we tell the workers? The socio-economic foundations of work and vocational education*. Boulder, CO: Westview.

Kincheloe, J., Steinberg, S., & Gresson A. (Eds.). (1996). *Measured lies: The bell curve examined*. New York: St. Martin's Press.

Kincheloe, J., Steinberg, S., & Hinchey, P. (1999). *The postformal reader: Cognition and education*. New York: Falmer.

Kincheloe, J., Steinberg, S., Rodriguez, N., & Chennault, R. (1998). *White reign: Deploying whiteness in America*. New York: St. Martin's Press.

McLaren, P. (2000). *Che Guevara, Paulo Freire, and the pedagogy of revolution*. Lanham, MD: Rowman and Littlefield.

Rodriguez, N., & Villaverde, L. (2000). *Dismantling whiteness*. New York: Peter Lang.

Weil, D. (1998). *Towards a critical multi-cultural literacy: Theory and practice for education for liberation*. New York: Peter Lang.

West, C. (1993). *Beyond eurocentrism and multiculturalism*. Monroe, ME: Common Courage Press.

Wilson, S. (1977). The use of ethnographic techniques in educational research. *Review of Educational Research, 47* (1), 245–265.

Preface

Alberto Bursztyn

The idea for this book was born in the context of our frequent conversations about teaching graduate students of education at Brooklyn College. As we considered the various texts addressing questions of ethnic and cultural diversity in schools, we could not find one that approached the subject from a variety of vantage points and confronted the inherent complexity of the topic. Although in the past decade much scholarship and an unprecedented number of books on multiculturalism and education have been published, many focus primarily on ways of promoting and implementing multiculturalism as curriculum in schools, while others address theoretical approaches and discourses with scant connection to research. The book we wanted to include in our syllabi would be a book that connected discourses on multiculturalism with how multiculturalism is lived in schools and experienced by children, teachers, families, and support professionals. Imagining such a book meant that we needed to bring in a variety of voices and research approaches. We hoped to be able to engage and challenge the reader with a multidimensional multiculturalism, an approach to the subject that was neither reductive nor simply celebratory.

We believe that the increasing human diversity of our public schools is a salient issue of our time. Multicultural concerns are likely to remain in the forefront of educational policy and curriculum simply because this country's population has never been as diverse as it is today and demographic trends point to a time in the not too distant future when no single group will compose the majority of the population. It would be naïve to suggest that this historic confluence of cultures, races, languages, and beliefs could be accepted, embraced, and incorporated into schools and curricula easily. The realities of school life are not unlike those of the rest of society; the tensions and conflicts inherent in a rapidly diversifying nation echo powerfully in classrooms, school corridors, cafeterias, and yards. Since their inception, public schools in the United States have had a mandate to forge a nation out of the waves of immigrants arriving to its shores. The myths of unproblematic and highly tolerant schools welcoming newcomers of all races and faith, dissolves quickly as we consider the struggles that followed *Brown v. Board of Education* in the 1950s, 1960s and beyond. Schools have been and continue to be the battlegrounds where conflicting ideals of nationhood are fought.

Multiculturalism is not simply a curricular approach; it is a description of our schools, particularly our urban schools. This was the type of multiculturalism we wanted to write about, one that did not shy away from tensions and ideological rifts. We wanted to create a book that told the story of children and adults living these same tensions and rifts. We anticipate that teachers and teacher candidates reading this book will recognize their own experiences in these case studies, gain new insight, and be better prepared to address their own multicultural classes.

An edited volume requires great perseverance and focus, we learned this lesson by doing, but we are most grateful to Nina Neimark, our editor, for her encouragement and guidance in every step of the process. We thank our contributors for their generosity in sharing their ideas and lived experiences. Finally, we thank our graduate students, who inspired us to embark on this project.

RETHINKING
MULTICULTURAL
EDUCATION

Introduction: Cultural Transitions and Curricular Transformations

Carol Korn

Cultural transition, as a result of immigration or movement between minority and majority cultures, is increasingly recognized as a salient component of children's lives. School is acknowledged as one of the places where different cultures meet and where cultural difference may be negotiated (Igoa, 1995; Liston & Zeichner, 1996) or, as a number of the contributors to this volume suggest, ignored and/or rejected. It is a place where children's home culture intersects with the dominant culture—what Madeleine Grumet (1988) referred to as the common culture—and is typically the first public audience before which children bring the artifacts and stories of their cultures of origin. Educators often seek to fill in the gaps between the cultures of home and school with multicultural curricula, creating occasions in which schools can recognize and honor different cultural communities, creating connections, and easing the transitions between the cultures of home and school.

The multicultural curriculum is best known for its celebration of diversity—a means of promoting children's and families' feelings of inclusion and social validation by the school, for the greater aim of promoting connection to the institution of school and to its values and practices. This approach to multiculturalism, characterized by its instrumental nature, deploys culture as a tool in the service of, and subjugated to, the overarching goal of school adjustment. As the national trend for high-stakes testing of schoolchildren increasingly comes to bear on the everyday life of schools, the vulnerability of an instrumental approach that links multicultural education directly to academic achievement becomes increasingly apparent. In a zeitgeist of truncated childhood accompanied by an equally harried pace of instruction, methodologies that promise efficient, direct delivery of skills, however decontextualized these may be, grow in popularity. Multicultural education as a route to increased school achievement is easily circumvented or pushed aside in the pressured atmosphere of high-stakes test preparation that currently pervades public education from the early childhood through the adolescent years.

In this, multicultural education shares with the arts in education similar risks and turning points. Like the arts, multicultural education can easily slide to the edges of classroom life and nudged into the hallways, where it assumes a decorative function in themed bulletin board displays. Like the arts, multiculturalism is also frequently called upon as a tool for skill development, for example, by providing topics for reading and writing activities. Commonly, multicultural education finds its niche in social studies, where it is often joined to art activities. What is often referred to as a *heroes and holidays approach* to multiculturalism is readily wedded to what passes as the arts in many schools and has given rise to countless turkeys and cutout snowflakes.

In the academic hierarchy of schools, multicultural education is situated below, and serves to enhance, the content areas, such as social studies and English language arts, while the arts, situated even lower than multicultural education on the school ladder, serve to enrich a heroes and holidays multicultural curriculum. In the increasingly high-pressure, competitive world of early childhood and elementary school classrooms, multicultural education, like the arts, provides what is widely perceived as a restful and entertaining respite from the rigors of drill and practice regimens. Both serve a decorative function, gracing hallway bulletin boards across the nation. Both are typically fit into time slots somewhere between lunch and dismissal, signaling their tenuous place within the curriculum and within the daily routines of schools. Indeed, the meager time slots that multicultural and arts education fill are increasingly usurped by test coaching and practice drills.

Associated with a respite from the tedium of schoolwork, multicultural education together with its partner, the arts, are eagerly welcomed by children, who happily light into the paste and construction paper cutouts their teachers provide. The children's delight with such respites cements a heroes and holidays approach to multicultural education—and a *decorative approach* to the arts—in the hearts of their well-intentioned teachers. It is not uncommon for multicultural activities accompanied by art activities to be held up as a carrot by teachers to encourage student compliance. The place and form of multicultural education, like the arts in education, cannot be considered in isolation from curriculum development and from an approach to teaching that privileges product over process and that places test preparation at the core of curriculum.

An *instrumental approach* to multiculturalism that centers celebration of cultural diversity through a heroes and holidays approach typically puts forth an uncritical and narrow view of culture (Cummins, 1989; Hoffman, 1996; Nieto, 1996). Such efforts, typical of what James Banks and Cherry McGee Banks (1993) refer to as an *additive approach* to multiculturalism, focus on cultural diversity as encoded in dress and food, tending toward prototypical cultural elements that border on the stereotypical. The additive approach to multicultural education, in which some new ideas and materials are included in the existing curriculum but without significantly altering it, is commonly critiqued for its maintenance of a traditional curricular structure unaltered by its contact with cultural difference. The ease with which this approach may be integrated into a school's existing curriculum and approach to teaching and learning, without raising questions about the culture of the school and about its pedagogy and mission, makes this a popular choice for many schools. With little incentive, and often facing administrative opposition to curricular change, teachers who draw upon this approach can lighten the academic burdens their students face. When, as earlier noted, the arts are included in the additive approach to multicultural education, the happy faces with which children welcome such a change of pace endear this approach to similarly bored and stifled teachers.

A second way in which multicultural education is taken up in the schools is through what Banks and Banks (1993) refer to as the *infusion approach* to multicultural education. The infusion approach widens the scope of multicultural content by threading new material throughout the existing curriculum, rather than providing solely add-ons, as in the additive approach. While the infusion approach takes a more holistic view toward curriculum development and seeks to integrate multiple perspectives throughout the curriculum, like the additive approach it too retains the structure, content, and underlying assumptions of the extant curriculum.

In neither of these two approaches are basic assumptions about the aims of education or about how classrooms are organized and curriculum constructed challenged. Both the additive and the infusion approaches serve what I earlier referred to as an instrumental approach to multiculturalism. While infusion of multicultural content furthers the representation of diverse cultural, ethnic, and racial groups in the curriculum and, like the additive approach, provides opportunity for children to identify with the heroes and holidays of their home cultures, it too serves the instrumental aim of delivering the extant curriculum and, in so doing, lending support to the pedagogical principles that undergird school practice.

In contrast, the *transformative approach* (Banks & Banks, 1993) to multicultural education adopts a more comprehensive and radical view and demands that the curriculum be fundamentally altered, to encourage student empowerment and social action. In applying a transformative

model to the cultural transitions that children make as they move between the cultures of home and school, we look at how cross-cultural
encounters between the school and home cultures can transform its participants. The school edifice, solid and imposing, demands, in the public
imagination, obeisance: if not filial devotion of its children, teachers, and
parents, then at the least, unquestioned compliance with its rules and
regulations. The solidity of its common brick façade, though, belies the
permeability that permits change to seep into its structures. The point at
which the cultures of school and home converge is also the nexus at
which the possibility of change is found.

The place in which the cultures of home and school intersect holds
potential as a site of mutual influence and transformation. Like all opportunities, it bears with it the risk of a hardening of positions on both
fronts. Such places are often filled with difference: different views, different beliefs, and different organizing values. Providing reflections of
difference in the curriculum, as in the additive approach to multicultural
education, is an important means of facilitating children's adjustment to
and assimilation within the common culture of school. While facilitating
children's adjustment to a new environment is critical to successful transition from home to school for all children, it is but one component in
the complex issues of cultural transition as enacted in schools across the
country.

A transformative approach to understanding the cultural transitions
that children make as they move from home to school calls for engagement with the questions and problematics that cross-cultural encounters
engender. It implies a responsive approach to pedagogy, in which critical
reflection and decision making lead to social action or to what Paolo
Freire (1970) called "praxis." Social action implies curricular change:
changes in how one thinks about and develops curriculum and in how
one understands, responds to, and teaches children. Such changes constitute major shifts in teaching praxis. They call upon teachers and other
education professionals to critically consider the assumptions that underlie educational practices and to explore the inconsistencies, contradictions, and silences that surround discussion of multicultural
curriculum and the role of the school in negotiating children's cultural
transitions.

Curriculum is never neutral; in deciding what is included and what is
left out teachers make decisions that are informed both by the positions
they take and by the social interests that are embedded in curricular
traditions. George S. Howard (1991) suggests that school is a place where
the dominant culture's stories are encoded and communicated and
where children learn the prevailing scientific, moral, mathematical, religious, historical, and political stories of the dominant culture. In Chapter
1 of this volume, "Silenced Voices: A Case of Racial and Cultural Intoler-

ance in the Schools," Deborah Nelson and Margaret Rogers offer an example of a school in a diverse urban school district whose population is 97 percent white and 3 percent Asian, Hispanic, and African American. The chapter tells the parallel stories of the narrator, the school's first African American school psychologist, and of Corey, a second-grade African American boy. Corey's spontaneous remark to his classmate, "I'm stupid because I'm black!" provokes the school psychologist's inquiry into the explicit and implicit messages transmitted to Corey through the curriculum and through his teachers' beliefs and expectations. It deepens her query, too, into her own position at the school and the quiet that greets her dissenting voice during conferences with teachers and parents.

The silence that enfolds the experiences of the minority children and families at this school reverberates in the silences that greet other aspects of children's cultural experiences, left, like the muddy boots of polite visitors, beyond the threshold of school. Religion, a central feature of the practices of diverse cultural and ethnic groups, and a highly significant part of the lives of many children, for example, is rarely a topic of discourse within communities of educators. It comes up in Nelson and Rogers' writing, in a critique of the school's sweeping disavowal of the rights of minority groups for inclusion of their holidays in the prevailing heroes and holidays curriculum or, at the very least, of their right to a nondiscriminatory policy toward observance of religious traditions.

A transformative approach to understanding cultural transitions calls for consideration of those practices that are part of children's lived experience within the home culture but that do not lend themselves easily to a heroes and holidays approach. Silence, for example, surrounds the chasm between the home cultural norms of gendered behavior and the values and expectations of the school culture, and also surrounds such familial and cultural practices as corporal punishment. These silences need to be explored if we are to be able to engage in meaningful dialogue about children's experiences of cultural transition and how these may be expressed and responded to at school. We need to explore how schools can address and respond to children's diverse cultural experiences while maintaining the historic ideal of schools as democratizing agents within American common culture.

In contrast to the school described earlier, Vernita Zubia and Beth Doll offer an example of a middle school program that worked to alter traditional cross-cultural interactions and, in so doing, began the slow process of re-culturing the school. Their chapter, "Redefining School Culture: Creating New Traditions for Bicultural Students," addresses a school's attempts to introduce culturally diverse students to the dominant culture while honoring the students' home cultures and practices, even when these diverge substantively from those of the school. On his fifteenth birthday, for example, Luis found himself, together with two older sisters, supporting their family of seven when his parents quit their jobs. It was, he explained, his turn to support the family.

Zubia and Doll found that the cultural transitions that bilingual and bicultural students faced were complicated by the socially exclusionary practices endemic to middle schools, here based upon collective ethnic identity, in addition to the ongoing negotiation between the values and traditions of the home and dominant cultures. This same boy observed, "Sometimes the other students made fun of me because, you know, how my Spanish is different than Mexican Spanish." Subtle cues that teachers emit regarding perceived student competence, long a topic of inquiry in education, are painfully responded to by children already struggling with the intense ambivalence that often attends cultural transitions.

The authors address the school's ongoing efforts to challenge the traditional structures in which English-language learners are constructed as needy, while native speakers of English provide the leftovers from which the newcomers gratefully nibble. Inequitable distribution of resources—of competent teachers, school/program choice, and career counseling—is taken up by the school in an attempt to redress the unequal power distribution among English-language learners and native speakers of English. The more oblique injuries, of inattention and averted gaze—what the authors refer to as "a dearth of social resources"—plague this middle school, as they do countless others. Noteworthy here is the work of this school to negotiate the cultural differences and distances between—and within—its native English-and Spanish-speaking cultural groups.

As change seeps into and begins to alter the ways that schools work, schools are called upon to identify and to make explicit the underlying assumptions and expectations of the dominant culture and to examine how these are negotiated within the culture of the particular school. In reconsidering their multicultural practices, schools need to be clear about how decisions are arrived at and whether such decisions enhance or restrict access for students. At the middle school described earlier, for example, parents of native speakers of English could opt in or out of a dual-language immersion program. Parents of English-language learners, in contrast, were not consulted.

Bridging the worlds of school and home/community cultures brings forth complicated questions about the multiple meanings that emerge from a meeting of diverse cultural worlds. It provokes questions about what gets talked about and what is silenced, what there is time for and what gets buried in the margins of classroom daily schedules. When curriculum is constructed around these intersections, differences between cultural experiences can be acknowledged and common ground located. Openings for understanding and for transformation are created when the problematics of such encounters between cultural worlds are explored. Hans Georg Gadamer (1967, 1975) speaks of a "fusion of horizons" that arises from this meeting of one's socially constructed horizon—here, the culture of home—with other possible worlds. The juncture at which cultures meet bears within it the potential for greater understanding, even as the assumptions that underlie a culture's traditions are illumined when these are considered from a different perspective. Understanding can be furthered insofar as differences between cultural perspectives are acknowledged and the meanings that inhere in these differences are explored.

An approach to multicultural education that has meaning at its core—that focuses on what difference means to children, teachers, and families—calls upon educators to examine their own positions in addressing or avoiding discussions of difference. To understand children's experiences of cultural transition as they move between the cultures of home and school, it is necessary to explore what the children's transitions mean to their teachers and how they too negotiate transitions as they move from home to school each day. Diversity does not allow for an uncomplicated relationship between the individual and society but, rather, engages us in continual renegotiation of the personal and social. The stories or case studies that the contributors bring to this volume reflect this shifting gaze—from child to teacher to parent—and take up the various relational configurations these three form between each other and among themselves.

These stories adopt a reflective lens, turning a critical eye toward instances of classroom practice and life within schools that serve to connect personal knowledge with school change. In some of the cases presented here, the authors draw directly on autobiographical material, linking these to a reflective approach to teaching (Jalongo & Isenberg, 1995; Schon, 1987). In exploring the impact of the educator—that is, her beliefs, attitudes, and ethics—on student learning and development, reflective practice links the autobiographical impulse to teaching and learning. As these autobiographical works enter the public domain of discourse, they are renegotiated, opening up possibilities for deeper understanding of how individual attitudes toward multiculturalism and diversity affect what happens in the classroom and in the community. The interactive matrix created by public discourse shapes individual attitudes and necessitates a revisiting of one's own subjective understanding, as arrived at through introspection and the self-reflective turn. Folding reflection and autobiographical understanding into the dialogic matrix of public discourse offers the hope of broadening understanding and the promise of negotiating larger scale, institutional change.

A transformative approach to multicultural education demands that teachers, like children, achieve greater familiarity with and respect for diverse human experience and the ability to consider their own life experiences within the context of culture, place, and time. Such work can feel risky. To explore the geology of schooling involves acknowledging and responding to that which lies right below the surface of classroom life, covered over by the silence that blankets unauthorized voices, their students' and their own. Although teacher voice is widely recognized in academic circles as critical to developing an understanding of educational experience and has become increasingly accepted as a methodology in teacher research (Connelley & Clandinin, 1988; Schon, 1983, 1987), on the local level, teacher talk continues to represent a marginalized discourse.

The perspectives of teachers that several contributors bring to this volume underline the critical role of teachers in developing a transformative approach to multicultural education and to working in diverse settings. Cheryl Holcomb-McCoy's "Issues of Class and Race in Education: A Personal Narrative" (see Chapter 3) moves between her own autobiographical notes of her childhood as a child of two African American schoolteachers, and her own first-year experience as a kindergarten teacher. She tells the story of Wayne, a five-year-old African American boy in her class, whose placement in the school's "gifted and talented" program she advocated over the objections of other members of the school staff.

In Chapter 4, "Crossing the Brooklyn Bridge: The Geography of Social and Cultural Transitions," I look at the experiences of teacher education students as they move between the cultures of what are often insular communities and Brooklyn College, a large, urban, and diverse institution, and between the college and several major New York City cultural arts organizations. I consider the developmental, social, and cultural transitions that students undergo as they become teachers and address the teacher's role as cultural mediator in the classroom.

In several of the cases presented in this book, literature becomes a screen against which teachers confront questions about working with children of diverse backgrounds. Storytelling, a staple of multicultural curricula, forms a backdrop for Korn's discussion of teacher as cultural mediator, listening to how individual listeners hear and respond to stories from the vantage point of their own cultural backgrounds and life experiences. In Chapter 5, "An Ecological Perspective on Preparing Teachers for Multicultural Classrooms," Helen Johnson responds to Camille, a graduate student in teacher education, who is irked by her fifth-grade students' interruption of her reading to ask questions. Camille interprets her African American students' interruptions as a challenge to her authority as a white teacher, rejecting the children's claim to voice as disrespectful of authority. Johnson eschews the traditional approach to preparing teachers to teach multicultural education that focuses exclusively on delivery of content about the history and practices of diverse groups and advocates for addressing the personal experiences and values from within which teachers approach their work in the classroom.

Drawing upon his own personal narrative to illumine the complexity of interest in multiculturalism and commitment to issues of equity, Peter Taubman, in Chapter 6, "Facing the Terror Within: Exploring the Personal in Multicultural Education," also addresses the role of the personal in teaching, focusing on the teacher as subject. Taking a psychoanalytic approach to thinking about multicultural curriculum and about teaching and learning in culturally, ethnically, and racially diverse classrooms, he calls upon the analytic concept of countertransference to explore, via his own personal narrative, a teacher's complex, subjective responses to diversity. Taubman outlines the multiple cultural, ethnic, and racial identities to which one may be called or hailed but that one may, or may not, elect to turn to. He speaks to how personal construction of a hybrid identity, comprised of overlapping and shifting layers of identification, impacts on how multiculturalism is addressed both within and outside of the classroom.

Construction of cultural identity is increasingly recognized as a dynamic process, negotiated from within the social and cultural frameworks that undergird and inform development (Darder, 1995). For minority children, in particular, this process is often complicated by what are experienced as conflicting pulls from the cultures of home and of the dominant society. In Chapter 7, "Transforming the Deficit Narrative: Race, Class, and Social Capital in Parent-School Relations," Hollyce C. Giles analyzes the transformation of a "parenting group" from one that was organized around what the school regarded as the parents' deficient parenting skills to one directed by the parents' interests, most notably in the kinds of social action that would be of direct benefit to their children.

In Chapter 1 "Silenced Voices: A Case of Racial and Cultural Intolerance in the Schools," Nelson and Rogers address the dangers of constructing the cultures of home and of school in exclusionary terms. Inevitably, the culture of home is denigrated and dismissed as inferior, and familial ways are deemed inimical to academic achievement. To participate in the culture of school in such circumstances demands a binary choice on the part of the child between the culture of home and the common culture of school. To identify with the school would signal abandonment of the culture of home, together with foreclosure of the lengthy and complicated process whereby cultural identity is constructed.

Language is closely bound to culture, and tied up with the construction of cultural identity. It has often served as a locus for debates around cultural transitions (Cummins, 1994; McKeon, 1994), especially regarding bilingualism. The arguments that surround bilingual education as a transitional methodology for learning English or as a means of maintaining bicultural identity speak to the ways in which language and culture are intertwined and, also, to the pulls between the culture of origin and the common culture of school. Schools though, Alberto Bursztyn observes in Chapter 8, "The Path to Academic Disability: Javier's School Experience," are slow to change.

Despite growing diversity in school populations, multiculturalism is increasingly marginalized as other highly politicized arguments around school choice, standards, and regulated curricula come to dominate the public forum. Bursztyn contends that the marginalization of multiculturalism hinders broader examination of how minority-culture children fare in public schools. Enrollment patterns in special education, he points out, reveal a disproportional identification and placement of culturally and linguistically diverse children in these classes. The case of Javier, a seven-year-old Hispanic boy, illustrates the particular vulnerability to labeling and subsequent placement in special education that culturally and linguistically diverse children face.

The space in which children move between cultures is located at the intersection of several of the key controversies and concerns that currently inform educational thinking, critique, and practice. Issues of language, culture, and disability emerge when questions are raised regarding referral and placement of culturally, ethnically, racially, and linguistically diverse children in special education and in the contested category of "gifted and talented." All schoolchildren are seasoned travelers of home-school cultural journeys. The particular journeys that children make as they move between the cultures of home and school, and educators' responses and reactions to the experience of transition and identity formation, in both their own lives and the lives of children, provide a working framework for the case studies that follow.

Honoring cultural transitions in schools calls for educators to be cognizant of the passages their students make as they move from home to school, and for appreciation of the role of their own perspectives and experiences and how these impact upon teaching praxis. It calls for a responsive pedagogy that identifies teaching and learning as mutually informed acts and that provides a place for teacher initiative and for perspectives of diverse communities to inform and contribute to the transformation of curriculum. The stories and case studies that follow offer vignettes from the classroom and from the preparation of teachers that illuminate the complicated nature of cultural transitions and the role and obligation of schools to create places in which children and families of diverse cultural, ethnic, and racial background can thrive. This book highlights the place of a multicultural curriculum that plays a transformative role within the lives of children and communities, that alters our thinking about what we teach and how, and that focuses attention on the members of our audience, the children.

REFERENCES

Banks, J. A., & Banks, C. A. M. (Eds.). (1993). *Multicultural education: Issues and perspectives* (2nd ed.). Boston, MA: Allyn & Bacon.

Connelley, F. M., & Clandinin, D. J. (1988). *Teachers as curriculum planners: Narratives of experience*. New York: Teachers College Press.

Cummins, J. (1994). Knowledge, power, and identity in teaching English as a second language. In F. Genesee (Ed.), *Educating second language children: The whole child, the whole curriculum, the whole community*. New York: Cambridge University Press.

————. (1989). *Empowering minority students*. Sacramento, CA: California Association for Bilingual Education.

Darder, A. (Ed.) (1995). *Critical perspectives on the bilcultural experience in the United States*. Westport, CT: Bergin & Garvey.

Freire, P. (1970). *Pedagogy of the oppressed*. New York: Seabury Press.

Gadamer, H. (1975). *Truth and method*. New York: Continuum.

————. (1967). On the scope and function of hermeneutical reflection. In D. E. Linge (Ed), *Philosophical Hermeneutics* (pp. 18–43). Berkeley: University of California Press.

Grumet, M. (1988). *Bitter milk: Women and teaching*. Amherst: University of Massachusetts Press.

Hoffman, D. M. (1996). Culture and self in multicultural education: Reflections on discourse, text, and practice. *American Educational Research Journal, 33*, 545–569.

Howard, S. G. (1991). Culture tales: A narrative approach to thinking, cross-cultural psychology, and psychotherapy. *American Psychologist, 46*, 187–197.

Igoa, C. (1995). *The inner world of the immigrant child*. New York: St. Martin's Press.

Jalongo, M. R., & Isenberg, J. (1995). *Teachers' stories: From personal narrative to professional insight*. San Francisco: Jossey-Bass.

Liston, D., & Zeichner, K. M. (1996). *Culture and teaching*. Mahwah, NJ: Lawrence Erlbaum Associates.

McKeon, D. (1994). Language, culture, and schooling. In F. Genesee (Ed.) *Educating second language children: The whole child, the whole curriculum, the whole community*. New York: Cambridge University Press.

Nieto, S. (1996). *Affirming diversity: The sociopolitical context of multicultural education* (2nd ed.). White Plains, NY: Longman Publishers.

Schon, D. (1987). *Educating the reflective practitioner*. San Francisco: Jossey-Bass.

————. (1983). *The reflective practitioner: How professionals think in action*. New York: Basic Books.

1

Silenced Voices: A Case of Racial and Cultural Intolerance in the Schools

Deborah Nelson and Margaret R. Rogers

As psychologists, we seek to attain the noblest of goals of our profession—that of improving the lives of those we serve. But what happens when our efforts to provide effective psychological services and create empowering educational environments are overshadowed by bigotry and intolerance? A major challenge for psychologists working in today's schools is to ensure that our clients' human rights are preserved. As we undertake this challenge, we must be continually mindful of the cultural assumptions that operate in the environments in which we serve and strive to educate others about the harmful consequences of erroneous beliefs, cultural misinformation, and prejudice. The present case describes the parallel experiences of an African American school psychologist and an African American student as they attempt to find their own ways in a largely white school setting. What follows begins with a description of the school setting and school staff as seen through the eyes of the psychologist, then relates observations of a second-grade child attending the school, and ends with an exploration of the implications of the case. As you read this case, consider whose voices ring out, are heard, valued, and respected in School E.

EASTLAKE SCHOOL: THE SETTING AND THE STAFF

"Deb, I've got to talk to you. You won't believe the experience I've just had." Mary, the school social worker, blurted out, her arms flailing to punctuate her emotions. I could tell by her mannerisms that she was angry and upset. Having worked closely with her at the urban elementary school where we were both assigned full-time for two years, we often shared stories of our daily adventures. "I was just upstairs passing by the fourth-grade classroom," she explained, "and I noticed the students were watching a film about Mount Vesuvio in Italy—you know the volcano—so I stopped to watch with them. You know I love anything Italian," she added. Indeed I did. As a twenty-year veteran of the field, Mary was tough, unerringly professional, straightforward, and as fiercely proud of her Italian heritage as I am of my African American heritage. I admired that about her and took great enjoyment in listening to her childhood remembrances of her hardworking, immigrant grandparents and their lively and spirited discussions around a Sunday dinner table laden with fresh-cooked pasta, homemade sauce, and rich desserts.

Knowing how much delight Mary took in experiences reflecting her cultural heritage, I was puzzled by her obvious distress. She continued her story by saying that she had heard several children snickering over the accents of the Italian natives in the film, over the foods that were eaten, and other depictions of an Italian lifestyle. Concerned, I asked, "What did the teacher do?" "That's exactly why I'm so mad, Deb. She didn't do a thing." Mary shook her head incredulously. "She didn't do a thing." But then that was the typical response of the thirty-person staff of our school when it came to addressing any issues of cultural conflict. They didn't do a thing. Nothing. Mary's account brought back memories of other incidents that had also disturbed me greatly. There was the time when a sweet-faced, blond-haired, blue-eyed third grader asked if liking me meant that she was a "niggerlover," like the "big kids said." Then there was the time when the school's secretary responded to a parent who inquired about the school's policy of not having celebrations of Christmas as a Christian holiday by saying, "Well, I don't know why they would want to take the joy out of Christmas for these children." When it was suggested that perhaps it was because Christmas was a celebration of a Christian holiday and that its acknowledgement would exclude those in the building who were Jewish and Moslem, she replied, "Well, that's part of being American. Those who don't like it should just go back to where they came from."

I remembered another incident involving a Moslem mother of two, who became distraught when two school staff members accused her of starving her children. Tearfully, she explained to me how the children (a second and a third grader) were celebrating Ramadan for the first time that year and were required to fast during the day. Although the experience was a new one for them, the boys were nevertheless proud of achieving this milestone in their religious development. She had asked for the school's support by requesting that they be occupied during lunchtime. Instead of providing the children with an alternate activity, they were sent to the office to sit in an area usually designated for acting-out students. During the entire period of the holiday, which lasted one month, she was criticized by staff members, who insisted that she be referred to Child Protective Services. The absolute shame of this incident was that one of the thematic units in third grade was Islam. What a wonderful opportunity it would have been to have these students' experiences validated by their school's curriculum.

When I mentioned some of these incidents to the assistant principal, emphasizing the racial slurs and bigoted language, she responded, "Don't get yourself so worked up. The students are just repeating what they hear every day in the community." Conversations with the principal about these same situations were also fruitless. While he admitted that they were serious, he nevertheless felt that little could be done to change the situation. "There isn't anything you can do to change bigotry. It's unfortunate, but it's true," he responded. In other words, from his perspective, it was acceptable to allow staff and students to promote cultural intolerance. Indeed, in this school it was a cultural norm.

How, I wondered, could a school located in a diverse, urban school district become so culturally encapsulated? Nestled between the city's trendy shopping district and large condemned factory warehouses, the school sat on one of the city's economic dividing lines, with 54 percent of the population receiving free lunch. Out of 450 students, 97 percent were white, while the other 3 percent were Asian, Hispanic, and African American. This demographic breakdown was highly unusual for a school situated in a large urban school district that is predominantly African American. My friends used to think I was joking when I said there were more African American staff members than students in the building. But this was actually true. There were only four African American students, but there were nine African American staff members, including the custodial and kitchen staff.

The fact that I am an African American female school psychologist was a common focus of conversation during my first months at the school. An African-American female school psychologist was apparently such a rarity that the majority of staff, white and African American alike, had never before encountered one. Most staff did not feel comfortable interacting with me in that capacity. My presence also highlighted other social and cultural divisions in the building. For example, although there were three major staff lounging areas in the building, one was frequented by white staff, the other by African American staff, and the other by the clinical staff, which before my assignment had been all white. In an attempt to familiarize myself with all staff members, I made the round of these lounges, and heard disturbing language coming from each of them. Labels like "stupid," "ugly," and "crazy" were often attached to children who were perceived as being different from the cultural "norm" of the building. "White trash," was a common moniker for students whose family incomes were below the poverty level, with families on welfare being called "lazy welfare trash."

However, it wasn't just students who were targets of these verbal barrages; members of the staff were targeted as well. In the first month of my employment, stories were related about the "crazy" fifth-grade teacher who had worked for two years in Sri Lanka ("Why on Earth would anybody go to a place where people have all those diseases and no toilets?"), the "cold" fourth-grade inclusion teacher who was "one of those Orthodox Jews" ("She's too good to eat with us. You know how they eat all that funny food. I don't know how she can stand it. You wouldn't catch me doing something like that. Do you think she wears a wig like the rest of them?"), the "black bitch" fifth-grade inclusion teacher who thought she "knew everything," and the "homo" principal ("You know he's married to a man, don't you? Just wait until you see that.")

Curiously, I never heard conversations mentioning ways to address the fact that 47 percent of the student population was reading below grade level, instruct the school's educationally diverse population, or handle children with difficult behaviors effectively without the verbal abuse or negative physical contact that I commonly observed. How, I wondered, would I begin to find a place in such a culturally constricting environment? It was a question made increasingly poignant as I began to interact more with the few children of color in the building. If I was struggling as an adult to find a level of emotional comfort within my surroundings, how much more must their struggle have been as children?

In her case study of a junior high school undergoing restructuring, Pauline Lipman (1997) discusses the dynamics of race, power, and ideology. She discovered that while race was salient in the dialogue of the teaching staff, with code words such as "low SES" and "at-risk" being synonymous with the African American student population, the school never directly addressed racial issues. She concluded that "a consequence of silencing public discussion of race was that educators disregarded African Americans' cultural identities and continued to normalize the institutional ideologies and practices that shaped their educational experiences" (p. 19). I felt that this was happening at my school.

But what was needed to bring about a discussion of culture and race in an authentic, unthreatening way? How could we begin to use the curriculum to empower and transform staff and students' thinking about issues of multicultural education and diversity? Looking to the work of James Banks (1996, 1993) provided me with a framework for viewing the situation more objectively. Multicultural education is a process that, if effective, has the potential to transform schools (Banks, 1996). But how do we transform schools in overburdened systems that are struggling at a basic level of survival and that provide few opportunities for reflective practice and positive growth? In order to better understand the situation, I considered Banks' (1993) five dimensions of multicultural education. They include (1) content integration, (2) the knowledge construction process, (3) prejudice reduction, (4) an equity pedagogy, and (5) an empowering school culture and social structure.

According to Banks (1993), *content integration* refers to the use of content and examples from different cultural groups to highlight concepts, principles, ideas, and theories in a subject area or discipline. The *knowledge construction process* describes ways in which teachers use activities, methods, and questions to help students "understand, investigate, and determine how implicit cultural assumptions, frames of reference, perspectives, and biases within a discipline influence the ways in which knowledge is constructed" (p. 21). When teachers attempt to help students develop democratic attitudes and values about racial attitudes through instructional strategies they are using *prejudice reduction*, and when teachers adapt their instructional methods in ways that promote the educational achievement of students from diverse cultural, racial, and gender groups, an *equity pedagogy* exists. An *empowering school culture and social structure* refers to the school as a complex social system that must be restructured in order to implement reform related to multiculturalism and diversity. I found that my experiences at this particular school touched on each of these areas.

I recall one specific incident that occurred as I was passing by a fourth-grade classroom that illustrated the content integration dimension. A group of about fifteen students sat engrossed as their teacher read an African folktale to them. After reading the first page, she turned the book to show the picture. Snickers, laughs, and whispers broke out among the small group. "She looks funny. Why is she dressed like that?" they inquired, referring to one of the main characters in the story, a little girl garbed in traditional African dress. Instead of taking the opportunity to talk about cultural differences in dress and lifestyle, the teacher just shrugged, "That's just how she's dressed" and continued to read the story. Scenes like this were not unusual; they reflected the difficulty many teachers have in accurately integrating unfamiliar cultural content into learning experiences.

Our school had fallen victim to what Diane Hoffman (1996) describes as "hallway multiculturalism." For instance, a few posters of children from diverse cultural backgrounds graced the walls, and the principal always made sure to include the accomplishments of African Americans and Hispanics in his morning announcement segment on "This Day in History," but few attempts were ever made to address any issue that would require reconceptualizing or restructuring of the present cultural code (Beckum & Zimney, 1991).

As I looked through the second-grade curriculum to see what other chances students had for learning about culturally diverse groups, I saw there were some learning opportunities. Yet little initiative was taken to integrate information over and above what was presented in the text. In some cases misinformation was delivered by the teacher. In one instance the teacher gave the class the wrong birthdate for baseball pioneer Jackie Robinson (she inadvertently used the date that he first played in the major leagues). At other times I heard the names of culturally different individuals in history mispronounced. I remember one such occasion. The special educator was listing facts on chart paper about Rosa Parks, when she mispronounced the civil rights activist's birthplace name. She repeated this mispronunciation several times throughout the lesson and even had the students repeat it after her. When I later explained this to her and informed her of the correct pronunciation, she shrugged and stated, "I thought I was pronouncing that name right. How was I supposed to know?" I understood the not knowing. What I was disturbed by was her lack of a desire to know. If the teacher was unaware and misinformed, couldn't she have found out by asking someone?

These were just instances that I observed. I began to wonder how often misinformation about cultural issues were delivered in this class and in the building. Can curriculum be truly used to transform and empower when there is no guarantee concerning how it will be transmitted and delivered to others? Around this time, I found myself wanting to learn more about the prejudice reduction activities that Banks (1993) mentions as another essential dimension of multicultural education. In an effort to find out what was available in our district, I made phone calls searching for systemwide programs that actively addressed issues of diversity and cultural intolerance. I began in the district school psychology office, asking the supervisor if he was aware of any such programs. He responded that there were none of which he was aware, and he advised me to try the Office of Guidance Services and the Office of Staff Development.

A call to the program facilitator of the Office of Guidance Services yielded little. The office sponsored just one program. Titled, "Proud to Be Me," the program was under the auspices of the "Drug Free Schools Project." The facilitator explained that it addressed topics such as families, feelings, risks and choices, and alcohol and other drugs. When I asked specifically about topics dealing with cultural intolerance or issues of diversity and related some of the incidents that had occurred at my school, the facilitator empathized and explained that they had never had a formal request to address those concerns. A call to the Office of Staff Development provided little more information. The office's director explained, "We used to do that kind of stuff in the 1970s, but we haven't gotten any requests for it lately." However, she remembered that there was a center that contracted with the city to do that kind of work, but the fee ranged from $100 to $500 per workshop and had to be paid out of school funds. Clearly the school district did not place a high priority on prejudice reduction programs or on programs that provide participants with skills for successfully negotiating cultural boundaries. I wondered whether it was possible that in a large school district that employed about ninety school psychologists that I alone detected the need for such work.

EASTLAKE SCHOOL: THE CASE OF COREY

As the year progressed, I would learn more about the struggles of one student, Corey, as he attempted to negotiate the cultural boundaries in his second-grade classroom. I still remember our first meeting. With sweat beading his seven-year-old brow, Corey bent laboriously over his seatwork. His was a lone brown face in a sea of white ones. Tightly clenching his pencil and pulling his bottom lip between his teeth, he paused in his language arts task of writing a letter to persuade Martin Luther King, Jr. to continue the Montgomery bus boycott. He leaned over and whispered to his neighbor David, "I can't spell this stuff." He worked at his task for a few more moments, then, exasperated, he slammed his pencil on his desk. "I'm stupid because I'm black!" he exclaimed. David turned to him, empathic and consoling. He, too, was struggling with the assignment. "Martin Luther King is black and he isn't stupid," he explained to Corey, with a shy smile as he peered intently through his thick lenses, satisfied that he had solved his classmate's dilemma. Corey, however, sighed loudly and retorted, "Yeah, but he doesn't go to my school." Oblivious to this exchange, Corey and David's teachers told them to get back to work.

As an observer in Corey's classroom that day, my stomach clenched painfully when I heard his words. Where had Corey learned that he was stupid, and how had he come to associate this with being black? What were the explicit and implicit messages that were being transmitted to Corey through the curriculum and his everyday interactions within the building that strengthened such beliefs? A sour bile rose in my throat. How could I convey Corey's perceptions to his teachers? What was my expectation about their reaction? Confronting them was a moment that I was dreading but that would become inevitable.

When I first spotted Corey at the beginning of the school year, I intuited that our paths would eventually cross. It was only a matter of time. The only questions remaining were when and for what reason. Driven by my own personal history, experiences, and perspectives, I followed the path laid by fate and nurtured by circumstance. In hindsight, these were what determined the outcome of Corey's and my own experience at the school. Corey and I were anomalies at the school. We were both part of a large metropolitan school district that boasted a student population that was 85.2 percent African American, 13.3 percent white, and 1.5 percent combined Asian, Indian, and Hispanic. Yet we both found ourselves in a school that was composed predominantly of white students and staff. Corey, as one of only two African American male students in the building, stood out in bold relief. I did too, as the school's first African American female school psychologist.

I had heard rumblings about Corey almost from the first day of school. He wasn't "that bright," was "too hyper," would do his class work only when he "felt like it," and "Oh, yeah, he's that kid of the mother that's on drugs and in jail." The experiences that I had at the school, along with declarations such as these about his ability and potential, helped me to understand where Corey got the message that his heritage (African American) was synonymous with a perceived level of intellectual incompetence ("stupid"). As a young African American male in a predominantly white school, his words indicated that he felt powerless to change his existing educational situation, a perception that was reinforced by his school environment.

Corey had no doubt learned from his teachers that labels could draw our attention away from the larger social, political, cultural, and economic situations that have created these labels (Marsh, 1993), and thereby put up smoke screens that make us feel less responsible for our individual responses toward others. It struck me that as adults we commonly participate in a socially defined reality that is designed to help make sense of the world and to organize our activity within it, yet there is little acknowledgement of the often arbitrary nature of that reality. Yet, I thought, if we have made it, can't we unmake it and remake it and ourselves differently so that all are included? Like Michael Apple (1990, p. 15), shouldn't we ask, "Whose knowledge, whose culture, whose commonsense is made legitimate in our educational institutions? Whose knowledge/voice is valued in the public school? The voice of the normal, middle-class?" How, I thought, might education and teaching/learning be changed if we equalized knowledge/voices? How might it be changed if we engaged in a discourse that would allow the reciprocal exchange needed to critically reconstruct the present reality (O'Loughlin, 1995)?

Leonard Beckum and Arlene Zimney (1991) stress that the educational process cannot be separated from the community or societal norms of which they are a part. The resulting norms, values, and beliefs that drive school and curriculum practices often support dominant, mainstream culture and further marginalize students who are already on the fringe because of race, ethnicity, or social class. How could we then empower the school culture to reconstruct its present reality to be more inclusive of students like Corey and staff such as myself? I searched for answers for both of us. I agreed with Hoffman (1996) that many of the concepts embedded in multiculturalism (e.g., "culture," "self," "identity," and "difference") are fraught with personal assumptions and colored by individual experience. So the task became to find common ground in a situation in which I was not common and was only reluctantly accommodated.

In his classroom, Corey was one of forty students in a second-grade inclusion class that was team taught by two white female teachers. Both had expressed reservations about inclusion to me and other staff previously. "It's not that I don't believe those other kids can't learn, but the smart ones shouldn't be held back because of them [the special education students]." Statements like these alerted me to the precarious situation that I was in. Furthermore, it also created another layer of difference between myself and the staff because, in addition to my other job titles and duties, I was also the facilitator of the school support team, which had just been funded to implement a systematic, data-driven, problem-solving model designed to reduce the number of referrals to special education and to promote the placement and maintenance of students in inclusive education environments. I was unaware of just how awkward a dilemma this posed for some staff until a teacher approached me nervously one day. "I know you believe in inclusion and all, but I got to tell you I don't think that works. My son was in a school that had that, and he wasn't learning nothing [sic] in that class with those dumb kids. He wasn't getting the attention he needed."

Corey's teachers shared similar sentiments. The regular education teacher in the classroom had been teaching for fifteen years and felt strongly that "some of these kids just can't make it in here no matter what we do." The special educator, who had been teaching for four years, was frustrated and overwhelmed. "I've tried everything with these kids and nothing works," she was heard to say on more than one occasion. In addition, they both felt that the school support team performed a gatekeeping function by preventing students from getting "real help" in special education environments.

Nevertheless, it was through the vehicle of the school-based support team that Corey's and my paths finally crossed. One of Corey's teachers cornered me one day after school and said; "Corey needs some help. He's way too hyper. We know he needs medication, but his mom just won't get it for him. You know she takes drugs and she was probably doing them when she was pregnant." When cautioned about making such pronouncements without further investigation, she responded, "When you've been teaching as long as I have, you just know things like that. He won't sit still long enough to do his work. He won't keep his mind on what he's doing." When we sat down to talk in more depth, it was revealed that Corey did complete some work, but "not enough." When asked whether or not he had the prerequisite academic skills required to complete all the assigned tasks, the teachers responded that he was capable of grade-level work, so they felt strongly that the issue was one of will (a condition controlled by Corey) and not skill (a condition controlled by and easily manipulated within the learning environment).

I agreed to observe Corey several times in the classroom in order to get a better idea of what was occurring. During two observations, he completed all the work that he was assigned in a timely manner. However, I did see other students who were out of their seats and/or talking to peers about matters not related to schoolwork during this independent seatwork time. Yet the teachers did not refer these students. At no time did Corey's teachers praise him for being on-task and completing his work independently. As a matter of fact, his teachers did not address him in any manner. His presence was not acknowledged at all. Later I shared these observations with the teachers. They explained, "He's not usually like that. He was probably just doing that to impress you. He likes you for some reason." I explained that even if he was trying to "impress me," the fact was he was able to complete his assigned work and remain on-task during the entire fifty-minute period. When the teachers were asked if they were having difficulty with any other students in the class, they responded, "Not really, the rest we can pretty much handle. Corey's our main behavioral problem."

On the third occasion when I observed Corey, he was working in his reading group of ten students. The teacher immediately berated him for not sitting "pretzel style" like the other students, although he was sitting on the carpeted area with the other students. When Corey did not comply immediately he was asked to go get a regular chair and bring it over to sit in because he could not "follow directions like the other students." Head and eyes lowered, Corey went to get his chair from his desk and bring it back to the group. He sat and began to fidget nervously with his fingers. His teacher looked up, "Corey, what are you doing?" She looked at me over the heads of the children seated before her and rolled her eyes and jerked her head toward Corey. "See what we were trying to tell you. He gets like this." Corey snaked down further in the seat as the other students in the reading group looked from me to Corey to the teacher, some also shaking their heads knowingly. "Please pay attention, Corey," she said. Obviously embarrassed, Corey began to fiddle with his shoelaces, untying them and twirling them between his fingers. Exasperated, his teacher looked up again, "Corey, if you can't sit still, you're going to have to leave the group and go back to your desk." As if on cue, and not unexpectedly, Corey's activity level increased. Although he never actually left his seat, he nevertheless managed to twirl his body into every conceivable contortion. His teacher looked up again and with a look of total frustration, closed her reading book and stopped the lesson. She walked over to Corey's chair and, with him in it, physically pushed it back to his desk. "You'll just have to sit by yourself until you can learn to sit quietly with the group."

Throughout this exchange other students in the reading group whispered and snickered. Others, distracted by the events, began to fidget also. Their actions went unnoticed. My heart broke for Corey. No wonder he felt he was stupid, and I could see why he felt it was because of his race. Other students were engaging in the exact same behaviors but were not reprimanded or isolated from the others. They fidgeted and talked when they weren't supposed to, but were still allowed to participate with the group. This observation was confirmed later when during a period of independent seatwork, many students were observed talking and getting out of their seats, yet only Corey and his tablemate David were singled out for inappropriate behavior.

Ironically, the thematic unit that the class was studying during the time of my interaction with Corey was the civil rights movement, particularly focusing on the Montgomery bus boycott and the roles of Rosa Parks and Dr. Martin Luther King, Jr. How was it possible to teach about equal rights and opportunities for all individuals regardless of race, ethnicity, gender, or economic status, and yet treat a student with such insensitivity that he had come to believe that he was stupid because he was black? Where was the knowledge construction process that Banks (1993) was writing about? Corey was learning how unexamined assumptions, dominant perspectives, and fundamental attribution errors disempower and imprison him instead of freeing him to understand more about himself and others.

Around this time, Corey's situation in the class worsened. He had begun to come late to school quite frequently. "I knew this would happen," his regular education teacher lamented, "He's not getting the help he needs, so he's not coming to school. He'll probably be a dropout." I was lamenting too. Where was Corey? He had never had a problem with his attendance before and was usually on time for school. The special educator in the classroom whispered to me conspiratorially one day, "You know his mom got put in jail again. I hope he's not using her as an example." When I talked to Corey I discovered that he had been hiding out at the side of school for several days, terrified to enter the building. He was reluctant to state the reason, but after a tension-filled hour of discussion, he revealed nervously that some fifth-grade boys were cornering him in the morning, throwing rocks at him, and calling him a "nigger." I was shocked and appalled.

I thought back to an incident with a parent of one of the students at school. The mother of the first-grade boy had come to our scheduled parent conference intoxicated. At one point in our conversation about her son's academic performance, she leaned over and abruptly changed the conversation. "You know it bothers some of the parents that you're black. They don't like Blacks much around here. That's why they don't like for the kids to go to Sage (the neighborhood high school which was predominantly African American). They say the kids up there is too street and always jump the white kids, but I don't blame you for that. That's not your fault. Just like slavery wasn't my fault."

Thrown off guard by this unexpected turn in events, I deftly turned the conversation back to the issue at hand. But I thought about that conversation later that night and long after that. Although I knew I was not what individuals from the community typically pictured when they thought of school psychologists (who in our district, as in many others, were mostly white females), I nevertheless didn't realize that others were so blatantly disturbed by my presence. After all, we weren't in a rural area with few opportunities for interactions with individuals from other cultures; we were in a major metropolitan city that was *predominately* African American. I expected individuals to have biases, limited awareness of other cultures, and some prejudices, but I never imagined that they might be expressed so overtly. I knew just how Corey must be feeling. I wasn't sure if others did, however, or if they cared.

I discussed Corey's dilemma involving racial epithets and taunts with the principal and asked that the situation be addressed. His solution was to make a general announcement to the student body that afternoon on the public address system, reminding them that "name calling" was not "effective for solving problems." I threw up my hands in frustration. Another opportunity for learning was bypassed in the name of convenience and personal comfort. How could we ever begin to challenge the biased norms and eliminate the cultural intolerance in the building?

When the reason for Corey's absences was shared with his teachers, they explained that they understood, but asked me to stress to Corey the importance of getting to school on time. My anger and disappointment with the situation were mounting. It was clear from what I had observed in connection with Corey in particular and in our school's culture in general that regardless of the information and assurances given to students and staff about multicultural education and diversity, cultural intolerance and differential treatment based on race, ethnicity, religion, gender, and racial bigotry were acceptable in interactions with other staff and students. Contributing to my feelings of isolation was the fact that I knew that this situation, like many others, did not go unnoticed. Others saw these same events occurring but chose to do nothing. As Lipman (1997) reminds us, "efforts for school change, and the participation and collaboration of teachers, occur in contexts neither neutral nor insulated from larger social forces" (p. 5).

I knew things would come to a head soon, very soon. The inevitable happened in one of the weekly Admission, Review, and Dismissal (ARD) team meetings held to assess the status of special education students. This was not a meeting held to discuss Corey, who was a regular education student. Nevertheless, it became a forum for expressing much of the simmering feelings regarding not just Corey, but the interaction between the teachers and myself.

Corey's teachers had referred a student for special education, and so both students were discussed at the meeting. Ironically, the student referred was David, Corey's tablemate. Having had the opportunity to observe David on numerous occasions when I was in the classroom, I felt confident that his difficulty originated from an instructional mismatch rather than from a disability. Reviewing his records and work samples confirmed this for me. In the meeting, I explained that while I had seen David struggle with his academic tasks and realized that he needed some intervention, I did not suspect that he had a learning disability. I suggested that we schedule a meeting to discuss the situation further and develop some appropriate instructional strategies. "But we've already tried everything. There's something wrong with him," the special educator said. Distressed, the regular educator turned to David's mother, who was also present at the meeting. "Look Ms. Rose, we know there is something wrong with your son, and you do too, but you're going to have to get a lawyer if you want him to get any help at this school." "Yeah," added the special education teacher, "they," she glanced quickly at me, "only like to help certain kids at this school."

Clenching my teeth tightly, I turned to the parent. "Ms. Rose, you certainly have the right at any time to do what you feel is best for your son. I'm just sharing my professional opinion that there is not enough evidence that your son has a learning disability or any disability that requires special education." The regular educator turned again to Ms. Rose; "I go home at night sometimes and cry about your son. I feel so bad for him," she sniffed tearfully, "I just know he needs more help than we could give him. Don't let anyone else tell you otherwise." A bitter bile rose high in my throat as I burned from my anger. It was clear to me that neither of these teachers trusted my professional opinion or me as a professional. All the work that we had completed together in the previous weeks with Corey meant little to them in terms of questioning and challenging their attitudes, instruction, and behavior toward the students in their class. Fuming, I remained silent for the remainder of the meeting. After the parent left, the regular educator threw one last glance my way. As she rose to leave, she said over her shoulder, "I got it figured out now. You only want to help the black kids." I walked to my office, in as carefully controlled a manner as possible, shut the door, and screamed.

Later, another member of the ARD team, who was present at the interaction, gave me her take. "Maybe she shouldn't have said some of the things she did, but don't take it personal. You shouldn't take things too personally around here." Then it occurred to me, she was right. I was taking things too personally. "I guess I do," I replied, "I certainly take bias, prejudice, and bigotry very personally. If I didn't, I couldn't walk in this building everyday and stay here for eight hours knowing that when I leave things will probably remain the same." An equity pedagogy (Banks & Banks, 1993) did not exist in our school. What I was beginning to realize was that one would never exist with the prevailing attitudes. Diversity was not acknowledged, so there was no need to change instructional style to meet the needs of something that did not exist.

After the incident at the ARD meeting, the rest of my interaction with Corey was anticlimactic. His teachers became "too busy" to dialogue about his progress. He was doing fine, they assured me, and since other students were starting to have difficulties, they found they did not need to spend as much time with him. At about this same time, however, I noticed that when I passed by the office, Corey would often be seated in the area designated for acting out students. He was effectively "timed out" from learning and participating in the mainstream culture. Had we both become cultural prisoners? Could Corey's teachers and I patch things up and continue to work with him to help him reach his academic potential? Should we? How would Corey's perception of himself as a powerless individual controlled by his environment ever change if we, the adults in the building, could not?

Sadly, Corey's teachers and I never reconciled our differences. Life at the school progressed as it always had. I found myself becoming skeptical that things would ever change, that others would ever question why things were the way they were. Would we ever have an opportunity as a school to experience ourselves as the empowered culture and social structure that Banks (1995) described? Time has put some distance between this incident and the present, but it continues to live with me, taunting me, challenging me. Where did I, we, go wrong? How could we have made it right?

IMPLICATIONS AND UNRESOLVED QUESTIONS

This situation with Corey raises several compelling questions. For example, what is the professional responsibility of educators—including school administrators and regular and special education teachers—to challenge social and racial inequities and personal and institutional structures of bias? Don't educators have a professional responsibility to examine their own assumptions, values, and beliefs about racial identity, gender, religion, and sexual orientation? How should educators deal with fellow professionals who exhibit racial intolerance? How will children learn to deal with racial and cultural conflict in an environment that does not honor and value alternative perspectives? How will children like Corey, racially isolated and vilified, cope within a system that so clearly misunderstands their experience? What will Corey learn about being a young African American male in a racially diverse society if the socially sanctioned authority figures in the school do not take action to critically examine their own belief systems and faulty attributions? Isn't it our challenge as professionals to find ways to create educational environments that are psychologically safe, just, and empowering?

Clearly, Corey's teachers had difficulty negotiating differences in the school environment, whether those differences were racial, ethnic, economic, or educational. And clearly, I had my own beliefs, prior history, and past experiences, which influenced my actions and which at some point became so rigid that, regardless of intent, it became impossible for me to work effectively with others. The path that I had originally perceived as linear turned out to be a circular one. When I came full circle, I realized that I too had difficulty negotiating difference within the school. I realized that my own philosophical beliefs about the nature of difference—race and racial differences—contrasted sharply with those held by many of the parents, teachers, and administrators in the school. Those different beliefs seemed to fuel separate realities for us, and as we became entrenched in our beliefs, the philosophical division seemed impossible for us to cross.

What could we have done differently? I often ask myself that question. Initially, I felt that what had been missing was open and honest dialogue about cultural beliefs, values, and expectations. However, now I believe that some important foundation work had not been laid. For example, I'm not even sure that the staff and parents saw a need for multicultural education at any level. Nestled in the neighborhood's cultural enclave, most residents stayed out of economic necessity or personal choice. Many residents had lived there for generations. Despite the city's growth and expansion, the community had remained virtually untouched by technological demands and changing social norms. In short, most community members liked the way things were and depended, in part, on the school to keep things that way.

Many of the staff felt similarly. I vividly remember asking about neighborhoods when I first began working at the school. At the time, my husband and I were thinking of buying a house and wanted to know more about different neighborhoods and communities in the area. After driving in one day, I remarked to a staff member that I had seen a beautiful house for sale in one of the neighborhoods. When I described the area, she remarked, "That's my neighborhood." Later that day, she pulled me aside and stammered nervously, "I need to warn you. They don't like black people in my neighborhood. It doesn't matter to me, but I just need to let you know." Most staff members had not grown up in the community, although about fifty percent of the school's teachers had taught there for fifteen years or longer, making them community members by proxy. Indeed, the school's master teacher, who had taught at the school for twenty-nine years, once told me that she firmly believed that the school's high test scores were attributable to the lack of "outsiders." There was no need to teach students to be tolerant of others because the expectation was that they wouldn't have to be. Many of the staff lived in homogeneous areas and were not accustomed to interacting with individuals from diverse backgrounds. They lived and worked in racially and ethnically homogeneous environments where their ability to interact with others from diverse backgrounds was rarely challenged.

I often think of Corey and his future. I can still see him as he was on the last day of school, proudly marching into closing exercises, and afterward coming over to give me a quick hug before rushing off to a leisurely summer. He survived that year, but what about the next? I survived that year, also, but chose not to return. Corey did not have that choice. I often wonder what he returned to and how he was subsequently shaped by those elementary school experiences. How was his worldview molded and how did it impact on how he interacted with others as he grew and developed?

REFERENCES

Apple, M. (1990). *Ideology and curriculum.* (2nd ed.) New York: Routledge.

Banks, J. A. (1996). Multicultural education and curriculum transformation. *Journal of Negro Education, 64,* 390–399.

———. (1993). Multicultural education: Characteristics and goals. In J. A. Banks & C. A. M. Banks (Eds.) *Multicultural education: Issues and perspectives* (2nd ed.) (pp. 3–28). Boston: Allyn & Bacon.

Banks, J. A., & Banks, C.A.M. (1993). *Multicultural education: Issues and perspectives* (2nd ed.) Boston: Allyn & Bacon.

Beckum, L. C., & Zimney, A. (1991). School culture in multicultural settings. In N. B. Wyner (Ed.), *Current perspectives on the culture of schools.* Brookline, MA: Brookline Books.

Hoffman, D. (1996). Culture and self in multicultural education: Reflections on discourse, text, and practice. *American Educational Research Journal, 33,* 545–569.

Lipman, P. (1997). Restructuring in context: A case study of teacher participation and the dynamics of ideology, race, and power. *American Educational Research Journal, 34,* 3–37.

Marsh, H. (1993). The multidimensional structure of academic self-concept invariance over gender and age. *American Education Research Journal, 30,* 841–860.

O'Loughlin, M. (1995). Daring the imagination: Unlocking the voices of dissent and possibility in teaching. *Theory into Practice, 34,* 107–116.

2

Redefining School Culture: Creating New Traditions for Bicultural Students

Vernita Zubia and Beth Doll

Schools play an essential role in introducing culturally diverse students to the dominant culture of their communities (Commins, 1992; Moll, 1991; Pastor, McCormick & Fine, 1996; Rotheram-Borus, Dopkins, Sabate & Lightfoot, 1996; Suarez-Orozco, 1991; Trueba, 1987). Optimal cultural introductions can enrich bicultural students' learning, language, and problem-solving opportunities; allow them to understand and engage in effective social interactions in both the dominant culture and their family culture; and enhance their opportunities for life success. Unsuccessful cultural introductions may inculcate stereotypical limitations by restricting students' internalized perspectives of their opportunities for success in the dominant culture. The appropriate balance between family culture and the dominant culture will be unique for each student, reflecting the events that shaped the student's introduction to the United States and the unique juxtaposition of home and community values that permits him or her to feel successful, respected, and comfortable in both cultures. (Rotheram-Borus, 1993; Waters, 1996).

This chapter discusses contextual features of schools that promote successful bicultural adaptation in students. We present the case of a culturally diverse middle school with a dual immersion bilingual program that seeks to alter the traditional cross-cultural interactions that occur within it. Descriptions of two Spanish-speaking students enrolled in the middle school are illustrative of a student who has evolved an effective bicultural identity and a second student who struggles to negotiate his identity. Particular attention is paid to school and classroom features that do and do not support these students' biculturalism. Finally, this case example raises questions about the degree to which schools can act independently of the community to support bicultural students sufficiently.

GUIDING THEORETICAL PERSPECTIVES

The premise of this chapter, and of the middle school that it describes, is that successful cultural introductions must attend simultaneously to the social, linguistic, and sociopolitical experiences of Spanish-speaking students and their families. The school's model has much in common with James Banks' (1999) Dimensions of Multicultural Education. In particular, the middle school drew upon the work of Lev Vygotsky (1962) to address Bank's Content Integration and Knowledge Construction dimensions. They drew upon the work of Erik Erikson (1968) to articulate the School Culture and Social Structure dimension. Finally, they drew upon the work of John Ogbu (1995) to design an equity pedagogy and address prejudice within the system.

Socially, middle school students are actively synthesizing their personal identities out of their childhood aspirations and the roles made available to them within their families and communities (Erikson, 1968). Thus, the community including the school is responsible for appropriating the attention, status, and high expectations that nurture *success identities* for students and that inspire students to explore multiple, challenging role options. Tension and conflict between cultural groups can create diametrical choices that require bicultural students to become either strongly ethnically defined or strongly defined by the dominant culture. However, schools ought to model bicultural roles that can be simultaneously valued by both the students' families and the dominant cultural community.

Just as important for bilingual students, the language experiences provided to students by families, schools, and communities are the raw materials that shape the students' intellectual potential. Contexts that constrain or enrich students' language experiences can limit or expand their capacity to use language effectively as an intellectual tool (Vygotsky, 1962). Moreover, the structural patterns of students' language come to represent the basic organization of their thought and reasoning. Thus, schools and communities must support the acquisition of English as a second language in ways that preserve the complexity of students' language patterns and extend their opportunities to use their language actively in intellectually constructive ways.

Students' school success must also be examined as products of the economic and political histories of their families (Ogbu, 1978, 1987, 1995). Where families have experienced rewards, prestige, and opportunities for behaving in school-compatible ways, students are likely to act consistently with these behaviors. Conversely, ways of behaving that have not benefited the students' families in the past are unlikely to be performed by students and may come to represent points of conflict between students and the school. Ogbu describes important features of this process for involuntary immigrants who arrive in the United States out of political or economic necessity and often struggle against unflattering stereotypes and social subordination. There may be major discrepancies between these families' expectations for success and those of the school, requiring that their children adjust their social identity in order to achieve academically. Ogbu suggests that the ways in which community and school inequities are addressed can lead students of involuntary immigrant families to see either equitable opportunities, creating incentives for them to stay engaged in school, or unfairly restricted opportunities, causing them to become resistant to school achievement.

As involuntary immigrants, the Spanish-speaking students in this middle school were negotiating bicultural identities against a backdrop of language differences, social role restrictions, and historical inequities. The middle school attempted to facilitate their acquisition of secure bicultural identities by identifying and modeling roles that were simultaneously valued within both dominant and family cultures, by providing language experiences that promoted intellectual sophistication in both primary and secondary languages, and by recognizing and addressing inequities in the school and even in the community.

CASE STUDY: THE MIDDLE SCHOOL

The middle school enrolls children from a neighborhood that includes subsidized housing, university student housing, and upscale private housing. The university student housing contributes international families who enroll their children in the public schools during the parents' studies at the community's nationally respected university. These children arrive in U.S. schools having received prior English language instruction and generally good academic preparation. The subsidized housing contributes involuntary immigrant families from rural Mexico and other Central American nations. These families value the skills needed for success in agrarian communities, skills that are very different from those needed for school and work in this country.

The area of subsidized housing is the part of the neighborhood where Luis and Antonio (pseudonyms) reside; they describe it as a "tough place." As one of them noted, "We even have our own police station." Both of their families, who belong to the involuntary immigrant community, identified drugs and violence as prevalent in their neighborhood, but they are left with few housing options. The average rent for private residences in the neighborhood often exceeds an immigrant family's total monthly income.

Despite the school's diversity, Antonio and Luis report very low levels of ethnic tension. Although a visitor to the school would notice more solidarity among children who share a common linguistic or ethnic background, cross-cultural friendships are not unusual. Membership in peer groups is situational and changes depending on the activity.

The middle school offers a dual-language immersion bilingual program that promotes simultaneous academic literacy in English and Spanish. At each grade level, a bilingual team enrolls a balanced mix of native Spanish speakers and native English speakers as students. Consequently, all students simultaneously can model their native language on that of other second-language learners and have native language models in their second language. All academic classes are conducted in one language or the other but never in both, and students take the core academic classes in either language. Teachers and students are encouraged to stay in the language of instruction for each class without relying on translation or repetition of content. Additional support is provided through second-language instruction, thematic teaching, and homework assistance. Ideally, the bilingual program provides initial literacy instruction in the primary grades and progressively introduces literacy and content instruction in the second language as the students move through elementary school. In practice, as the only middle school in the neighborhood providing bilingual programming, students enter the program at all grades with varying levels of skill in their native and second languages. (For further reading regarding programming for dual language learners, see Miramontes, 1993; Miramontes, Nadeau, & Commins, 1997.)

The middle school has been less successful in fostering social integration among the students' families. Two separate parent leadership groups have been formed: the English-speaking Site-based Improvement Team (SIT) and the Spanish-speaking Latino Parents Group. Initial efforts to have Spanish-speaking parents participate in the Site Improvement Team (SIT) were not successful. Originally, the SIT meetings were conducted in English with Spanish-speaking translators, but the Spanish-speaking parents were left on the periphery of the SIT discussions and decision making. More important, the Spanish-speaking parents were uncomfortable with the assertive manner with which English-speaking parents made demands on the school. Subsequently, the Latino Parents Group was started, facilitated by a Mexican American mother employed by the school as a parent liaison. That group shared strategies for raising a family in the United States without the supportive network of relatives and friends customary in their countries of origin, and sought ways to support their children as they reconciled family and school expectations. Still, the separation of these two parent groups exacerbated rather than diminished the social barriers between the Spanish-speaking and the English-speaking school communities.

Antonio

Twelve-year-old Antonio is a soft-spoken, confident seventh grader in
the middle school. His bronze skin and dark shimmering eyes accentuate
his Mexican heritage. Antonio immigrated to the United States with his
family when he was four years old. The family had moved from rural
Mexico, where long days in the field paid off when rains were plentiful
but did not when droughts dried up the crops. They reluctantly left
behind their close, extended family so that their children might have a
better life in the United States.

Antonio is the second oldest in the family, with an older brother and
two younger sisters. He proudly talks about his parents' respected positions. "My father is a chef in a really nice restaurant. A lot of people
here know him. My mother takes care of children in our home"—work
to which Antonio respectfully refers as *"como una maestra"* (just like a
teacher). He spends most of his time at home being the *hermano mayor*
(big brother), a caretaker and a model for his younger sisters. "I like to
read them books, take them to the park to play, and fix them something
to eat. Sometimes I even have to talk to them at night when they are
scared." Because they worry about the neighborhood, Antonio's parents
have encouraged his involvement in organized community sports, and
he has become extremely competitive in soccer, basketball, and football.
He also attends supervised "teen nights" at the community's recreation
center.

Antonio's best friend of six years is a white student, with whom he
shares such common interests as fishing and football. They spend most
of their time together at his friend's house. "I help him in Spanish class
because he is just learning Spanish, but he helps me out sometimes in
English class too." This special friendship also brings together other students in the school. "At school, my other Mexican friends and his friends
sometimes hang out all together. It's easy for all of us because most of
us can speak Spanish and English, so we get along good."

His good-natured manner contributes to Antonio's positive relationships with teachers and peers. "I get along good with my teachers because I don't get in trouble and I do what I'm supposed to do." Enrolled
in the dual immersion bilingual program since kindergarten, Antonio
received primary literacy instruction in Spanish through second grade
and began learning more English in the second and third grades. By sixth
grade, he was reading, writing, and speaking above grade level in both
Spanish and English. His social and academic skills have earned Antonio
considerable recognition. His awards in sixth grade include an *Aprove-
chamiento Award* (Achievement Award) given to students who distinguish themselves in both English and Spanish classes. Antonio was

elected to be the student government representative in seventh grade and served on the interview committee to hire a new assistant principal.

Antonio's mother is a core member of the Latino Parents Group and a consistent participant in school activities. "I think it is important for me to go to the meetings and programs at school. Sometimes I have to take the bus to school, and then I ask one of the teachers to give me a ride home. I do what I can to show Antonio that school is very important." Still, the family's story is not without its adversities. Antonio's sixteen-year-old brother has had trouble with the law, was retained one grade, dropped out of school, and is the father of a one-year-old child. The girlfriend and baby currently live with Antonio's family.

Luis

Luis is a fifteen-year-old eighth grader at the middle school. His stocky stature and bold, dark features resemble those of his noble Mayan ancestors of Guatemala. Luis is the third of five children in his family, with older sisters and younger brothers. His sisters describe him as *el genio* (the genius) and add, "Ever since he was little, he would be taking things apart just to see how they worked. He always has to be doing something." Luis' oldest sister is majoring in Computer Studies at a local university, while his second sister recently graduated from high school. Luis describes his favorite family activity: "Most of all, I love playing with my little brothers. I take them out to play so they don't get tired of being in the house." When Luis turned fifteen, his parents quit their primary jobs and began to depend on him and his two sisters to work. Luis explained, "Since they have always taken care of us, it is time that we take care of them now." Although his parents work at occasional jobs (cleaning, factory work, and general labor), the children's earnings pay the rent and the car payment.

Luis was eight years old when his mother immigrated to the United States and was eleven years old when he moved with the rest of his family to join her. Guatemala was then in the throes of a civil war and Luis describes at least one incident in which he was held at gunpoint by military forces. Luis was left with anxious feelings related to his traumatic war and immigration experiences, for which he has received services from a school-based mental health therapist. Now, four years later, his fear resurfaces in the form of overly nervous behavior, unfocused thinking, inattention, and discomfort speaking in class.

Luis' school success has been mixed. At eleven his limited English skills resulted in his being enrolled in the third grade, where he completed the year with peers three years younger than he. Luis attributes his rapid acquisition of English to a classmate who became his friend.

Luis was subsequently moved ahead to the middle school's sixth grade, based on his strong academic foundation in Spanish, his English fluency, and his age. To help him feel connected to the classroom, his sixth-grade teachers gave him preferential seating, validated his contributions to discussions, helped him monitor his attention level, and assigned him to work with other students in small groups. He remembers this as a strong year for him, during which he received good grades and completed an advanced math class. In seventh grade, his grades and attendance dropped immediately when his teachers stopped giving him the extra attention and stopped monitoring his interactions with peers. When his nervous behavior resurfaced in his advanced math class, he was subsequently transferred to a basic math class. "There were other kids in that class that were doing the same things that I was doing, but she would help them. With me, she just said that I don't think this is the right class for you and then I was taken out of her class and put in an easy math class."

Luis' experiences with both peers and teachers have frequently left him feeling alienated and unvalued. He could not name any students at school who were his friends. "I don't really have one person that is my friend. I guess I just try to get along with everybody." His nervous behavior and different dialect seemed awkward to the other students. "Sometimes the other students made fun of me because you know how my Spanish is different than Mexican Spanish. Most of the time I just speak English so they won't make fun of my Spanish." Luis' experience with the math class was only one example of mistreatment that he perceived as blatant racism. One exception was a teacher from Chile, who Luis admired after she defended his Guatemalan Spanish. "One day I said a word in class, and all of the kids in my group were making fun of me and saying that I didn't know how to speak Spanish. She heard them and came over and explained that I was using the right word and talked about how different countries that speak Spanish use different words for the same thing. You know, it wasn't really wrong how I said it, but the other kids didn't understand. Anyway I respected the teacher for sticking up for me."

Like Luis, his parents feel that the middle school is an unfriendly place, and they have sought out other resources in the community. His parents reported, "We tell our children that school is the most important way to achieving a better life in the United States." Despite several invitations, Luis' parents have not become involved in the Latino Parents Group because, they explain, "Well, we felt out of place. Everybody already knew each other, and they talk about different things that aren't important for us. We go to church instead where there are other families from Guatemala, and we talk to our children here at home about school." Luis has become a frequent visitor to his neighborhood learning center and is a member of his church youth group.

The middle school teachers, administrators, and families are seeking to create unique systems of support that will allow students like Luis and Antonio to negotiate successful and satisfying bicultural futures. Doing so will require that the school make fundamental changes to its bicultural operation and communication, and is complicated by the fact that, like Luis and Antonio, different students will need very different kinds of support. Moreover, the school's experiences to date have convinced the staff and parents that they cannot accomplish this task without concurrent support and broad changes in the larger school system and the community where its students live, work, and play. These challenges have raised new questions in the minds of the middle school staff and participating community members.

How Can the Middle School Facilitate Effective Bicultural Identities for Students?

The exploration of one's ethnic identity is an important component of the identity development process for bicultural adolescents. Many bicultural students express their ethnicity by forming a collective identity that unites their cultural group through shared ethnic symbols, music, art, and dress. Ogbu (1987) reminds us that minority students may use such a collective identity to resist the dominant society. Still, collective ethnic identities need not imply resistance to school and education. Schools that build trust among students, create cultural respect, and share cultural power can promote a collective ethnic identity that fosters academic achievement and minimizes ethnic tension (Matute-Bianchi, 1991).

While the middle school teachers view trust building as a primary contribution to identity formation, both Antonio and Luis illustrate the challenges they face in earning the trust of bicultural families. Antonio remembers all of his teachers as trustworthy: "I can't remember any teacher that I didn't trust. I've had all good teachers." In contrast, Luis felt that some of his teachers betrayed him: "Some teachers look at me and then they think that I'm probably not smart. It's hard for me to learn from teachers if they think I'm not smart. So I just wouldn't do anything." Luis is a critical observer of teachers' eye contact, tone of voice, and how they expectantly await responses to questions. These were subtle but powerful indicators that Luis used to decide whether the teacher recognized his competence (Moll, 1991). His advanced math teacher failed this test when he was transferred out of her class, and thereafter he lacked the trust needed to try another advanced math class. Luis' successful teachers found an important place for him in their classrooms, and he eventually became the student they knew he could be. When uncomfortable in his classes, Luis' anxious behavior increased and his attendance faltered.

Because identity formation is also a function of peer interactions (Erikson, 1968), the middle school teachers were careful to model respect for all students so that other students could internalize the behavior of the teacher toward their peers. They did this by arranging cross-cultural learning structures, seating native-language models with second-language learners, planning for students to work together on cooperative projects and rotating team roles. Such structures communicated implicit norms that all levels of language proficiency and dialects are acceptable and that everybody has value to contribute to a group. Antonio noticed these efforts when he explained, "I most of all like the way that teachers put me in groups to help other students in Spanish. It made me feel like my language was important and that I could help others. They sometimes tell the students when they ask for help, 'Go ask Antonio. He knows how to do that.' " Luis also noted, "It worked best for me when teachers put me with other students that they knew would work well with me. Sometimes if there were problems in working together, I would just leave the group and work by myself."

Collective identities are most potent if modeled by all school staff. For example, one bilingual teacher periodically gathered Spanish-speaking students to talk about being Mexican and being a good student. She inspired students to celebrate their bilingual literacy as an important way to take pride in their ethnic heritage and simultaneously demanded that students model the excellence that Mexican American students were capable of. Another teacher recognized students for their special talents in singing Mexican songs, reciting Spanish poetry, or drawing horses and other cultural symbols. Still, divisive attitudes sometimes interrupted the middle school's bicultural models. For example, one heated discussion occurred when the English-speaking teachers described feeling intimidated when students conversed in Spanish, worried that they might be talking about teachers or other students. The Spanish-speaking teachers reframed these situations as examples of the students' collective identity, and noted that the students' interdependence could be used to enhance cooperative learning. Finally, the Spanish-speaking teachers challenged the staff to consider how they would view groups of English-speaking students learning in Mexican schools. Would they worry that mutual group support would interrupt learning? Through these collegial discussions, the middle school teachers challenged each other's inherent biases and the impact those biases had on students.

The visibility of minority adults with professional positions is another important determinant of bicultural students' identities, as these perceptions color students' expectations of the social rewards available to them through education (Ogbu, 1978). The middle school worked to raise students' expectations by recruiting minority mentors, tutors, and classroom presenters to extend the students' bank of ethnic role models. Even so, Luis observed, "I don't see very many people in this town that are like me and have the kind of jobs that I want. I would like to know some [ethnic role models]; like, I want to be a lawyer but I don't know any Guatemalan lawyers." In this case, a mentorship project through the local university was created for Luis, who had difficulty making connections in school. By highlighting community models, the school could also help to expand his life visions to include professional career goals.

Bicultural adolescents need to explore their social identities as ethnic group members and as students (Erikson, 1968). A special challenge is to foster this dual identity without polarizing dominant and minority cultural groups into oppositional views of schooling (Ogbu, 1978).

How Can the Middle School Integrate the Language and Culture of Bicultural Students?

The middle school has come to understand that its commitment to a dual immersion bilingual program represents only a first step toward a fully inclusive learning environment for bicultural students (Banks, 1999). Students whose home culture differs markedly from the school and dominant community culture have distinctive life histories that must be confronted within daily interactions where verbal and nonverbal actions can inadvertently restrict language experiences, limit understanding, and convey stereotypical role expectations (Vygotsky, 1962). Thus, the school seeks to link its daily curriculum to the life experiences of bicultural students as well as those of students from the dominant culture.

Instructional activities provide the most obvious way for the school to link experiences of bicultural students with those of the dominant culture. For example, a social studies lesson on "Neighbors" prepared students to study relationships between neighboring countries. The lesson began with a local comparison of the needs of a community and the important services that create interdependent relationships among its members. The teacher highlighted Antonio's parents as important service providers in the neighborhood: a chef and a child care worker and also included other parents' roles. The resulting classroom discussion invoked the individual pride that all people have for their neighborhood. Linkages were also created through a poetry unit in which a teacher helped the students see how Luis' traumatic experiences had given him special insight into the potent feelings of fear, loss, sadness, and confusion.

Conducting important tasks of governance in both languages strengthens cultural linkages. Both Luis and Antonio participated in a Latino group in which they made suggestions for school changes and developed action plans to achieve those changes. For example, one early suggestion was to have a soccer team in the school. Through community service, the group earned city funds to purchase the uniforms and equipment. This activity created important opportunities for the students to solve a problem, depend on each other, and enjoy the results.

The middle school's efforts successfully reduced cultural barriers for Antonio as he grew increasingly comfortable within the dominant culture. In part, his trust for his teachers developed out of the history and ethnicity that he shared with the Spanish-speaking community. Conversely, the middle school failed to notice when their new traditions added new barriers for students like Luis who did not easily access either the Spanish-or English-speaking groups. In a bicultural school community, the linkages created must be transactional to acknowledge the strengths of all social subgroups.

How Can the Middle School Confront Discrimination and Social Stratification?

In sixth grade, Luis and Antonio both wrote personal essays on the question, "Why is it important to be bilingual?" This assignment was preceded by in-class discussions of articles presenting different perspectives on bilingual education. Several of the articles were quite racist while others celebrated the richness of a pluralistic country. Accustomed to hearing only the benefits of bilingual education, students were initially taken aback in the face of detractors' harsh words. However, the safety of the classroom allowed all students to consider how to react to acts of social discrimination. This and similar discussions established a common vocabulary about human rights, respect, dignity, oppression, discrimination, and racism.

For Luis, social discrimination was a very real and unfair part of his life. He recalled an incident at a restaurant in which he regretted not speaking up and advocating for himself: "I was waiting in line with my father at this fast-food restaurant. We had been waiting a long time and finally we were next. The salesclerk called several customers over from another line instead of waiting on us. I felt so angry and I wanted to say something, but my father told me, 'Let's just go,' and we never went back to that place. She was racist, is what it was. I wish she knew what that felt like." Luis added, "Yeah, things like that happen to me and my family every day—at school, the store, on the bus." It limited the way he was able to interact with other students and teachers, it cut at the family pride that his parents tried to maintain, and it caused him a great deal of internal distress.

Luis talked with his parents about discrimination and how to deal with it. His mother shared her own experiences: "I tell Luis about things that happen to me like: just the other day when I was in the grocery store and I took a number at the deli like you are supposed to do. I stood there waiting and then when my number came up, a lady just walked up and started to take a number and the man behind the counter just told her that he could help her. Well, I went up there and told him with my poor English that there is a process here and to be fair to everybody; that he needs to follow the process. I don't care if my English isn't good, but I tell my kids that you have to stand up for yourself." Luis understands the personal distress caused by social unfairness and has a personal goal to be a "good lawyer" who helps people defend their rights.

Classroom interactions provide teachable moments in which the teacher can show students how their own actions can promote social discrimination. For example, one middle school teacher noticed that all of the Spanish-speaking boys were together in the back of her classroom, all of the white boys were sitting in a group up front, and the girls were divided similarly. The teacher asked the students, "Look around and tell me what a guest speaker will think about how students in this school learn." From this concrete example, students were able to articulate that a visitor might think that students learn in separate ethnic, language, and gender groups; that there are real differences among these groups; and that some learners are either less interested or more interested than others. Then, they quickly rearranged themselves.

Another example occurred in Luis' sixth-grade music class. Several students told the music teacher that they did not speak English and so could not write a critical response to musical pieces in her class. Consequently, she had Spanish-speaking students color a picture while the other students wrote their critique. On learning of the incident, the bilingual teacher observed that most of the students were beautifully bilingual and all of them had sufficient English skills to do the assignment. She used a chart to show her class how the different groups of students had been affected. Some bicultural students were pleased because they got to do less work, but Luis and others were humiliated by having to color while other students in the class were writing. A negative consequence for all of the Latino students was that the others viewed them as being less capable. Further discussions examined how to deal with teachers' low expectations for students and the collective responsibility that ethnic group members have to each other.

To be truly successful in their bicultural identities, students must become self-advocates, transferring their academic and social skills to situations outside the protected environment of the school. To facilitate this, the middle school teachers connected pairs of students to a staff person at the beginning of sixth grade. Luis and Antonio were assigned to interview the staff members about their role in the school. The pairs of students then introduced these important people in the school to their classmates as resources to help with different problems and needs. Pictures of the students with the staff members and final copies of the students' reports were bound in a classroom resource book for student use. Through the interview process, students were provided with a supportive network within which to practice their self-advocacy skills.

The school provides an important place to address the fundamental issues of social discrimination and stratification. In part, this is because schools gather together the different social groups of students during their formative years, while they are still learning about interacting within a culturally diverse setting.

What Is Necessary to Foster Family-School Collaboration with Bicultural Families?

Both Luis' and Antonio's parents were educated and socialized in agrarian societies. Ways to survive as *trabajadores* or working class families in Mexico and Guatemala included having large supportive family networks, assigning jobs so that even children contributed to the household, and keeping children close to home. Even after these two families chose to move to the United States, their agrarian family survival strategies continued to shape their understanding of successful parenting and schooling (Suarez-Orozco, 1991; Valdez, 1996).

Simply applying the Spanish language to conventional U.S. pedagogy would have undermined the middle school's ability to provide bicultural students with what their parents believed to be a quality academic program. Instead, so that their teaching would be consistent with the Spanish-speaking parents' values about education (Erickson, 1987), middle school teachers had been selected because of their thorough understanding of teaching approaches familiar to Mexican schools. For example, when students carried home their daily learning in neat *cuadernos* (spiral notebooks), parents had familiar access to their children's learning. The use of direct instruction, guided reading, outline note taking, and dictation were meaningful evidence of learning for many Mexican parents.

Still, it would be a disservice if bicultural students were not also taught in ways that prepared them for learning opportunities outside of the bilingual program. Toward this end, Luis and Antonio also learned problem-solving approaches in which they inductively searched for information relevant to a problem, applied critical reading strategies in analyzing literature, utilized the writing process to create original literary pieces and defended their points of view through Socratic seminars. Without preparation, Spanish-speaking parents would have questioned the rigor of such exploratory learning experiences. So that parents could anticipate these different educational practices, the middle school provided the Latino Parents' Group with explanations of how these unfamiliar learning experiences could prepare their children for high school, university, future careers, and work.

For example, one middle school activity invited parents to compare the expectations their own parents had held for them with the goals they had for their children in the United States. A rich discussion took place when the parents saw how different their own adolescent goals had been and began to seek new information so that they could support their children's success in unfamiliar life tasks. Topics included: What classes and credits does my son/daughter need to be accepted in a university? What are the cultural issues that interfere with school success? How do I involve my son/daughter in setting limits and consequences for behavior? The strength of this collaborative activity was that parents selected the topics that they were ready to learn about and felt were most important.

Still, a comparison of Antonio's and Luis' families shows that not all Spanish-speaking families felt comfortable in the Latino Parents' Group. Antonio's mother became a core member of the Latino Parent meetings and was very effective in rallying other parents to participate, while Luis' mother did not feel this same affiliation. Not only did Antonio's mother have more in common with the predominantly Mexican families of the middle school, but she also had been building friendships with them since Antonio began school in kindergarten. In contrast, Luis had only been in the United States for four years and had only recently transferred to the middle school from a school that lacked Spanish-speaking resources. It is also possible that cultural animosity may had contributed to Luis' mother's alienation, as the family had suffered some unpleasant incidents with Mexican immigration authorities during their trip through Mexico to the United States. Consequently, while Antonio's mother received support from the school's Latino Parents' Group, Luis' mother sought out the support of other Guatemalan parents, who reinforced the parenting strategies that had been effective in their own country of origin.

In the course of dealing with immigrant families, the middle school had come to recognize that the parents' own cultural knowledge about good parenting could differ in important ways from the school's expectations. Luis' mother described her parental role: "I think it is my job to send my son to school ready to learn and well behaved. I tell him to respect his teachers." Unable to read the English letters and newsletters from Luis' previous school, she carefully organized the papers in a box just in case she needed them some day. The family's resources were too meagre to expect it to make donations to the school or to buy books at the monthly book sales. The school environment was too intimidating for Luis' mother to be a classroom volunteer. Yet, even on his worst day at school, her interest rejuvenated Luis and gave him the willpower to return the next day. Luis and Antonio's mothers beamed with pride when told, "*Ustedes estan haciendo un buen trabajo con sus ninos porque son respetuosos en la escuela y son bien educados.*" (You are doing a great job raising your children because they are respectful in school and they are well disciplined.) Luis' responsibility for financial support of his parents was a more challenging difference for the school to accept. This responsibility might have interfered with his school progress, but eventually he was helped to find a job at a university working with computers that permitted him to receive academic mentoring while still meeting his obligations. It is especially important to respect such cultural boundaries when involving parents in schools (Delgado-Gaitan, 1992).

It would be too simplistic to suggest that Antonio's family, clearly more accustomed to the middle school community, will ultimately prove more successful than that of Luis. In fact, while Antonio has had considerable success in school to date, his older brother left without completing high school. In contrast, Luis, for all of his social alienation, has two older sisters who are actively studying for professional careers at a local university. Where Antonio's parents had become actively engaged in the school's bicultural community, Luis' parents continue to demand a tight family unit and teach strongly ethnically defined standards. It is critical that the school's work with parents include a respect for both kinds of families.

How Can the Middle School Negotiate Equitable Access to Its Own Resources?

The most difficult challenge for schools is to develop a willingness to release control over resources to those students and families who have traditionally been disempowered. Access to such resources as quality teachers, advanced courses, technology, social opportunities, and allocation of school funds is often restricted despite the school's positive intentions. Still, such restrictions perpetuate the dependence of minority families on the dominant cultural group for management of important life decisions.

In a monolingual English program, second language learners are always in the "needing help" role. This leaves them dependent on native English speakers to make learning accessible and inadvertently reproduces the stratification of social groups. Luis felt "lucky" to have a friend that helped him to learn English when he was in an English-only school. He remembers, "If it wasn't for her, I would have never have learned English. To this day I don't know why she helped me, but I guess she felt sorry for me." On the other hand, Antonio's opportunities to be a leader and help teach English-speaking students in his Spanish classes balanced his need to seek help as a second-language learner in his English classes. This shared cultural competence shifted the power so that both language groups depended on each other.

At the middle school, the students, families, and teachers continued to struggle to overcome unequal access to social and material resources. In one instance, an incompetent teacher was left to teach a class for an entire school year. Most English-speaking students whose parents complained were transferred to other classes, but the Spanish-speaking students were left in the class despite continuous parent complaints from the Latino community. Clearly, the middle school needed to become more cognizant of such equity issues.

Small steps can be important in addressing barriers to shared access of school resources. In the middle school, one critical change was giving Spanish-speaking parents clearer explanations of their educational options for their children. The dual immersion bilingual program required written parental consent to enroll students. English-speaking parents made an informed decision to place their child in the program, but Spanish-speaking parents were often given consent forms to sign without a thorough explanation of the program and without knowing that they had other choices. When challenged by the bilingual staff, the process was changed to provide a native Spanish speaker to talk with all incoming Spanish-speaking parents and students and fully inform them of their options and rights in any program for a second-language student.

The implicit codes and rules in schools are evidence of a "culture of power" (Delpit, 1988). Luis' and Antonio's families lacked sufficient understanding of the system, which handicapped their access to resources because they were not part of the dominant group. The middle school worked to teach minority families about the "keys to the system" that would enable them to share in the resources available in schools and communities.

SUMMARY

Antonio's and Luis' personal stories provide examples of the many ways that the middle school challenged traditional school structures to promote healthier learning communities and maximize the potential of each bicultural student. The case study describes the middle school's attempt to put into practice the theoretical framework that it used to understand bicultural education: Vygotsky's recommendation to infuse language into learning within the social and instructional interactions in school; Erikson's demand to attend to the bicultural identity that schools create and model for the student; and Ogbu's invitation to challenge student expectations for their futures and attend to the community context within which learning occurs. Redefining school culture in this way can create new school traditions that intentionally prepare bicultural students to live in a pluralistic society. The case study shows how the same program was received differently by Antonio, for whom it was highly successful, and by Luis, who presented greater challenges for the staff. Finally, the case study also provides several examples of where the middle school's efforts came up short, typically because they overlooked some cultural factor that was important to Antonio and Luis and to their families. The critical point is that the middle school noticed, reflected, regrouped, and revised its approach to be more responsive. Creating effective schools for bicultural communities is a constantly changing endeavor constructed in concert with its community, a connection that is clearly called for in order to change school and community structures that have traditionally burdened the bicultural student.

REFERENCES

Banks, J. A. (1999). *An introduction to multicultural education* (2nd ed.). Boston: Allyn & Bacon.

Commins, N. L. (1992). Parents and public schools: The experiences of four Mexican immigrant families. *Equity and Choice, 8,* 40–45.

Delgado-Gaitan, E. (1992). School matters in the Mexican-American home. *American Educational Research Journal, 29,* 495–513.

Delpit, L. D. (1988). The silenced dialogue: Power and pedagogy in educating other people's children. *Harvard Educational Review, 58,* 280–298.

Erickson, E. H. (1968). *Identity: Youth and crisis.* New York: Norton.

Erickson, F. (1987). Transformation and school success: The politics and culture of education and achievement. *Anthropology & Education Quarterly, 18,* 335–356.

Matute-Bianchi, M. E. (1991). Situational patterns of school performance among immigrant and nonimmigrant Mexican-descent students. In M. A. Gibson & J. U. Ogbu (Eds.), *Minority status and schooling: A comparative study of immigrant and involuntary minorities* (pp. 205–248). New York: Garland Publishing.

Miramontes, O. B. (1993). ESL policies and school restructuring: Risks and opportunities for language minority students. *Journal of Education Issues of Language Minority Students, 12,* 77–96.

Miramontes, O. B., Nadeau, A., & Commins, N. L. (1996). *Restructuring schools for linguistic diversity: Linking decision making to effective programs.* New York: Teachers College Press.

Moll, L. C. (1991). Social and instructional issues in literacy instruction for "disadvantaged" students. In M. S. Knapp and P. M. Shields (Eds.), *Better schooling for the children of poverty: Alternatives to conventional wisdom* (pp. 61–84). Berkley, CA: McCutchan Publishing.

Ogbu, J. U. (1978). *Minority education and caste: The American system in cross-cultural perspective.* New York: Harcourt Brace Jovanovich.

———. (1987). Variability in minority school performance: A problem in search of an explanation. *Anthropology & Education Quarterly, 18*, 312–334.

———. (1995). Understanding cultural adversity and learning. In Banks, J. A. & C. A. McGee-Banks (Eds.), *Handbook of research on multicultural education* (pp. 582–595). New York: Macmillan.

Pastor, J., McCormick, J., & Fine, M. (1996). Makin' homes: An urban girl thing. In B. J. Ross-Leadbeater & N. Way (Eds.). *Urban girls: Resisting stereotypes, creating identities* (pp. 15–34). New York: New York University Press.

Rotheram-Borus, M. J. (1993). Biculturalism among adolescents. In M. E. Bernal & G. P. Knight (Eds.), *Ethnic identity: Formation and transmission among Hispanics and other minorities* (pp. 81–104). Albany: State University of New York Press.

Rotheram-Borus, M. J., Dopkins, S., Sabate, N., & Lightfoot, M. (1996). Personal and ethnic identity, values and self-esteem among black and Latino adolescent girls. In B. J. Ross-Leadbeater & N. Way (Eds.), *Urban girls: Resisting stereotypes, creating identities.* (pp. 35–52). New York: New York University Press.

Suarez-Orozco, M. (1991). Immigrant adaptation to schooling: A Hispanic case. In M. A. Gibson & J. U. Ogbu (Eds.), *Minority status and schooling: A comparative study of immigrant and involuntary minorities* (pp. 37–62). New York: Garland Publishing.

Trueba, H. T. (1987). *Raising silent voices: Educating the linguistic minorities for the 21st century.* New York: Newbury House.

Valdez, G. (1996). *Con respeto: Bridging the distances between culturally diverse families and schools: An ethnographic portrait.* New York: Teachers College Press.

Vygotsky, L. S. (1962). *Thought and language.* Cambridge: MIT Press.

Waters, M. C. (1996). The intersection of gender, race, and ethnicity in identity development of Caribbean American teens. In B. J. Ross-Leadbeater & N. Way (Eds.), *Urban girls: Resisting stereotypes, creating identities* (pp. 65–81). New York: New York University Press.

3

Issues of Class and Race in Education: A Personal Narrative

Cheryl C. Holcomb-McCoy

> When we, as educators, allow our pedagogy to be radically changed
> by our recognition of a multicultural world, we can give students
> the education they desire and deserve.
>
> —bell hooks (1994)

Historically, education has been viewed as an instrument not only for personal development but also for social equality. Most American parents believe that the outcome of twelve years of public education is an accumulation of the knowledge and skills needed for responsibility in the workplace or for undertaking postsecondary educational training (Winters, 1993). This perception is misleading, however. Equal access to education for all children does not exist in the United States, and children of different social classes continue to attend different types of schools, to receive different types of instruction, and to study different curricula (Persell, 1989). Students from low-income and minority backgrounds, who tend to live in urban and rural areas, frequently attend schools with fewer resources and inadequate facilities. In his poignant book *Savage Inequities*, Jonathan Kozol (1991) noted that urban schools in low-income neighborhoods are not only overcrowded and less well-funded than other schools, but they are also disproportionately staffed by inexperienced and unprepared teachers. Indeed, these vast discrepancies between schools reinforce racial and class gaps in achievement and inhibit progress toward social equality.

While the inequities between poor children's schools and affluent children's schools persist, attaining an education has been cited as a precondition for upward mobility in our society. According to Linda Darling-Hammond (1998), "those who do not succeed in school are becoming part of a growing underclass, cut off from productive engagement in society." Most new jobs require formal education, including specific certifications and degrees. It is this power of credentialing that affords educational institutions a preeminent responsibility for dismantling ethnic and social class divisions. For some time, public schools have shaped and determined access to certain programs that, in turn, provide preparation for particular jobs and occupations. It has been well documented that student performance on college admissions tests has served as a barrier for ethnic minority and low-income students when they apply to colleges and universities. Cardine Persell (1989) purports that assessment instruments tend to discriminate against ethnic minorities and are "tools for sorting students into unequal categories." It appears, therefore, that schools have served or can serve as "gatekeepers" to economic as well as academic achievement.

While multicultural education has traditionally promoted cultural diversity and the modification of curriculum to include cultural issues, it is important for us, as educators, to revisit and discuss the way in which social class and racial inequalities influence student outcomes. More than two decades ago Samuel Bowles and Herbert Gintis (1976) suggested that schools reproduce the class and racial structures of the community by encouraging the distribution of ownership, dominance, and subordination among the various groups in the working population—men and women, Blacks and Whites, white-collar and blue-collar workers, immigrant and nonimmigrant. According to Bowles and Gintis, "students learn attitudes and modes of behavior suited to that level in the production process that they will ultimately occupy." They argued that educational messages are differentially distributed in schools based on students' racial and class background. For instance, blacks and other oppressed groups often attend schools where coercive authority structures persist and attention to following the instructions of others is emphasized. In contrast, White and affluent children generally attend schools where student participation is favored and students are encouraged to take initiative and to be independent in their decision making. It is this difference in educational messages, argue Bowles and Gintis, that creates a reproduction of the class and racial stratifications of our society.

Unlike Bowles and Gintis, who focus on the role of schools in the maintenance of class and racial inequities, John Ogbu (1988) holds that the inferior status of African Americans and many other minorities is permanently determined at birth by skin color and/or racial group membership. He argues that African Americans with equal educational status and income will still receive fewer rewards because of the discrimination against their ethnic group. The basis of his argument lies in the individual's racial background and ethnic identity development. Minority students, according to Ogbu, develop an oppositional identity that contributes to their lack of achievement in school.

Another perspective, voiced by Julius Wilson (1978), contends that African Americans' and other ethnic minority groups' opportunities and successes have more to do with class position than race. Wilson points out that poverty is at the core of most school failures, while access to higher paying jobs is increasingly based on education. He adds that the increased social mobility of ethnic minorities has increased their class consciousness and decreased their race consciousness.

My own perspective is that race and class interact and are both determinants of social inequality. The narrative in this chapter highlights this perspective and focuses on my experiences as a middle-class, black, first-year teacher in a predominately working-class minority school in a suburb of Washington, D.C. Although I currently teach graduate students, I can easily recollect the emotions and events of my first year as a kindergarten teacher. The year was a turning point not only in my career but also in my own racial identity development. My thoughts and beliefs as to what it means to be a black woman and a black teacher were intensified and challenged during this year.

My position regarding the effect of race and class in the U.S. public educational system builds on four claims: First, I am convinced that faulty beliefs held by educators about minority and poor students are damaging to student educational outcomes and access to opportunities. While this is not a new concept, it is highly relevant and significant to my narrative. Second, I argue that certain practices and programs implemented in American schools encourage and maintain our social class and racial structure. It is uncertain whether educators intentionally or unintentionally promote class stratification through special programming (e.g., programs for the gifted and talented). My argument, however, is that multicultural educators must explore the extent to which special programs promote class and racial divisions and determine how these programs should be restructured to meet the needs of all students. Third, I claim that as educators, we bring our own racial and class attitudes to bear on our work and in our interactions with each other. In this chapter I hope to illustrate the dynamics of class and race in a faculty's interactions. I take the position that we are long overdue in beginning racial and class discourse. We must find the courage to speak and to break the "code of silence" that exists in our schools. And lastly, I believe that educators must ensure that parents, of all backgrounds, have a "voice" in the education of their children. Poor and minority parents often feel silenced by educators and other parents from more privileged backgrounds. This tendency of poor and minority parents to feel less empowered inhibits them from speaking up and attaining resources for their children. I argue that it is our responsibility as educators to empower minority and low-income parents to play a more active role in the education of their children.

When envisioning this chapter, it was not my intention to write for an academic audience. Rather, I wanted to talk to parents, teachers, and community members who grapple with racial and class issues on a daily basis. I wanted to make this narrative accessible to a wide audience while at the same time maintaining the integrity of the ideas put forth. I am hopeful that the readers will find that they can use the ideas discussed in this chapter in their daily conversations with colleagues, family, friends, and neighbors.

THE NARRATIVE

This chapter draws upon my experiences in the school and community where I taught for the first time. In order for the reader to understand my perceptions of the school, I feel that it is necessary to describe my background and the varied influences on my behavior and thoughts during that crucial year. In this section I first describe my own family background, and then describe, as seen through my eyes, the community, parents, and staff of Spring School (a fictional name).

The Teacher: My Background

I am a child of southern, black, Baptist parents. Born in Hampton, Virginia, at the height of the civil rights movement, oddly enough I don't remember very many civil rights events. The day Martin Luther King, Jr., was assassinated stands out in my mind because of my parents' emotional response. Beyond that day, I remember very little about the movement. Although I realize now the omnipresent reality of race in my childhood community, my parents sheltered me from this reality as much as possible.

Hampton, situated on the Atlantic coast, was a predominately military and working-class city in the 1970s. Neighborhoods were divided to some extent by class and definitely by race. Aberdeen, my neighborhood, was entirely African American and consisted of mainly working-class and middle-income Blacks. Because my parents were teachers, we were considered a part of Hampton's black middle class. Most of my parents' friends were educators, entrepreneurs, and professionals of various kinds. Despite their middle-class pretensions, most of the middle-class Blacks were barely two or three paychecks away from poverty.

In the early 1970s many of the college-educated black middle class began to purchase homes on the outskirts of Aberdeen. Poorer black families lived in downtown Hampton or closer to the Newport News Shipyard, where a majority of black men and women worked. Although there were striking similarities between the living conditions of the black working class and the white working class, the groups coexisted in a parallel fashion, each with its own set of religious institutions, cultural activities, social centers, and schools.

In 1972 the schools in Hampton were forced to integrate, and black elementary students were bused to schools in white neighborhoods while white secondary students were bused to predominately black schools. Although my parents taught in a neighboring school district and had friends in the Hampton school system, they were terribly uneasy about my attending a "white" school. I vividly recall my parents discussing their distrust of white teachers and their fear for my safety. Unbeknownst to me at that time, this was my first encounter with racism.

Today many of my white acquaintances comment, "You grew up in a middle class family. You had a privileged lifestyle!" Although my family possessed material resources, I remember the "sting" of not possessing racial privileges. As a child, for example, I remember observing my mother being ignored by sales clerks in department stores and eating in cars rather than inside of restaurants. Even though Blacks in Hampton were treated far differently when it was clear that they lacked money or material resources, middle-class Blacks still experienced prejudicial behavior by Whites, but in a less extreme form. This recognition of class status within the black and white communities gave my family a buffer from the worst forms of discrimination, but despite this relative privilege, I never felt equal to my white peers.

The experiences and stories of my mother and father shaped much of my race and class consciousness. Both of my parents grew up in rural areas where hard work was a necessity and education was a luxury. My maternal grandfather was a minister and worked in the Newport News Shipyard. My paternal grandfather managed a tobacco farm. Along with other black rural families, they experienced racism in hundreds of different ways, which shaped the basic framework of their existence. Their experiences ranged from being denied the vote to being limited to unequal and segregated schools. The common message from my grandparents was "work hard and get an education!"—that is, they strongly believed that education was a means to escape poverty and oppression as well as a means to attain power and privilege. In many ways this belief was the framework for my parents' goals for me. My parents encouraged me to study for long hours, to be persistent, to never give up, and to always achieve beyond the expected. But most important, I remember feeling pressured by my mother's intense desire for me to excel beyond my white peers. This was evidenced when I received a higher mark than a "smart white student." My mother would literally jump for joy! I now understand that in my parents' eyes, my ability to compete with white students was symbolic of my mastery of the "white system."

When I began teaching at the age of twenty-one, I brought with me my black middle-class parents' perception that schools and schooling are the American vehicle of upward mobility. Behaving in ways and displaying the skills, abilities, and credentials traditionally associated with white Americans had been encouraged and embraced by my family. This way of thinking permeated my school behavior and academic effort when I was a child. It was also this perception that led me to believe that despite racial differences and social inequity, education had given me an equal opportunity to succeed and, thus, was the social and intellectual equalizer for my students.

During my first year of teaching, my thoughts changed. I began to understand the impact of race and social class on education in a broader sense and wondered how to combat these inequities in education. As I observed my students interacting and participating in class, I recalled my own school experiences. I remembered not being called on in class and having to watch white students receive the unspoken privilege and advantage of responding at will. I understood the fear of asking too many questions and thus being labeled as unintelligent or "stupid." As a result of my experiences, I made a conscious decision to ensure that my students would never experience the same inequities. Although I grew up in what bell hooks (1994) calls a "materially privileged background," I found that my experiences based on racial differences were similar to those of students in my class who were from low-income backgrounds. During my first year of teaching I often thought about how my students were encouraged to betray their class and race origins by conforming to acceptable white, middle-class behaviors and norms, just as I had been. This had been a struggle for me, and I wanted to shelter my students from having to cope with such unfortunate situations. I came to learn, however, that these experiences contributed to my own feelings of self-doubt, anger, and frustration, and I hated the fact that my minority and low-income students were beginning their long struggle with the same feelings.

The Spring School Community

Over ten years ago I started my teaching career at Spring School, a school located in a predominately poor, working-class, African American and Hispanic community in a suburb of Washington, D.C. Interestingly, I didn't choose to teach at Spring School. Spring School's principal, an African American woman, chose me from a long list of new teachers.

When she offered me a teaching position, I immediately jumped at the opportunity without asking many questions about the school or about her expectations.

Spring School is the center of the community both geographically and culturally. The Spring School community consists of an admixture of homes, including large apartment buildings, and numerous fast food restaurants. Detached single-family homes with small cluttered yards are adjacent to the school, and several small businesses are in close proximity. Residents of other District of Columbia suburbs often perceive residents in this community negatively because the media regularly publicizes violent crimes that are committed there. Children from this community are often viewed as lazy, irresponsible, and unable to interact cooperatively with adults and their peers. This key reaction on the part of those persons who are not members of the Spring School community negatively influences Spring School students' identity and ultimately their motivation to achieve academically. Many older students in the community often spoke of their community as the "hood" or described themselves in terms of their toughness or streetwise abilities rather than their intellect or academic abilities.

Spring School, a "magnet school," was considered to be one of the best schools in the district because of its nongraded curriculum and Gifted and Talented (GT) program. For those parents who desired private school education for their children, it was the next best thing. About one-third of the students traveled from other communities to attend Spring School, and about seventy-five percent of those students were identified as gifted and talented. The students who traveled to participate in Spring School's special programs were overwhelmingly white and middle to upper middle class. This disproportionate number of white gifted and talented students created anger among many community residents because they perceived the school system as placing special programs in the school only to attract white students. It was not uncommon to hear community residents make comments such as: "What about us?" "That school is racist!" "We are the real community—not them!" These tension-producing attitudes not only caused wide divisions among community residents and the white middle-class parents but also set the tone for a polarized school environment.

The GT program was a highly valued program within the school, one that symbolized "power." By power I mean that the GT students received access to special resources (i.e., computer labs, extra textbooks), more responsive teachers, and more creative and challenging curricula. These children were challenged to explore, to think, and to create. In addition, there were special privileges for those associated with the GT program, whose students were for the most part isolated from the general education students. Though virtually all students would benefit from being similarly challenged, this program was restricted to those students who met such subjective criteria as intelligence, appearance, racial/ethnic background, and/or parental occupation(s). These restrictions made the program very attractive to many of middle- and upper-class white parents who wanted a "private school-type" education for a "public school price."

Although I do believe that there were parents of the gifted and talented students who truly wanted their children to be enriched by a multicultural school experience, these parents were in the minority. Not surprisingly, the comments regarding the school community that I heard from numerous parents of children identified as gifted and talented were primarily negative. Comments such as "I would bring (my child) back to school tonight if I felt it were safe" and "I would prefer my daughter to stay in the gifted class for all subjects, rather than mixing with the others for art, music, and PE" were commonplace. My impression was that these comments invoked anger and resentment among the poorer minority parents who lived in the community.

Spring School Parent Association. Given the school's special curriculum and structure, the Parent Association was often a sounding board for parents' curricular and programming concerns. Job flexibility and the large number of "stay-at-home moms" provided many of the white and middle-class parents with the ability to attend these meetings and ultimately to lead the organization. In essence, these meetings became their "voice." The agendas usually focused on the gifted and talented curriculum, safety issues, and the hiring of teachers. The nonwhite and working-class parents, on the other hand, were often "silenced" at these meetings. Many of the community parents commented on their discomfort voicing their opinions, ideas, and feelings. I believe they feared the possibility of having to challenge or confront the middle-class or more privileged parents. As a result, many community parents came to believe that the Parent Association was useless and, in turn, became even more distrustful of the school and its personnel.

The Spring School Staff. The staff of Spring School consisted of mostly young, middle-class white women. The principal, in contrast, was a middle-aged, middle-class, African American woman. Although it was never discussed, I believe that this configuration of a person-of-color in authority created great hostility and discomfort among many white staff members. It was common for teachers to challenge the principal on her decisions and authority. She, however, never shied away from using her authority, and on many occasions she would flaunt her power. When staff members challenged her, she responded intensely, oftentimes invoking fear among the staff. For instance, as part of her system of monitoring the school's curriculum, the principal required the submission of weekly lesson plans on Monday mornings. Feeling pressured and not

trusted, a group of experienced teachers challenged the principal on this
policy at a faculty meeting. Without any discussion or input from staff,
the principal announced that if any individual had a problem with the
policy, he/she should get on the transfer list immediately. This announcement shocked the staff and added even more hostility to an already tense environment. I, too, was shocked and amazed at this power
play. Encouraging teachers to transfer if they disliked her policy was
somewhat understandable, but the fact that she was unwilling to listen
to an opposing argument or to invite input from teachers was a "power
statement." Furthermore, it was apparent that we were expected to suc-
cumb to her power. I too became alienated from the principal, and more
important, felt as if I had lost a potential source of support.

The principal's propensity to exert her power contributed to a feeling
among white teachers that the principal was "the enemy." One African
American teacher shared with me a conversation she overheard between
two white teachers. One of the women exclaimed that she was sickened
to the stomach to think that "this woman" was her boss. They went on
to further discuss their disdain for her extravagant and "colorful" appearance. These types of comments caused me to wonder whether the
basis for the teachers' dislike of the principal was her leadership style,
race, class, or possibly gender?

Because I thought race and class were sources of tension among our
staff, I often attempted to discuss these issues with other teachers. I remember trying to initiate a conversation with a white colleague on the
topic. She commented that "there is too much talk about race and racism
in the schools." Her view was that "personality differences" instead of
race were the source of tension. White teachers often used such coded
language to speak of sensitive racial and class situations. For instance,
phrases such as "the community parents," "the apartment people," and
"those people who don't speak English" were often used to describe
minority parents. It was perceived as inappropriate or dangerous to use
the word "race" or "racism" in faculty discussions. I believe that many
of the white staff members felt that they might be viewed as racist or
prejudiced if they truly discussed their beliefs and perceptions of what
was happening in our school among staff and parents.

As an African American middle-class woman in a school with these
faculty dynamics, I felt awkward and uncomfortable. My reactions to the
school environment stemmed from two perspectives: one, that of young,
naive, first-year teacher, and two, that of an African American woman.
As a first-year teacher and a novice to the politics of educational settings,
I felt as if I had to silence my opinions regarding educational programs
and community tension for fear that I would somehow be penalized for
having an opinion but no experience. As an African American, I was
angry at the racist and biased opinions of my colleagues, but at the same

time, I was confused. How should I confront my colleagues' seemingly racist attitudes? I also questioned my surprising identification with both groups, the privileged and the less privileged. The principal, for instance, reminded me of my parents and their middle-class black friends. As Beverly Daniel Tatum (1997) said, "many of us are both dominant and subordinate." I observed how the principal's attitudes and behaviors reflected privileged ideals while her skin color denoted an unprivileged status. I, too, experienced this conflict that stemmed from my identification with both the stance of a more privileged class and a less-privileged racial group.

When interacting with the three teachers-of-color at Spring School, I often felt isolated and alone. It was apparent that previous negative experiences had tainted their perceptions regarding the education of minority students. Feeling helpless and powerless, they often advised me to "get your paycheck and go home. . . . You can't change this system!" Like the minority and poor parents in the community, they felt powerless within the school system. In addition, the fact that there were only three ethnic minority teachers in a school with a large population of students-of-color created a situation in which these teachers felt pressured to be the minority voice. They declined to be that voice, and I became annoyed by their lack of motivation and tendency to avoid conflict. I could only think of the many opportunities for students that were missed because of their refusal to speak up on pertinent issues that directly affected the lives of children, particularly ethnic minority students. My greatest fear was that I might become like them.

This interplay of class and racial tension among staff and parents set the stage for the following case study. Wayne, a student in my class, was an exceptionally bright African American kindergartner. Wayne's story is important to highlight because it illustrates how power and privilege can play a critical role in a student's access to resources and educational opportunities. Furthermore, the dynamics between parents such as Wayne's and the GT specialist are also critical elements when considering the roles of parents and educators in the process of acquiring educational opportunities and resources for students. The case of Wayne within the context of Spring School not only illustrates how inequities are maintained in schools but also how one event can impact the perceptions of an energetic, naïve first-year teacher.

The Case of Wayne

Wayne is the oldest child in a working-class African American family. His mother, Mrs. S., a housekeeper at a local hotel, is a quiet and patient person who finished high school with honors. She explained that although she was an honor student, her teachers never encouraged her to attend college. Therefore, immediately after high school she married and started a family. Wayne's father (Mr. S.), a bus driver in Washington, D.C., is outspoken, witty and a bit "rough around the edges." His sense of humor and loud laugh made him a popular visitor in the school office.

Wayne's home life was stable and his lifestyle that of a typical five-year-old. Although he did not have expensive toys and gadgets like many of my middle-class students, Wayne was happy and energetic. He loved books and was very proficient at computer games. Oftentimes, Wayne was louder than most of the children, especially when he was excited. Also, he frequently interrupted others while they were speaking. My hypothesis was that he was modeling the behavior of his father. This upset my white teacher's assistant, who was also a member of the school's Parent Association. She thought that he was rude, and I thought it was interesting that she never acknowledged Wayne's academic strengths. I found myself constantly affirming his accomplishments when this teacher's aide was in the classroom, hoping that she would see his incredible talents and intelligence. This, however, never happened.

During the spring of Wayne's kindergarten year, I met with his parents to discuss his progress and educational opportunities for the next year. Most important, I wanted to recommend him for the GT program. In my opinion, Wayne was a perfect candidate for the program. He was reading three years above grade level, and his math and reasoning skills were advanced for a five-year-old. I was also impressed with Wayne's creativity and analytical skills.

Wayne's parents were both pleased and a bit apprehensive by my recommendation. Although they wanted Wayne to be challenged academically, they were concerned about his placement in a program that they perceived as being "for white folks." Furthermore, they were concerned about the costs associated with the program. I assured them that there were no costs and that if Wayne felt uncomfortable in the program, they had the power to take him out. They then requested a meeting with Ms. D., the GT specialist to discuss the gifted/talented process of identification.

The dynamics of the meeting with Ms. D. were reflective of the class and race differences in Spring School. During the meeting, when Mr. S. spoke in his usual loud and aggressive tone, frequently using grammatically incorrect words, I noticed Ms. D.'s tense posture. For many individuals from less privileged backgrounds, Mr. S.'s loud voice and language would not have been disturbing. For Ms. D., however, these seemed both disturbing and bothersome.

In addition to Ms. D.'s obvious discomfort with Mr. S., her remarks to me regarding Wayne's work were condescending and her disbelief in his abilities, insulting. "Did he do this without any help from you, Ms. Holcomb?" and "I can't believe that he is reading so well at such an

early age!" I described Wayne's strengths and the rationale for my recommendation and was again shocked when she asked for more examples of his work and recommendations from specialist teachers (e.g.,
physical education, art). I commented to Ms. D. that she had not requested additional work samples from other (i.e., white) students in my
class. Her reply was that she needed more than one sample of Wayne's
work and that this was to ensure his appropriate placement, emphasizing "appropriate." To me, she had not only questioned Wayne's academic appropriateness but also his racial and class appropriateness for
this program. Although my interpretation might seem extreme, my reaction arises from observing and experiencing the inequitable and unfair
criteria historically used to exclude minority and low-socioeconomic individuals from special opportunities.

Ms. D. exemplified biased behavior further in her focus on Wayne's
social skill mastery instead of on his academic strengths. Her comments
consisted of statements such as: "He is a very nice child," "He understands and follows directions well," and "His work is really neat." This
emphasis on Wayne's social competence and willingness to follow the
directions of others illustrated Ms. D.'s belief that minority and underclass students are typically socially incompetent. Furthermore, I really
understood at that point that class and race could truly determine student success if there was no one to intervene or stop a biased process.

Wayne's parents' reaction to the conference was puzzling, however.
They were neither bothered nor angry about Ms. D.'s behavior. I wondered if they were choosing to ignore her behavior or maybe they were
merely accustomed to being treated in such a manner. Since many persons from oppressed backgrounds suppress their anger as a technique
for survival, I also wondered if they were merely hiding their anger for
fear of destroying an opportunity for Wayne. In my mind, I kept asking,
"These are bright people; why aren't they reacting to Ms. D.'s behavior?"
"Why aren't they more demanding like the white, middle-class parents?"
I understand now that Wayne's parents were merely reflecting attitudes
and behaviors developed as a consequence of social isolation and repeated denial of opportunities and dreams. Passivity and resignation are
the result of the ongoing denial and manipulation of access and opportunities that poor and minority people confront.

Despite the GT specialist's apprehensions, I proceeded with the identification process. Wayne's scores on the GT assessments were overwhelmingly positive. Surprised at Wayne's scores, Ms. D. notified me of
his acceptance into the program. Her lack of enthusiasm made it apparent that she was not pleased. My reactions to her announcement were
mixed. On one hand, I was thrilled that Wayne had demonstrated his
abilities and had proven Ms. D. wrong. On the other hand, I was disappointed by the way in which the GT program gave faculty members

the authority to differentiate between and categorize students. It was apparent that Wayne had crossed a line and had entered a "forbidden zone." He was neither white nor privileged by class—that is, he didn't fit the pattern or prototype for the program. Wayne's entrance into the GT program signified, in my mind, that he would receive the same quality of education that "other" children received. This was a powerful moment for me because I knew that our educational system had probably failed significant numbers of talented minority and poor children. Perhaps, I thought, I had saved one!

DISCUSSION

Despite the above narrative's focus on one episode at Spring School, my hope is that the dynamics of Spring School's staff and community along with Wayne's case emphasize the serious dilemmas regarding class and racial divisions in schools. Although I feel fortunate to have helped Wayne acquire access to an educational opportunity, I am angry about the social inequities and tension that I encountered at Spring School. In general, I am angry at the way in which race and class were used as determinants of students' accessibility to resources but never openly discussed. Every teacher, school counselor, and administrator should also be angry. We must ask ourselves, "What do we do to reduce racial and class divisions in our schools?" And then we must ask, "What am I willing to do to prevent this from happening at my school?"

As stated previously, in order to acquire multicultural and equitable environments for students, we must challenge the barriers that block less-privileged students like Wayne from access to educational resources. In particular, we must talk about racism and classism in the nation's schools. I often wonder what Spring School would have been like if we had discussed the racial and class tensions in our school and community. Would we have benefited from dialogue or, better yet, did we need to be confronted about our misperceptions and biases? One of the most important things I believe that could have been done to make our school more multicultural and equitable would have been to break the silence concerning issues of race and class. Many teachers, like the teachers at Spring School, fear that exposure of their class and racial biases many endanger their status or privilege. Moreover, I believe that many teachers, both white and black, fear that they will be isolated or rejected by fellow staff members if they speak openly about issues of race and class.

The notion that schools should be at the forefront of social change requires that teachers change not only classroom structures but also attitudes. According to Geneva Gay (1989), when teachers unconsciously form different expectations about students of different social class backgrounds, they tend to spend more time interacting and praising those students from privileged backgrounds. For instance, the GT specialist in this narrative seemed to have formed low expectations for African American and low-income students. For this reason, she was reluctant to accept Wayne into a program in which she couldn't envision him having a role or being successful. These are the beliefs that we must challenge and discuss openly. Educators talk of how we want our students to be more open and accepting of differences, yet we very rarely discuss our own perceptions, biases, and prejudices regarding our students. This silence only fosters and perpetuates more inequities and unfair educational practices. In essence, I believe that being silent results in the loss of human potential.

Although the politics and procedures related to specialized programs, such as GT programs, are beyond the scope of this paper, I believe that educators must revisit the goals and intentions of programs designed to enhance the education of special student populations. While these programs are intended to be of benefit to students, they nevertheless act as a means of distributing unequal resources. Educational equality for less privileged students cannot be achieved without modifying those educational programs and practices which tend to separate and stratify groups based on race and class. If not monitored for potential discriminatory practices, educational programs for the gifted and talented, and for other students with special needs, can close rather than open paths to social and academic advancement by assigning some students early on to an educational underclass. Minority and poor students in Spring School were virtually cut off from a highly valued and powerful program that would have ultimately created more opportunities for social equality. Parents as well as community leaders should work with teachers to decide who participates in such programs.

Parents whose perceptions and beliefs reflect social class and race stratifications further reinforce the educational inequities in teacher attitudes and classroom interactions. This can be problematic, as was evidenced in the composition of the Spring School's Parent Association and by Wayne's parents' apprehensiveness about his participation in a program for "white folks." When parents are divided by racial and class lines, educational equality is reduced. Ultimately, ethnic minority and low-income students suffer because of their parents' sense of powerlessness. Their parents perceive themselves as having no voice, and many feel that their opinions will not affect outcomes. Furthermore, many ethnic minority and low-income parents are reluctant to take part in school activities because of their lack of know-how in negotiating the school bureaucracy. Decades of educational abandonment have instilled this sense of powerlessness in many parents; school personnel should aim to create schools that encourage the participation of all parents. We must realize that numerous parents in disadvantaged communities portray a passive stance that is the result of a long history of meaninglessness in society. Wendy Glascow Winters (1993) maintains that meaninglessness among African American parents occurs when social situations are so unclear and muddled that parents become less confident in themselves and in the schooling process. By developing a policy of parental involvement, school personnel can extend access to social as well as educational opportunities to parents who might otherwise feel powerless, meaningless, and isolated from mainstream society.

Creating change in schools undoubtedly requires courage. How can educators find the courage to remedy issues of equalizing opportunities and access to resources for all students? This is the question I ask myself continuously because I too struggle with fear and feelings of inferiority. How will my colleagues perceive me if I challenge their biased beliefs and attitudes? Am I truly able to create change in schools? Am I qualified? I learned one thing from my experiences at Spring School and that is, I can't fix the entire school system but I can make a difference for one child. Tatum (1997, p. 204) offers this wisdom about being a change agent: "While many people experience themselves as powerless, everyone has some sphere of influence in which they can work for change, even if it is just in their own personal network of family and friends." In writing this chapter, I hope to ignite some interest in parents and teachers to ask themselves: What dialogue is taking place in my children's school regarding the maintenance of class and racial divisions? How can I help to dismantle racism and classism in my school or my child's school?

School reform efforts should begin by redefining the mission of multicultural education to include providing equal access to quality schooling for all students, regardless of race or class. Quality, in turn, should be determined by the degree to which students from all income levels and racial backgrounds are engaged in learning and determined also by the educational outcomes of all students.

REFERENCES

Bowles, S., & Gintis, H. (1976). *Schooling in capitalist America*. New York: Basic Books.
Darling-Hammond, L. (1998). New standards, old inequities: The current challenge for African American education. In L. Daniels (Ed.), *The state of black America 1998*. Washington, DC: National Urban League.
Gay, G. (1989). Ethnic minorities and educational equality. In J. A. Banks & C. A. M. Banks (Eds). *Multicultural education: Issues and perspectives* (2nd ed.) (pp. 167–187). Needham Heights, MA: Allyn & Bacon.
hooks, b. (1994). *Teaching to transgress*. New York: Routledge.
Kozol, J. (1991). *Savage inequities: Children in America's schools*. New York: Crown.

Ogbu, J. U. (1988). Class stratification, racial stratification, and schooling. In L. Weis (Ed.), *Class, race, and gender in American education* (pp. 163–182). Albany: State University of New York Press.

Persell, C. H. (1989). Social class and educational equality. In J. A. Banks & C. A. M. Banks (Eds.), *Multicultural education: Issues and perspectives* (2nd ed.) (pp. 68–86). Needham Heights, MA: Allyn & Bacon.

Tatum, B. D. (1997). *Why are all the black kids sitting together in the cafeteria? and other conversations about race.* New York: Basic Books.

Wilson, W. J. (1978). *The declining significance of race: Black and changing American institutions.* Chicago: University of Chicago Press.

Winters, W. G. (1993). *African American mothers and urban schools.* New York: Lexington Books.

4

Crossing the Brooklyn Bridge: The Geography of Social and Cultural Transitions

Carol Korn

Imagination, creativity, and the arts in education are celebrated for the fresh perspectives these can offer familiar experience and for the opportunities they present to engage the unfamiliar, creating links between the known and the novel (Egan, 1992; Eisner, 1992; Greene, 1978; Jagla, 1994; Sarason, 1990). Creativity and the arts in teacher education can serve yet another function: that of awakening students to the cultural lives they already have in their diverse communities, while connecting them to other possible worlds and ways of being. This chapter takes up the transitions that teacher education students make in coming to Brooklyn College, and examines the borders they cross in their journeys from home to school and from school to New York City's cultural institutions.

In this chapter, I call upon the oral history/storytelling project that I developed for an undergraduate course, *Education and Literacy*, to illustrate the role of transitions in the students' lives and in the lives of those whose stories they tell, as well as the place of cultural stories in the classroom. This chapter draws, also, on the collaborative work between the teacher education program at Brooklyn College and the Lincoln Center Institute for the Arts in Education (LCI). The students' experiences with this initiative call upon the kinds of transitions to the wider cultural and social worlds they will, in turn, introduce to their own students when they become teachers.

In connecting students to the local cultural institutions, folklore, and wisdom that reside within Brooklyn's communities as well as to such major cultural institutions as Lincoln Center and the Museum of Modern Art, with which LCI partnered, we ask our students to traverse the geography of New York City in ways both literal and figurative. The journeys they take turn, alternately, on taking leave of and returning to the culturally distinctive communities in which they reside rather than representing the kinds of linear trajectories commonly associated with developmental gains. The first journey that students make is in coming to Brooklyn College, a large, liberal arts college situated in a residential area a of Brooklyn, a borough of New York City with a very large immigrant population. In their daily commute to and from Brooklyn College, students move between the culture of home, in what is likely to be a culturally, socially, and ethnically homogeneous community, and the culture(s) of the Brooklyn College campus, more than one half of whose students are immigrants or the children of immigrants.

The second journey we ask our teacher education students to make is between what are often experienced as widely disparate worlds: the world of home and the cultural communities in which they reside, and the common culture of New York City, as represented by its major cultural institutions. In moving between their home communities and the college, and between the college and Lincoln Center, for example, Brooklyn College students traverse what are often experienced as broad social, cultural, economic, and racial divides.

The Brooklyn Bridge spans both of these worlds, connecting the Brooklyn of home culture and home cooking with the Manhattan of commerce and achievement. Two statues—one representing Brooklyn and the other New York City (Manhattan)—that once graced the foot of the Manhattan Bridge, the Brooklyn Bridge's younger and less graceful sibling, and were relocated some years later to the entrance of the Brooklyn Museum of Art, capture this study in contrasts. Brooklyn is depicted as a mother bent over a book reading to her child, while New York City's gaze is turned confidently outward, toward the horizon. The tension between the familiar and the comfortable that Brooklyn represents, and the energy and sophistication that Manhattan claims in the local imagination are evoked in this iconography and also, perhaps, in the transitions we ask our students to make when they come to Lincoln Center.

In this chapter I take up the developmental, social, and cultural transitions that students make as they become teachers, and consider how these transitions are further complicated when the students are recent arrivals to the United States. This chapter addresses the chasm between student expectations regarding place and continuity of experience, and faculty desire to transform classrooms from fixed places into spaces for exploration and transformation. Student experiences of the place of creativity and the arts in their own learning frame a discussion of the tensions that arise from negotiating the spaces between familiar and new places and suggest how the classroom can become a site for exploring student experience and its connection to pedagogy and for negotiating the transitions implicated in learning.

I begin with a description of the students' research in Brooklyn's communities and the applied work in literacy development, and I then discuss the collaborative work with the Lincoln Center Institute. The students' experiences moving between familiar and new social and cultural experiences frame the discussion of these curricular events.

MOVING BETWEEN HOME AND SCHOOL: THE ORAL HISTORY/STORYTELLING PROJECT

The Brooklyn College oral history/storytelling project was designed to help teacher education students understand and appreciate the diverse cultural communities in which they will teach. Employing the methodologies of oral history interviewing and critical reflection, the students interview migrants and immigrants; the stories they record provide material for writing books for children and young people. In conducting this research in Brooklyn's neighborhoods, the students must struggle with how to represent themselves and those they interview. The students keep journals of their research and writing experiences and read drafts of their work-in-progress to children in schools, engaging their audiences in conversation. Often the children assist in illustrating the books; the interactions between the children and the teacher education students during the process of storytelling and writing provide both the children and the students with the experience of writing and thinking about stories.

The oral history/storytelling project illustrates a means of connecting students to the art forms and literary expressions that reside within their home communities, while developing critical awareness of the complicated nature of transitions which mark passages in their own lives and in the lives of others. Critical awareness is especially salient to developing an approach to teaching which not only celebrates the contributions that varied cultural experiences bring to our lives, but appreciates the ambiguities, tensions, and sensitivities that attend major transitions, including the transitions that occur when stories cross cultures and gain new audiences. Such tensions are often revealed in the stories that are gathered and in the dilemmas created for the storytellers.

Stories, and especially their resolutions, are sedimented within a web of belief and value specific to a particular culture. The traditions and common understandings of a culture are communicated intergenerationally through shared social practice, especially language. Cultural stories suggest paradigmatic dilemmas and offer solutions that draw upon prevailing cultural beliefs and meanings. One is reminded here of the anthropologist Clifford Geertz's (1973) observations that the stories a society tells are an important means in which the culture's frame of reference and traditional folk wisdom are applied to everyday problems. Jerome Bruner (1990) adds that a culture's beliefs enter into the narratives that it tells about human plights. These narratives tell not about the way things are, Bruner reminds us, but rather about how they should be. Folktales are such stories. Steeped within a particular culture, they are repositories of cultural beliefs and traditions, and as such, they may be psychologically distant for the culturally different audience. In the absence of shared meaning, a story might be experienced as an interesting anthropological artifact rather than as part of one's lived experience, as would happen if both storyteller and audience shared a common history and culture.

Stories bear the imprimatur of the storyteller's voice; her understanding lends shape and form to the story. Like the story she tells, the storyteller is situated within a particular cultural and historical frame bound to the culture and to the time in which the story is told. The meanings that a folktale holds for a culturally diverse audience is likely to be very different from the way in which the tale is understood when the gap between the story and the lived experience is narrower. Yet it is only when the story is re-examined, held up to the light of the "new" culture, that differences in understanding and meaning emerge. The middle ground, the disputed space between the story's meaning in the culture of origin and its meaning for a contemporary New York City audience, becomes the site of negotiated meanings. The embeddedness of stories and storytellers within a culture is underlined when story and storyteller cross cultural borders in the act of telling stories. When stories assume a curricular role as a bridge between cultures—a common practice in multicultural education—we need to consider how stories that encode a culture's beliefs and ways of living in the world will be perceived through different, and more critical, lenses.

In the oral history/storytelling project described here, the teacher education students are close to the stories they record and work with. Often they turn to their own families for stories; for most, these are familiar tales, heard time and again in childhood. They encode particular ways of being in the world, capture dim memories of historic events, or present typical dilemmas and their culturally sanctioned solutions. An example of the dilemma created when stories cross cultural borders was provided by a student of Dominican background who presented a cultural tale, *The Magical Orange Seed*, familiar from her own childhood—one that had been passed down to her mother by her grandmother. According to the student, it is an oft-told tale, one primarily told by women to girls.

The Magical Orange Seed

A young boy, Kico, and his mother, Dona Tata, endure maltreatment at the hands of the boy's stepfather, Don Esteban, who is jealous of their loving relationship. The boy is compelled to perform menial, backbreaking labor while the stepfather's lazy son, Panchito, mocks him. Don Esteban deprives Kico of food; Dona

Tata comes to her son's aid, bringing bread and milk to him in the fields. One day, Panchito spies Dona Tata bringing food to Kico. Don Esteban beats Kico; Dona Tata faints.

Kico escapes to the forest. Alone, he cries for his dead father and prays. An old man dressed in white and illumined by a mysterious light visits him. The old man gives him an orange seed, instructing him that if he plants the seed and sings to it with love, the seed will provide him with food. Kico soon puts on weight, arousing the suspicions of Don Esteban and his son, Panchito. They spy on him and uncover his secret. Panchito steals the orange seed.

Kico discovers Don Esteban and Panchito in the orange tree; its growth unchecked by Kico's song, the tree has reached alarming heights. He sings to the seed, asking it to transform the pair by rendering them "good," and adds that he "loves" them. Frightened by the tree's height, Don Esteban and Panchito beg Kico for forgiveness and agree to be "good." Father and son are cured of their cruelty, and all live happily ever after, their home "filled with laughter and love." The old man in white reappears one final time: he comes to reclaim the seed from Kico so that he can give it to yet another desperate child.

The tale of *The Magical Orange Seed* invokes assumptions about domestic violence, religious faith, and the place of memory. The story is grounded on belief in the role of religious faith and prayer in ameliorating untenable situations and the role of the miracle in effecting cures of social ills—in this case, abuse. The tale additionally assumes that memory can be obliterated and that the aggrieved woman and child will forgive and forget. The resolution of the story turns on the transformative nature of love, belief, and faith and on the role of the son in caring for the mother. The retreat of personal memory in the service of family harmony is unquestioned; forgiveness obliterates memory. The social and cultural horizons of this story are bounded by the role of [Christian] religious faith and, concomitantly, by the powerlessness of women and children.

When stories are re-examined through what I have earlier referred to as "the middle ground," that disputed space between a story's meaning in the culture of origin and its meaning for a contemporary New York City audience (Korn, 1997), that in-between space becomes a site of negotiated meanings. In crossing these invisible borders, culturally determined meaning enters into dialogue with the socially constructed meanings that stories hold for audiences. The assumptions that underlie the stories that a culture tells are brought into relief when they are considered from a different cultural perspective. Hans Georg Gadamer (1967, 1975) speaks of a fusion of horizons arising from the meeting of one's socially constructed horizon with other possible worlds (Sass, 1989; Warnke, 1987). Neither story, storyteller, nor audience holds a definitive interpretation; rather, all three participate in this coming together of different layers of meaning. Multiple meanings of stories for which only shared meaning once existed are created out of the difference between story, storyteller, and audience.

Difference provides opportunities to ask questions that might not have been raised in a shared cultural world and highlights the ways in which culture informs and shapes the stories that we tell. Contemporary multiculturalism assumes diversity, a multiplicity of stories and views, in which the stories that comprise a culture are celebrated for their uniqueness and for the meanings they offer that can cut across cultural difference. When stories cross cultures and cultural frames of reference, the following questions are raised:

- How do diverse audiences hear and respond to cultural stories?
- What meanings do they hold for diverse listeners?
- How do these meanings differ from the story's intended meaning and function?

In a diverse society storytellers are not endowed with the authoritative stance they can assume within a culturally homogeneous group. Their stories are filtered through the lenses of their listeners as they respond to both the story and to the storyteller. A single story will yield multiple meanings, each imbued with the culture, history, and language of the listener. The storyteller's task becomes one of negotiating the cultural meanings that the tale may call up in its audience.

The various audiences of *The Magical Orange Seed*, for example, heard the story differently as it was filtered through the sieve of the cultural and social expectations of each set of listeners. The student/storyteller's mother, who heard it told by her own mother and grandmother, experienced it as an affirmation of faith's ability to overcome what can seem to be insoluble problems. For her daughter, steeped in the traditions of both the Dominican Republic and contemporary American society, additional layers of meaning accrued in the telling of the tale. For the storyteller hearing a retelling of the story in the company of her Brooklyn College colleagues, the story was filtered through the audience's acculturation to the shared social valuation of autonomy. Furthermore, this student audience called upon a feminist perspective regarding women's social position and analyzed the story in light of what they knew about domestic violence, including child maltreatment.

The task of crafting these oral history interviews into books for young people often involved re-examining the taken for granted in the students' own social and cultural lives. These writers were additionally called upon to anticipate how their intended youthful audiences might hear their stories. When these teacher education students become classroom teachers, they will need to not only listen to the cultural stories their students will bring to school, but also listen for and address the problematics that moving between cultural worlds, each with its own set of beliefs and values, call forth.

MOVING BETWEEN THE CULTURES OF HOME
AND SCHOOL

The oral history/storytelling project identifies a role for the bio-graphical and autobiographical in connecting curriculum to the lives of students and teachers (Aitken & Mildon, 1992; Denzin, 1989; Goodson, 1992; Lincoln, 1993). It describes a process that yokes biography to autobiography, connecting curriculum development to the lives of students, and to a teacher's life, as well. It demonstrates, also, a process by which preservice teachers can begin to conduct teacher research within their own communities, learning to look again at the taken for granted within their own lives, defamiliarizing that which feels familiar, and dig-nifying the lives and cultural experiences of family and community members. It serves as a reminder, too, that the lives of the children our students will teach will be as varied as the narratives they and their classmates will hear. In many instances these are likely to recall their own stories.

In researching their own family histories and in hearing each other's stories, these preservice teachers gain new understanding and appreci-ation of their own family backgrounds, as well as of the cultures and backgrounds of those they view as different. A number of students com-mented on the poignancy of hearing stories that reflected the lives of their fellow student/researchers and that provided a point of entry into communities and cultures that seemed remote in their difference. Robin wrote: "I was moved by many of the books, especially the ones that reflected on the author's life. Our class consists of so many different races and ethnicities, which privileged me to learn about so many new cul-tures. There are so many similarities that Indian, Jamaican, Russian, Cu-ban and Puerto Rican cultures have with my Jewish religion. I was fascinated to learn this."

Ellen reflected on the transitions she has made from a racially and ethnically homogeneous neighborhood and school environment to Brooklyn College. Paradoxically, she notes, studying with classmates she sees as different has given rise to feelings of closeness that eluded her in her prior school experience in a homogeneous setting. She observes, too, that this new environment of difference provokes critical thinking about perceptions and perspectives, leading to both personal growth and pedagogic considerations: "I feel that we have all formed a close unit and gained a lot from our interactions. Throughout my years of school-ing I had the same children in my classes and we never bonded. Being exposed to such different ideas and perspectives I had to maintain an open mind and choose my words carefully. I realized that we are judged and stereotyped based on perceptions, and I did not want to perpetuate this error—or be on the receiving end of it."

The transition from the culture of home to the culture of school is further complicated for many of our students by their own immigration experiences. Barbara, who emigrated from Poland five years earlier, reflected on her experience of difference within New York and within Brooklyn College. As she grappled with difference and learning within a diverse setting, she also challenged assumptions about herself: "Brooklyn College is different from a Polish college. It is big and beautiful, but at the same time kind of mysterious. There are many different people, different cultures and religions on campus. In my country there were not that many foreign people, the main religion was Catholicism, and the main culture was Polish. Meeting different people let me understand a lot of things. Even though I was considered in Poland a very open-minded person, here I have learned that it is not enough for this country."

Growing awareness of the historical value of the personal narratives and folkloric literature they were gathering encouraged students to examine the libraries at the schools where they student taught or held part-time positions. Often they were surprised to find how few materials were available on the specific cultures they were researching, despite the wide cultural, ethnic, and racial diversity of schoolchildren in New York City. This was especially the case in the area of folklore and narratives of Asian cultures, where a dearth of children's literature in English has been identified (Russell, 1997).

TELLING TALES: BIOGRAPHY, AUTOBIOGRAPHY, AND PEDAGOGIC PRACTICE

The task of connecting audiences and storytellers to the oral histories of diverse cultures—oral histories in which narrative and folklore overlay the geographic, social, and cultural maps traversed—calls for authorial presence in the work. Students, as researchers and as writers, situate themselves in the work, both when they present the personal meaning the cultural stories hold for them and when they make pedagogic decisions as they retell their stories to others. Engaged and responsive pedagogic practice implies that teachers will search for ways in which to connect curriculum to students' lives, helping children to locate themselves within curricular events and texts and to develop a sense of ownership of their own learning.

The relationship of the teacher to the curriculum, though, is one that is often easily overlooked. As I read my students' journals and engaged in conversation with them about their work, I became intrigued by the questions of how teachers connect to the curriculum they teach and what personal meanings, if any, the curriculum and teaching hold for them. Barbara reflected on her affinity for the imagination of childhood, on the role that dreaming and imagining have played in her own life. She also reflected on the bittersweet experience of learning that while the imagination can open up possibilities in the real world, such possibilities are suffused with the tensions between that which lies ahead and that which is left behind.

As a child I always dreamed of going abroad, of meeting other people, of getting to know other cultures, religions, languages. It was a beautiful day. I took a newspaper and the first thing I saw was the advertisement about the lottery to win a visa to the United States. I wrote a letter, forgot about it, and went on with my studies. A few months later [me and my immediate family] we received a letter from the embassy informing us that we were one of the lucky winners. We were so happy; we were supposed to go to America, the land where dreams come true, where people live happily, where it is easier to do anything. That was the myth about America then. We came to America five years ago. . . . Soon all charm burst. I had to start working. My whole life I did not have to worry about money; the only obligation I had was to go to school. I became very homesick. I missed everybody there: family, friends, food. I felt very lonely.

I too began to think about the oral histories I had never gathered: from my father, whose stories always left out more, it seemed, than they revealed; from my mother, who died before I had the courage to ask; and from her shrinking circle of friends, aging women who had grown up in the same Central European town, survived the ghetto and a succession of concentration camps together, and finally settled within walking distance of each other in New York. Like my students, I too began the process of gathering oral histories. Like them, I started to hear stories I had never heard before; in the listening, too, familiar stories shed their familiarity and took on a newness, a strangeness borne of close listening, working with text, and positioning oneself in the audience. Like those students who interviewed family members, I too was a privileged audience, privy to gossip and to the intimate details reserved only for familiar audiences. Like my students, I struggled to deal with what was told and what was held back, and finally, with where we, as intergenerational narrators, locate ourselves within these stories.

My work with stories arising from and/or deeply connected to particular cultural backgrounds raises questions for me about developing curriculum that is meaningful not only for students but also for teachers. It suggests that teachers can gain understanding of the dilemmas and of the passages that students face by drawing upon their own autobiographical and biographical knowledge and by their own engagement with the curricular initiatives that they introduce to their students. When teachers are engaged in the curriculum alongside their students, learning becomes shared enterprise that calls upon the creative processes of both teachers and students. This requires that teachers invoke their imaginations as they consider their own lives, as well as those of others.

Responsive pedagogy identifies teachers as curriculum innovators and as catalysts for cognitive and emotional connections to text and other curricular forms that can promote student learning. It assumes the value of students' emotional and cognitive connections to curriculum, implicating these in student learning. I propose here that a responsive pedagogy needs to ask how and where teachers can locate themselves within the process of teaching and curriculum development, and how teaching and the curriculum can be made meaningful for teachers as well as for their students. Yasmin, an undergraduate student of Puerto Rican background and the first in her family to attend college, connected creativity in teaching with understanding the lives of others and with examining one's own beliefs and responsibilities to others:

Most importantly I learned the characteristic of being a creative teacher: identifying with others, treating children with respect, honesty, knowing what we believe, and being aware of your responsibility. [My book] about a staff member at Brooklyn College changed my view of the people that work here, because it made me see a person who succeeded in life by overcoming many obstacles. And I thought to myself, how many other professors and staff members struggled to get where they are today? As I learned about the children in my neighborhood, I came to a decision that I wanted to teach in my community.

Yasmin's words imply an association between creative teaching and social responsibility, as well as a growing awareness of and appreciation for the transitions that others have made before her. She was surprised by her discovery that achievement does not always follow a predetermined and predictable trajectory. Yasmin described a sense of obligation toward her community, together with a keen appreciation for the classroom as a site of ambition and achievement, a place for considering possibilities for herself and for the children she will teach.

CROSSING THE BRIDGE: THE WORK WITH THE LINCOLN CENTER INSTITUTE

The students' research within Brooklyn's communities reminds us of our obligation to honor the homes and communities that contribute to children's foundational experiences and also recalls our pedagogic responsibility to expand children's as well as our own, range of experiences and expectations beyond the familiar. In our work with the Lincoln Center Institute (LCI), we call upon the arts to bring a freshness and an acuteness of vision to our everyday experiences; we also gave consideration to how the arts can be woven into curricular events, introducing children to new ways of thinking about the world and about the possibilities in their own lives. The collaborative work between the School of Education at Brooklyn College and the Lincoln Center Institute seeks to identify and create connections between the arts, curriculum, and pedagogic practice and at the same time to connect preservice teacher education students to the cultural institutions of New York City. This project requires teacher education and liberal arts faculty to work closely with LCI teaching artists in planning and implementing workshops on campus and at Lincoln Center and the Museum of Modern Art (MOMA). The workshops take as their focal point a work or group of works of art: a painting, sculpture or installation, or a performance piece in theater, dance, or music.

Extending the work of the classroom to include cultural institutions signals to our students that learning may be situated in places other than the classroom. It leads students away from the familiar classroom site of learning, challenging them to engage in new experiences and bring critical approaches to learning to bear on less familiar forms of representation (i.e., the arts). The workshops call upon an approach to learning that views questioning and reflection as learning tools (Korn & Toth, 1998), and that invites multiple perspectives regarding both works of art as well as work within the disciplines. The arts have long been recognized for their role in fostering a multiperspectival approach to learning and problem solving (Cochran-Smith, 1984; Eisner, 1992, 1993; Greene, 1978, Grumet, 1995, Heath, 1993) and recognized as providing a point of entry into the lives of others (Dambekalns, 1994; Dilger, 1994). In this regard, the work with the arts mirrors the research in which the students are engaged.

Conversation around specific works of art deepened the students' appreciation for the different perspectives each brought to what was, ostensibly, the same experience and led to reflections about the role of others in developing one's own understanding. The students returned to these themes again and again in their writing.

Olga wrote: "To visit a museum is more interesting in a group than alone. You look at the same painting from different perspectives, and suddenly you start to see in this painting something you didn't see before, and you would never come up with being alone." Yvonne commented:

What struck me most was that neither the MOMA nor the LCI workshops demanded that we interpret the themes in this or that way. Interpretation came from our own experiences. It is essential to give students dough and allow them to bake bread, give them some ideas to play with and make use of. That is why we should expose children to these kinds of experiences, so they can learn to be responsible for what they have and what they know.

Nancy, conversely, was surprised at how her personal reaction differed from the reactions of her classmates. She expressed pleasure at this discovery, and appreciation for the views of others: "As a result of this experience I have learned that my reaction to art can be so different from others'. My reaction is something that is very personal, and I was amazed at the various reactions that were heard. I think that it is wonderful to be able to experience art through other people's interpretations." For Juan, the uncertainty of responding to an unfamiliar work of art was not unlike meeting a new group of children for the first time, a challenge that calls upon a teacher's ability to understand and respond to others: "Looking at an abstract painting is like going into a class for the first time, because in the painting you try to see and understand the painter's meaning and ideas, and when you first walk into class you don't know how the children will react. Teachers need to get to know and understand the children; I believe I felt the same way when I walked into a classroom for the first time."

The tenuousness and concomitant challenge that Juan alludes to in describing his feelings when looking at an unfamiliar work of art or looking upon a new class of children for the first time is repeated in the questions and anxieties that surround what for many students are their first excursions to New York City's major cultural institutions. The anxiety that attends these initial forays first surfaces as questions of geography and travel. Navigating public transportation is a major concern for some of the students who usually drive or travel by bus, but rarely use the subway; those students who are regular subway riders—some take two or three different subway lines to school—enjoy sharing their expertise and subway maps with their colleagues. Catherine wrote: "When I woke up in the morning, I was so anxious to be going to the city to meet for class. I wasn't really sure how to get to the museum. I just knew that I was taking the B train, but I didn't know which way I was supposed to go. When I got off the train, I asked someone which way Fifth Avenue was, so that I wouldn't be lost in the city."

One year, at the beginning of the collaboration, a number of students arrived at Lincoln Center for a workshop with mothers and boyfriends in tow, signaling to us their apprehension and our need to address their misgivings early on, before the start of the workshops. Recognizing the place of uncertainty in change and growth, and the need for teachers to rise to challenges if they are to encourage their students to do so as well, Dominique wrote:

I think that I was feeling very sheltered within my college life and was challenged by the idea of moving outside of the school environment and into the city scene during school hours. I did realize, though, the importance of stretching oneself beyond what is comfortable and moving toward new experiences. This is a difficult concept for children. When they are very young, and have to leave the safety and comfort of their mothers' presence to move on to school, the transition is not always an easy one. The school scene poses the same challenge for the young as moving beyond the college territory posed for me.

Midway through the first of two workshops at MOMA, Takesha, usually lively and energetic, grew increasingly tired and restless and became eager to leave. This puzzled her, as she reported finding the workshop interesting. She recalled, though, an earlier experience at another major New York City museum, which she had visited for the first time the previous semester on a college assignment. Leaning over to more closely inspect a painting, Takesha inadvertently triggered an alarm. She recalled her humiliation when a guard reprimanded her and other museum goers looked her way. By the second workshop at MOMA, Takesha felt more at ease in the museum and had greater confidence in her ability to be an active participant in what was initially experienced as an intimidating place in which she did not belong:

On the second visit I felt a little more relaxed and I think it showed by the way I was very expressive about what the art was making me feel. I actually did not think that my filing analogy [response to Mondrian's work] would have been so widely accepted, and I am glad that I spoke up instead of shying away like I sometimes do. I think Cindy described what I meant about people looking at art according to their life experiences. She felt very strongly about making each picture into a story. I, on the other hand, did not tell stories from the artwork, but I put myself into the art and said what I was feeling using elements from the painting—the straight lines, the use of color and space. Still, I just kept thinking that the only way I could use this museum was by talking about the way people look at things differently because of their different experiences, beliefs, and feelings.

Dionne directly addressed the distance she has felt from what she called "traditional art museums," in which she expected to see neither herself nor her experiences represented. She mused on her responsibilities toward her own children as well as those she will teach. Like Takesha, she drew from the work at MOMA increased confidence in her ability to find meaning in the art in its galleries while helping children to do so, too:

I have always shied away from taking my children to art museums because I thought they would be bored and uninterested. As a child, I was interested in folk art because of the various colors, and I guess also because it depicted people of color. I was not into abstract art because no one helped pique my interest, but now I know that children can like and appreciate art of all kinds if only it is presented to them in an interesting and fun way. I am very excited about taking my children. . . . I love hearing their interpretations, descriptions, likes and dislikes . . . it's my pedagogic responsibility to expand my children's and my future students' experiences beyond what we may have thought as standard for them.

Acknowledging the risks that inhere in teachers trying on new ways of being in the classroom, Christine called attention to her own struggles, connecting these with the kinds of classroom experiences she hoped one day to offer the children she would teach. She pointed, too, to the need for teaching communities, in which teachers' efforts find mutual support, leading to school change:

I hope that there will be a critical mass of teachers who will come together and make change for children. It is very important to me to become a teacher who is not afraid to take risks. I want my students to take risks and risk new ways of learning. We can do this together and help each other. I hope that this work will have a domino effect among other teachers. If other teachers begin to see the potential, we can find the strength to be free enough to bring these things into the classroom.

DISCUSSION

In claiming the space between students' lived experience and their future, imagined selves as teachers, we ask that our students venture from a place of familiar ideas, beliefs, and ways of being to a place of uncertainty and difference. This place of risk and challenge marks the site of transformative learning, a site that we hope will be re-created in the classrooms and schools in which our students will teach. In demanding that the college classroom constitute a space in which comfortable places and assumptions be reconsidered, we breach our students' expectations as well as current educational lore that the ideal transition from home to school, at any age, at any time, and at any place, be "seamless."

Seamless transition between curricular domains and between school experiences assumes a blend of experience, a merger so successful that the contours of transition vanish. Seamlessness erases the traces of particular journeys, collapsing these into prototypic experience, a one-size-fits-all model. It calls to mind the misshapen blouse, cut from a whole piece of shiny turquoise cloth, I sewed in my seventh-grade home economics class. Despite this demonstrated lack of talent, it was apparent to me, a dressmaker's daughter, that the blouse's absurdity lay in its total absence of seams. From my mother I learned that it is in the skillful stitching of seams that artistry resides, and that seams not only hold fragments together, but also make alterations possible. In identifying the seams that mark the transitions that our students make, we identify, too, the possibilities for alterations, for different ways of being.

The mapping of our students' journeys makes the paths they have traversed visible; the geography of their migrations provides a context within which their history, in the form of biography and autobiography, may take root. This work calls for curriculum to be considered in light of its relation to the lives of students and teachers and acknowledges teachers' responsibility to create the kinds of pedagogic, personal, and creative connections that facilitate learning and that animate teaching. It describes a way of thinking about the cultural lives of schools and communities, introducing nuance to consideration of how different cultural experiences can enter into the lives of classrooms.

This work asks of us that we broaden the cultural horizon of schools to include a space for stories that represent different ways of being in the world. Bridging the worlds of school and home/community cultures calls forth necessary and complicated problematics, requiring a shift from an emphasis on techniques of implementation to an examination of the complexities and possibilities of working and living with different cultural worlds in the same classroom. The work with the oral history/ storytelling project and with the Lincoln Center Institute recalls our pedagogic responsibility to expand our students' and our own range of experiences and expectations beyond the familiar and expected. To that end we attend, as we wish our students to do with the children they will teach, to the transitions which inhere in moving between the cultures of home and school and also between school and the world beyond.

The work in the arts reminds us of the importance of familiarizing children with that which feels different, preparing them to risk transitions to unfamiliar worlds, expanding the possibilities that their lives hold for them. In connecting our teacher education students to local forms of culture as well as to New York City's major cultural and arts institutions, we signal their responsibility to recreate these possibilities for the children that they, too, will teach.

REFERENCES

Aitken, J. L. & Mildon, D. A. (1992). Teacher education and the developing teacher: The role of personal knowledge. In M. Fullan & A. Hargreaves (Eds.), *Teacher Development and Educational Change*. London: Falmer Press.

Bruner, J. S. (1990). *Acts of meaning*. Cambridge, MA: Harvard University Press.

Cochran-Smith, M. (1984). *The making of a reader*. Norwood, NJ: Ablex.

Dambekalns, L. (1994). Challenging notions of curriculum development: Questions of multicultural context and content in how we encourage students to learn. *Visual Arts Research, 20* (1), 84–90.

Denzin, N. (1989). *Interpretive biography*. Newbury Park, CA: Sage Publications.

Dilger, S. (1994). Developing policy and programs for multicultural art education: Curriculum and instruction responsive to cultural diversity. *Art Education, 47* (4), 49–53.

Egan, K. (1992). *Imagination in teaching and learning.* London: Routledge.

Eisner, E. (1993). The education of vision. *Educational Horizons, 71*(2), 80–85.

———. (1992). The misunderstood role of the arts in human development. *Phi Delta Kappan, 73* (8), 591–595.

Gadamer, H. (1975). *Truth and method.* New York: Continuum.

———. (1967). On the scope and function of hermeneutical reflection. In D. E. Linge (Ed.), *Philosophical hermeneutics* (pp. 18–43). Berkeley: University of California Press.

Geertz, C. (1973). *The interpretation of cultures: Selected essays.* New York: Basic Books.

Goodson, I. G. (1992). *Studying teachers' lives.* New York: Teachers College Press.

Greene, M. (1978). *Landscapes of learning.* New York: Teachers College Press.

Grumet, M. (1995). Somewhere under the rainbow. The postmodern politics of art education. *Educational Theory, 45* (1), 35–42.

Heath, S. B. (1993). Inner city life through drama: Imagining the language classroom. *TESOL Quarterly, 27* (2), 177–192.

Jagla, V. M. (1994). *Teachers' everyday use of imagination and intuition: In pursuit of the elusive image.* Albany: State University of New York Press.

Korn, C. (1997). Translating stories across cultures. *Education and Culture: The Journal of the John Dewey Society, 41* (1), 18–23.

Korn, C., & Toth, J. (1998). Tools and techne: Reclaiming the language of art in education. Paper presented to American Educational Research Association Annual Meeting, San Diego, April 1998.

Lincoln, Y. S. (1993). I and thou: Method, voice, and roles in research with the silenced. In D. McLaughlin & W. G. Tierney (Eds.) *Naming silenced lives* (pp. 29–45). New York: Routledge.

Russell, D. L. (1997). *Literature for children: A short introduction.* New York: Longman.

Sarason, S. (1990). *The challenge of art to psychology.* New Haven, CT: Yale University Press.

Sass, L. A. (1989). Humanism, hermeneutics, and humanistic psychoanalysis: Differing conceptions of subjectivity. *Psychoanalysis and Contemporary Thought, 12*, 433–504.

Warnke, G. (1987). *Gadamer: Hermeneutics, tradition and reason.* Stanford, CA: Stanford University Press.

5

An Ecological Perspective on Preparing Teachers for Multicultural Classrooms

Helen Johnson

Stimulated by the seminal work of Uri Bronfenbrenner (1979), social scientists have increasingly acknowledged the importance of examining phenomena in context. At any point in time, the behavior of the individual is situated within multiple ecological niches, and accordingly, efforts to implement change must consider these intersecting spheres of influence. The ecological approach stresses, moreover, that each sphere of influence constitutes a complex, multilayered unit in its own right, so that influences do not operate in a simple linear manner (Bronfenbrenner, 1979, 1986). This chapter applies an ecological perspective to illuminate some of the conflicting forces underlying current efforts to create positive multicultural classrooms.

Discussions of multicultural education generally center on the importance of broadening students' understanding and appreciation of diverse cultures. The pedagogical issues deal with what materials and experiences are best suited to children of different ages and backgrounds. The role of the teacher is recognized as critical to achieving multicultural understanding; in the ecology of the classroom, she is identified as the primary change agent, the source of influence that operates to increase multicultural understanding and acceptance. Unlike psychology, which devotes considerable attention to the dynamics of the practitioner's involvement in the therapeutic process, in education we too often treat the teacher's commitment to externally identified goals and objectives such as multicultural education as a constant and unanalyzed unit. Efforts to enhance teacher effectiveness center on providing teachers with additional information, materials, and activities. Missing from this analysis is consideration of the factors that influence teachers' participation in the process of multicultural education, including the beliefs and values that she herself brings to the task.

The importance of such personal factors in shaping the individual teacher's acceptance and implementation of models of multicultural education was apparent in the teachers enrolled in a graduate course titled *Stories, Families, and Literacy*. This chapter examines the responses of one of the teachers in the group, Camille and, drawing upon ecological and field theory, considers the challenges such cases present for models of multicultural education.

Camille was a first-year teacher in a fifth-grade classroom in a public school in New York City. She was from an Irish American working-class background and had one older sister who had been teaching in public schools for several years. In her literacy autobiography, Camille identified early reading experiences with her mother as extremely important. Although not a high school graduate, her mother read regularly to Camille and her sister, and they both developed a love for reading and stories. Camille credited the accomplishments of herself and her sister to their mother's involvement and encouragement. She strongly believed that adults must tell children what to do and that children should do as they're told.

Camille had worked as a teacher's aide for twelve years before completing the coursework for provisional teacher certification. She received her teaching assignment three weeks before the beginning of the semester. The school to which she was assigned is located in a neighborhood that is predominantly low-income African American, with rates of unemployment and drug-related crime that substantially exceed the city averages. Because of the low proportion of its students performing at grade level, the school had been placed on the NYC School Chancellor's list of schools under registration review (SURR). Within these schools, there is great pressure to meet citywide standards for academic achievement by improving students' performance on standardized tests. Camille had hoped to be placed in a school closer to her home and in a neighborhood more similar to her own. But although she was disappointed with the placement, Camille was pleased to finally be in the position of teacher rather than aide and viewed this job as a chance to begin working her way toward the one that she really wanted. Before school started, Camille hurried to prepare lesson plans and materials for her class.

At the same time that she started her first teaching assignment, Camille enrolled in my graduate course *Stories, Families, and Literacy* to begin earning credits toward the masters degree required for permanent certification. In this course, an elective in the masters program in Elementary and Early Childhood Education, we examined the contribution of stories and family practices to the development of literacy. One of the primary objectives of the course was to strengthen teachers' appreciation for diverse paths to literacy by highlighting the embeddedness of stories and family literacy practices within culture. Class discussions and writing assignments frequently required students to draw upon their teaching experiences and memories of their childhood and early schooling.

During the first class, students read *Tell Me a Story Mama*, a picture book by Angela Johnson (1989). The book offers a vivid example of how the repetitiveness and familiarity of family stories are valued by children and provide a basis for their engagement in verbal interchanges. It also beautifully illustrates the pleasure that children take in sharing stories and the storytelling process itself. Camille, however, responded to the book with some impatience. The child knew the story already, so why was she bothering her mother with questions about it? Why didn't the mother insist that her daughter talk less and let her mother tell the story? That child needed to learn to be a better listener. Other students in the class challenged Camille's remarks, suggesting that the mother was actually scaffolding her child's language development through storytelling. Camille dismissed these comments with a smile and wave of her hand.

The next class reading, an article by Shirley Brice Heath (1989), provoked heated reactions from the class. Many felt that Heath's criticisms of American schools for failing to accommodate African American children's style of oral communication were unfair and outdated. They recounted ways in which their own classes were organized to incorporate oral sharing of personal experiences and to include multiple and varied assessments of student skills. Camille's response was different. She did not consider it her responsibility to accommodate the individual learning styles of her students; it was their job to follow her instructions. Camille expressed frustration with her students' poor academic skills. They had difficulty following her lessons, and their homework, when they did it, was sloppy and incorrect. Although Camille had prepared a clear schedule of work and lesson plans before school began, the class was not keeping up with it. She was impatient: how would they get through the material if she allowed all their questions and digressions? Camille did not accept notions of cultural or individual differences in language and learning styles. She attributed her students' slow progress with her lessons to a lack of effort on their part and to a lack of discipline on the part of their parents and former teachers.

The following week, we viewed a videotape of teenage parents who were participating in a family literacy project by reading to younger children. In the discussion that followed, I emphasized the engagement that the teens showed in their reading as a potential motivator for subsequent reading achievement (Johnson, Pflaum, Sherman, Taylor, & Poole, 1996). Camille, however, was extremely critical of the poor reading skills that the teens displayed. Her reaction centered on the fact that the teens were not performing at grade level and were reading children's books. Other students argued that the level of the teens' performance was less important than their active involvement in the reading process and the fact that their level of skill, although delayed, was improving. Again, Camille dismissed these comments with a smile and wave of her hand.

In the weeks that followed, Camille's response to materials in the *Stories, Families, and Literacy* class remained fairly consistent. She rejected classroom approaches that encouraged teachers to draw on children's personal experiences (Dyson, 1994, Miller & Mehler, 1994), and she talked repeatedly about how little her students seemed to be learning and how little she felt she could expect to accomplish, given their poor skills. She was particularly critical of the parents of her students, commenting frequently on their lack of involvement. Although she sent many letters home about problems in class, few parents came in to meet with her. With parents like these, she concluded, "what could you expect" from the students?

Camille's teacher preparation courses had emphasized the importance of creating a culturally sensitive and respectful classroom environment. She had been careful to include books representing the experiences of different groups in her class library and was planning a "food day," for which students would bring their families' traditional foods to share. But at the same time as she was implementing these multicultural activities in her classroom, Camille's approach to many of her students and their families was fundamentally one of mistrust and disrespect. If one were to draw a graphic representation of the individuals and influences in Camille's classroom, her function in classroom exchanges would be difficult to portray because of the discrepancies between surface and underlying messages. On the surface, Camille solicited participation and sharing. But she also communicated more subtle messages that devalued the students and their families; what they had to share was considered strange or inferior. Camille did not convey the interest and respect that encourage genuine dialogue and engagement. A student in this class environment faces a dilemma: the teacher is requesting participation, but participation requires that the student breach the family's and cultural group's sanctions about privacy and, in so doing, will expose his or her family to derision. Although Camille intended to implement good practices, her rigid conceptions of appropriate behavior were reflected in the tone of her questions and her responses to student disclosures. It is certainly possible that under these circumstances, students might choose not to participate; the risks associated with participating were quite salient, and the rewards less so. Unfortunately, the students' reticence and lack of responsiveness to Camille's bids for participation fueled her own negative beliefs about their motivation and encouraged her to lower her expectations further. In this way, instructing a teacher such as Camille in techniques that potentially can be used to increase multicultural awareness may backfire and, inadvertantly, reinforce the barriers to understanding.

In his field theory of human relations, Kurt Lewin (1935) proposed that the laws of the physical world also operate in the realm of intra- and interpersonal behavior. According to Lewin's Galilean model, it is not possible to adequately study the forces, or in his terms, vectors, operating in a situation apart from the situation itself. "The whole situation," he argued, "changes with the process" (1935, p. 33). At first glance, this point may seem obvious. But this recognition of the ongoing dynamic between forces within an environmental context or field is actually a critical departure from traditional linear models and lies at the core of ecological (Bronfenbrenner, 1979) and transactional (Sameroff, 1989; Sameroff & Chandler, 1975) accounts of development. In the typical additive model of development, the impact of a particular variable is measured in relation to its appearance or operation at a specific point in time. Critical aspects of the variable, such as size, intensity, duration, may be quantified, as may its impact. Each of these impacts, moreover, is a discrete event, with an onset and an endpoint. The process of development entails the gradual accumulation of these influences and is essentially passive. But in the ecological approach, individual variables are subsumed within spheres of influence, or ecological niches, which exist in an ongoing dynamic. The impact of variables is determined through their relationship to one another, which means that the significance of a particular variable cannot be defined independently of the environment within which it is occurring.

Clearly, in discussions that seek to compare effects across cultures, this point is particularly important, for variables will operate differently and have different meaning in different cultural contexts. The work of Beth Harry (1991) provides powerful evidence of this point, documenting the influence of culture-specific views of family on the response of parents to identification of their children's "special needs." Moreover, the relative importance of variables in a situation is due partly to their placement relative to other variables in the field; for example, proximal variables will have more influence than distal ones. Development involves the constant interplay and shifting balance between these influences, for learning is a fundamentally interactive process. Within the classroom environment, at any point in time, there are intersecting valences from the students and teachers and their families and cultures, as well as from the school and the larger community it represents. Thus the meaning of a particular behavior will vary across contexts and cannot be defined independently of them.

In multicultural education, ongoing exchanges between all the individuals in the classroom frame the content of the curriculum. James

Banks and Cherry Banks (1995) have proposed five dimensions to consider in describing approaches to multicultural education. *Content integration* concerns teachers' use of information and examples from diverse cultural groups to illustrate concepts presented in the classroom. *Knowledge construction* relates to the reliance on culturally bound assumptions in the generation of knowledge within the social and natural sciences. *Prejudice reduction* deals with children's views regarding race, as well as strategies for fostering the development of attitudes that are more open and accepting. *An equity pedagogy* refers to teachers' use of methods that facilitate the academic achievement of ethnically and racially diverse students. Finally, *an empowering school culture and social structure* concerns restructuring the school culture and organization to provide experiences of educational equality and cultural empowerment for ethnically and racially diverse students. These dimensions reflect qualitative differences in perspectives on multicultural education rather than a quantitative continuum. However, the creation of *an empowering school culture and social structure* clearly requires content integration, knowledge construction, prejudice reduction and an equity pedagogy, so that these four dimensions may be viewed as necessary, but not sufficient, conditions for effective systemic implementation of multicultural education. This point is of particular concern for teacher education programs, which too often confine their work on multicultural education to the more circumscribed issues of content integration and prejudice reduction.

Banks and Banks also describe four discrete stages in the evolution of multicultural education. In early work, the emphasis was on *ethnic studies* and the incorporation of theories and concepts from diverse cultural groups into school and teacher education curricula. As the limits of this approach became apparent, scholars and educators adopted an approach of *multiethnic education*, which sought to increase educational equality by modifying educational procedures to accommodate cultural differences. More recently, concerns about representation and equity have been extended to other groups who have experienced discrimination, such as women and people with disabilities. This work has generated the current emphasis on "development of theory, research, and practice that interrelate variables connected to race, class, and gender" (Banks & Banks, 1995, p. 11). It is precisely these types of complex interrelationships between variables that the ecological approach addresses.

One important aspect of the ecological approach is the recognition that each source of influence is itself multilayered. Consequently, it is not sufficient to simply talk about the teacher's influence as a unitary force; her influence is a composite of many factors, some of which may operate at cross-purposes. Moreover, because of the transactional nature of development, each influence is continually modified by its encounters with other forces in the environment (Sameroff, 1989, 1997). For multicultural education, the primary spheres of influence are the children and their families, the teacher, and the school. What follows is a brief consideration of the layers of influences operating within each of these domains and a discussion of the implications for preparing teachers for multicultural education.

Each individual child brings to the class a set of personal values and beliefs about schools, about learning, about play, about family, and about the hierarchy of interpersonal relationships. These beliefs grow out of personal experience and are grounded within the individual's family history, culture, and social class (Gutierrez & Sameroff, 1990, Holloway, 1988, Lin & Fu, 1990, Stevenson, Chen, & Uttal, 1990). For the child of teachers, for example, school is an extension of family: it is the place where mommy and/or daddy work, and the teachers are people who care about me, like mommy and daddy. But for the child of recent immigrants with limited schooling and knowledge of English, school may be a disavowal of family: it may be a place where people do things in ways that mommy and daddy don't understand, and teachers may be people who expect me to learn these new ways and who don't value what I have learned before (Korn, 1997). Delpit (1995) observed this disjuncture between home and school for African American children attending an alternative school located on the border between two neighborhoods. "All the African American kids had to literally and figuratively leave their community in order to come to school. . . . Just as the school opened only to Society Hill, what happened inside was in great part an expression of Society Hill culture. On their trip every morning to the other side of the building, the South Side children were asked to leave what they knew and who they were behind, and to become someone else" (p. 35).

There are also cultural differences in views of the teacher and of the role that parents should play in their children's education. For example, many Asian cultures emphasize the mother's role in instructing children to be obedient and conscientious students (Chao, 1994). Moreover, children understand from an early age that their academic performance is important not just for their own success but to maintain the honor of their family (Caplan, Choy, & Whitmore, 1992). But many Latinos, particularly those who are isolated from the mainstream culture by both ethnicity and social class, view schooling as a domain completely separate from family, one in which parents should not interfere. Children's school performance is the responsibility of the teacher; it would be inappropriate for the parent to become involved. Reviewing studies on Hispanic families' involvement in schools, Harry (1991) concludes,

The most common research interpretation emerging from documented empirical studies has been that many minority parents tend to place their trust in the school and do not expect to play an influential role. . . . cultural attitudes such as trust in and respect for educational authorities, as well as difficulties in communicating and identifying with the dominant culture, have a negative influence on parents' interaction with the school. . . . participation may carry a different meaning for parents holding traditional Hispanic cultural values. (p. 102)

Thus, for some children, performance is linked to the goals and activities of the family; for others, there is a tension between these domains. These basic orientations frame the child's engagement in the class.

The process of learning requires that children encounter novelty and use it to build their understanding of the world. In this sense, school requires change from all children: each child must become a partner in a new series of social exchanges and must accommodate, in the Piagetian sense, the opportunities, demands, and constraints of the classroom. For some children, this new environment stretches the dimensions of what is already known; there is continuity between home and school that supports the child's forays into the community of the school. For other children, however, there is a sharp disjuncture between home and school; the gap between home and school means that "school ways" may be quite strange and unfamiliar to the child and also that the child may feel a tension between home and school, which may impede engagement. With a child who is experiencing this conflict, the teacher's offer of an opportunity to "share" may not be helpful; the child may hesitate to bridge the gap between home and school and may find it difficult to translate experience from home into the language and format of the classroom.

Just as the children come to the class with various degrees of familiarity with what will become the shared culture of the school, the teacher also comes with a personal background and history that overlap with some aspects of the school's culture and are discrepant from others. As the teacher moves to establish class procedures and structures, she draws upon what she has been taught, but her actions are always framed within her own values and experiences. For her, too, there will be greater familiarity with the experiences of some of the children than with those of others, and she will understand the difficulties of some of the children more readily than others. This is evident in the work of Courtney Cazden (1994), who has documented differences in teachers' responsiveness to the stories of children whose backgrounds are more or less similar to their own. The use of culturally sensitive activities and materials does not ensure that the teacher herself understands the gaps she is being asked to bridge or has a constructive perspective on the differences between children in her classroom (Horning & Kruse, 1991).

Banks and Banks (1995) describe four approaches to multicultural curriculum reform. The first, the *contributions* approach, incorporates information about heroes and heroines, holidays, and special cultural characteristics. The second, the *additive* approach, involves adding content, themes, and perspectives to the existing curriculum without changing its basic organization. The third, the *transformation* approach, entails actually changing the curriculum to highlight knowledge construction and the perspectives of diverse cultural groups. The fourth, the *social action* approach, builds upon *transformation*, linking the knowledge that has been socially constructed to positive action within the community. The *contributions* and *additive* approaches are fairly straightforward. In order to implement them, teachers need only introduce some additional information and perhaps acquire additional classroom materials. But the *transformation* and *social action* approaches require that the teacher rethink her classroom structure and practice and develop links to the families and community of her students. Teachers do not typically receive much preparation for these types of tasks. In fact, as in the case of Camille, they may be subjected to many competing pressures that discourage these efforts.

Much of the emphasis in teacher preparation for multicultural education has followed the *contributions* and *additive* approaches, focusing on *facts* about different countries and groups and *methods* for teaching children about differences. By now, for example, most teachers know that eye contact is considered disrespectful in some cultures and that it's a good idea to offer children opportunities to share information about their family practices and cultural traditions in school. These general pointers fail to prepare teachers, however, for the more subtle ways in which family and cultural differences will affect children's responses to "perfectly good" lesson plans. And more important, they do not provide an opportunity for teachers to fully examine their own feelings about these differences.

What does the teacher herself bring to the classroom? She comes with her own personal history: her family's view of education and involvement with her schooling, the positive and negative aspects of her own schooling, her sense of her own effectiveness as a learner. In the *Families, Stories, and Literacy* class described earlier, many of the teachers described very powerful negative memories of their own early school experiences: the anxiety evoked by round robin reading lessons, the discouragement stemming from not being placed in the top reading group, the embarrassment of not understanding what the teacher said. These memories led to greater compassion and empathy in some teachers; they remembered how hard they had tried to do well and how much it had hurt when their efforts weren't acknowledged. These teachers were trying hard not to repeat the practices that had been so painful to them as children. But other teachers in the group had a different reaction. Sure, there had been some tough times in school, but they had survived, and "taking some lumps" was good preparation for life. Schools should not be expected to coddle children and cater to differences, and teachers could not be expected to operate with the flexibility that more individualized approaches would require.

Beyond their memories about their own schooling, though, teachers also bring their own experience with cultural differences, which is critical in shaping their response to the variability in their students. During a recent class discussion, teachers who are nonnative speakers of English recalled the difficulty of being submerged in a language environment that they could not decipher. But others, native speakers with backgrounds similar to Camille's, recalled instead their feelings of resentment about the special services and activities that had been made available for students who were nonnative English speakers. Several of these teachers complained bitterly that they themselves had received less attention and fewer opportunities because in a school system with limited resources, their needs and interests had been deferred to those of non-English-speaking students. They resented these students and blamed the parents for failing to prepare their children to function in English-speaking classrooms.

While these teachers talked frequently about the importance of "respect for every child" and planned class activities to promote cultural understanding, they harbored deep feelings of distrust and resentment that undoubtedly constrained the sharing that occurred in their classrooms. Their feelings toward the families of their students were especially problematic. They expected the parents not to support their children's schooling and were rigid and unreflective about the ways in which they solicited family involvement. They interpreted families' lack of response to traditional participation opportunities—open school night, PTA meetings—as a lack of concern. There was no understanding that group functions might be intimidating for parents unfamiliar with the language and activities of the American school. What emerged instead was a view that whatever was accomplished with this child would be *without* and even *despite* the family. In this way, the teacher's good intentions are implemented through the lens of her past experience, and her attitudes create a barrier between school and family that the child must continually negotiate.

At the same time that each student and teacher brings personal values and beliefs to the classroom, the school itself embodies a set of expectations about what should be learned, when it should be learned, how that learning should be demonstrated and assessed, and how the process of learning should look and sound in a classroom. These values, like those of the children and adults in the classroom, are also grounded within culture and class. There is a growing emphasis in early childhood and elementary education on outcomes, assessment, and technology.

Starting at an increasingly early age, the school curriculum stipulates clear standards for knowledge and skills that all children should demonstrate. Despite frequent references to child-centered approaches, there is very little consideration of developmental processes or the contribution of individual, familial, and cultural differences to variations in how these processes unfold. Perhaps most troubling is the disproportionate representation of minority children in special education classes, which reflects the pervasiveness of cultural bias in the school agenda and assessments. Translating materials into different languages does not mean that the lessons are culturally sensitive. Indeed, even the "style" of classrooms—the emphasis on individual performance and the heavy reliance on competitive, timed activities—reflects specific cultural values.

At the same time that schools ask teachers to create "culturally sensitive" classrooms, they also ask teachers to complete certain tasks with their students within specific timeframes. The messages about cultural sensitivity are distinct from the messages about academic goals; they are not presented as interrelated. In fact, the "multicultural piece" is generally an add-on feature. Like expressive arts, it is treated as an extra unit rather than as an integral part of curriculum and teaching. Under these circumstances, "multicultural activities" are a deflection from the teacher's primary goals. No wonder, then, that under pressure to have students perform adequately on citywide and statewide exams, teachers may show little inclination to accommodate the diversity of their students.

Failure to embed multiculturalism within the teaching process begins in teacher preparation programs. A special course such as *Multicultural Education* may provide students with much valuable information about the history and practices of different groups, but positioning the information in this way, apart from coursework on teaching methods and theory, gives prospective teachers the sense that these are separate domains—there's teaching and there's multicultural education. To help teachers develop truly welcoming classrooms, teachers must receive training that integrates the perspectives of specialists in development, curriculum, and multicultural studies. They must experience the connections in their own training so that they can implement them in their practice.

Beyond needing adequate knowledge of the content areas, prospective teachers need an understanding of developmental process and the range of normal development, and they need exposure to models of teaching and learning that can accommodate student variability. Most important, teachers must be given an opportunity to work with this knowledge in situ and then reflect on the efficacy of their efforts. Reflective writing and discussion within a context that provides supportive feedback can encourage teachers to stretch their own understanding. In a very real sense, this is what the enterprise of multicultural education requires of them: to go beyond what is immediately known and understood using an approach that is positive and respectful. Luis Moll's work (1998) offers a powerful model for helping teachers extend their understanding of their students' lives.

There are two primary components to this model: qualitative research conducted by teachers with the families of their students, and regularly scheduled teacher study group meetings to discuss what they are learning through their research and their teaching. More specifically, elementary school teachers visit the families of their students and talk with them about the strategies and skills that the family utilizes to support its members. These discussions highlight the "funds of knowledge" embedded in the everyday functioning of students' families. Through this experience, teachers come to genuinely appreciate the families' knowledge and skills, and recognize the families as resources for classroom activities. In this way, teachers come to understand culture "from a more dynamic, 'processual' view, not as a group of traits, folk celebrations, foods or artifacts, but as the lived practices and knowledge of the students and their families" (Moll, 1998, p. 72). The teachers, together with researchers, also meet regularly as a study group to discuss what they are learning through their visits with families and to reflect on its implications for their teaching. Having time that is specifically designated for thinking and talking about practice enables teachers to begin to stretch their ideas of what is acceptable and possible in their classrooms. In this reflective context, teachers support one another's efforts to extend their teaching to be more responsive and inclusive.

The case of Camille illustrates the complexity of preparing teachers for culturally diverse classrooms. She had received training in multicultural education and believed, based on her own experience, that education plays a critical role for individuals from diverse backgrounds. However, forces within multiple ecological domains were operating against her implementation of a positive model of multicultural education. The strong support she received from her own mother, which had been a positive influence in her own school achievement, had given Camille a clear but rigid view of the parent's role and significance in promoting school success. This led her to lower her expectations for children whose parents did not conform to this model and also to adopt an antagonistic approach toward these parents. Thus, within the *personal domain*, there were influences opposing both the establishment of an open and respectful classroom environment and the formation of teacher-parent alliances.

In addition, although the students in Camille's predominantly African American class were eager to tell stories and share information about their lives, they had very poor academic skills and had difficulty completing their work. The eagerness they showed to talk about personal experiences, which could have been helpful for increasing interpersonal understanding, occurred throughout lessons and during time that Camille had allocated for structured work. Camille, frustrated by the students' poor performance, viewed student-initiated discussions as a threat to the class's academic progress. Thus, within the *classroom domain*, there were influences opposing both acknowledgement of student disclosures and encouragement of spontaneous dialogue.

Finally, the school in which Camille was teaching placed a heavy emphasis on getting students to perform at grade level, regardless of teaching method. The pressure to get through the curriculum led Camille to feel very uncomfortable with any digressions from her lesson plans and to be impatient with students who needed extra time or help. In this way, within the *domain of the school*, there were influences opposing both open-ended class activities and formative evaluations of student work.

From an ecological perspective, there were many conflicting forces impacting on Camille as she defined her approach to the diverse backgrounds and skills of her students. Camille genuinely wanted to be an effective teacher. In her view, an effective teacher was one whose classroom was quiet and whose students completed their work on time. This view, combined with pressures from the school to emphasize standardized measures of achievement, led Camille to see the diversity of her students as a problem to be managed rather than as a source of richness for the class. Camille also was troubled by the behavior of the families of her students. She felt that their lack of participation in school events and failure to respond to her notes indicated a lack of concern for their children's education and a lack of respect for her. As the semester wore on, these attitudes accelerated into a cycle of self-fulfilling negative effects. The students did poorly on Camille's assignments, she became angry and discouraged, and decided that it was not worth putting much effort into her teaching. Unfortunately, this sequence occurs all too often with teachers who are uncomfortable with their students. The initial gaps in understanding become magnified over time, negative attitudes become hardened, and expectations for the children's learning are lowered.

Given its self-perpetuating nature, it is extremely difficult to disrupt this chain of negative teacher-student-family transactions. However, some suggestion of how to accomplish this can be gleaned from the case of Camille. One aspect of Camille's responses to her students and their parents that was particularly striking was her tendency to personalize their actions. Thus, her students' diversity was experienced as *her* management problem, rather than as *their* personal backgrounds and characteristics. Similarly, their parents' lack of responsiveness was viewed as lack of respect for *her* rather than as an expression of *their* feelings about school and their own adequacy as learners.

One evening toward the end of the semester, Camille came into our graduate class extremely elated. She had been absent from school for several days because of illness. When she returned, her students had written her letters telling her how much they had missed her and how much they preferred *her* way of doing things to the substitute's. One of the parents had come by the school to see if she had returned. This recognition led to a change in Camille's attitude. The expressions of affection and acknowledgement of her efforts encouraged her to try a little more. She began to think that there might be some value in allowing the students to talk and write about their own experiences and interests. Camille was a new teacher who had been thrust into a school environment that stressed performance standards, with a class of students whose approach to learning was less structured than her own. She expressed concern about her ability to achieve the standards and impatience with her students' apparent lack of response to her. The responses of the students and parents to her absence gave Camille a sense that she was valued and that what happened in her classroom mattered. She began to realize that even though her students talked a lot and didn't always follow her lesson plans, they were paying attention and learning in their own way. Hopefully, this was the beginning of a positive cycle of transactions between Camille, her students, and their parents.

But this is not presented as a "happily ever after" story; rather, it is presented as an illustration of how, in a transactional model, changes in feedback at one point in time can alter the trajectory of an evolving classroom dynamic. Student and parent responses to Camille's absence played a critical role in moving her toward a more constructive approach to her students. Through these responses, Camille received personal recognition and validation from her students; and she learned that the families of her students really did care about the children's schooling and did appreciate her efforts. Camille's tendency to personalize the events in her classroom is not that unusual, especially for a new teacher. However, because of it, the experiences of personal validation were particularly powerful. This suggests that part of the solution to teachers' ambivalence toward multicultural education may lie in helping them identify and recognize affirmation of their efforts when that affirmation comes in forms that may not be familiar to them. In Camille's case, the students' eagerness to talk about their personal experiences, which she initially had viewed as simply avoidance of the work she had assigned, was in fact an indication of their positive feelings for her. Hopefully, recognizing this enabled Camille to acknowledge their disclosures more positively and to incorporate their stories into the discourse of learning in her classroom.

In Camille's case, the changes in classroom dynamics were triggered by feedback from the students and their parents, whose responses told Camille that her efforts were valued. But sometimes, it is precisely when teachers are not receiving positive feedback that they need to reflect on and modify their practice. As teacher educators, we must seek to develop a reflective, problem-solving approach to teaching that incorporates self-evaluation and revision as ongoing processes. Allen Black and Paul Ammon (1992) have identified five discrete stages in the development of teachers' pedagogical thinking, moving from associationist and behaviorist conceptions (levels 1 and 2) to constructivist conceptions that, at first, are quite global (level 3) but eventually become more differentiated and integrated (levels 4 and 5) (p. 331).

In the Development Teacher Education model outlined by Black and Ammon, key topics are discussed "repeatedly and hierarchically," so that teachers develop increasingly complex and differentiated understanding of classroom theory and practice. This approach shares Moll's emphasis on the value of providing regular opportunities for teachers to meet with peers to discuss what is going on in their classrooms and how it fits with what they are learning about their students and the larger school community. It would seem, then, that a critical aspect of strengthening teachers' efficacy is to acknowledge and accommodate their need for time to reflect on and consider their practice in a supportive and nonthreatening setting. Each teacher needs a sense that she is not functioning in isolation and that her concerns are not a reflection of personal inadequacy.

What the ecological approach suggests, then, is that efforts to prepare teachers for multicultural education must consider more carefully the complex influences operating within every classroom. The community, the school environment, the students and their families all exert multi-dimensional and often contradictory pressures. The teacher must make sense out of these influences, but she must do this always within the context and limits of her own experience and values. Pushing teachers to go beyond what they understand can lead to a cycle of negative transactions that only reinforces barriers between teacher, student, and family. What is needed instead are more opportunities for teachers to be reflective about how they are feeling and what they are trying to accomplish in their classrooms. Starting from these reflections, from what they truly know, teachers can begin to stretch their understanding as they reach out to build connections with their students and their families. Acknowledging and building on the strengths of all participants—teacher, student, family, community—will move the educational enterprise beyond static additive models toward the transformational and social constructivist engagement that Banks, Black and Ammon, and others have envisioned. In this way, the potential for positive multicultural education can be fulfilled.

REFERENCES

Banks, J. A., & Banks, C. M. (1995). *Handbook of research on multicultural education.* New York: Simon & Schuster, Macmillan.

Black, A., & Ammon, P. (1992). A developmental-constructivist approach to teacher education. *Journal of Teacher Education, 43,* 323–335.

Bronfenbrenner, U. (1979). *The ecology of human development.* Cambridge, MA: Harvard University Press.

Bronfenbrenner, U. (1986). Ecology of the family as a context for human development: Research perspectives. *Developmental Psychology, 22,* 723–742.

Caplan, N., Choy, M. H., & Whitmore, J. K. (1992). Indochinese refugeee families and academic achievement. *Scientific American, 266,* 36–42.

Cazden, C. (1994). What is sharing time for? In A.H. Dyson & C. Genishi (Eds.), *The need for story: Cultural diversity in classroom and community* (pp. 72–79). Urbana, IL: National Council of Teachers of English.

Chao, R. K. (1994). Beyond parental control and authoritarian parenting style: Understanding Chinese parenting through the cultural notion of training. *Child Development, 65,* 1111–1119.

Delpit, L. (1995). I just want to be myself: Discovering what students bring to school "in their blood." In W. Ayers (Ed.), *To become a teacher* (pp. 34–48). New York: Teachers College Press.

Dyson, A. H. (1994). "I'm gonna express myself": The politics of story in the children's worlds. In A. H. Dyson & C. Genishi (Eds.), *The need for story: Cultural diversity in classroom and community* (pp. 155–171). Urbana, IL: National Council of Teachers of English.

Gutierrez, J., & Sameroff, A. J. (1990). Determinants of complexity in Mexican-American and Anglo-American mothers' conceptions of child development. *Child Development, 61,* 384–394.

Harry, B. (1991). *Cultural diversity, families, and the special education system.* New York: Teachers College.

Heath, S. B. (1989). Oral and literate traditions among black Americans living in poverty. *American Psychologist, 44,* 367–373.

Holloway, S. D. (1988). Concepts of ability and effort in Japan and the United States. *Review of Educational Research, 58,* 327–345.

Horning, K. T., & Kruse, G. M. (1991). Looking into the mirror: Considerations behind the reflections. In M. V. Lindgren, (Ed.), *The multicolored mirror: Cultural substance in literature for children and young adults* (pp. 1–13). Fort Atkinson, WI: Highsmith Press.

Johnson, A. (1989). *Tell me a story Mama.* New York: Orchard Books/Franklin Watts.

Johnson, H. L., Pflaum, S., Sherman, E., Taylor, P., & Poole, P. (1996). Focus on teenage parents: Using children's literature to strengthen teenage literacy. *Journal of Adolescent and Adult Literacy, 39,* 290–296.

Korn, C. (1997). "I used to be so smart": Children talk about immigration. *Education and Culture, 14,* 17–24.

Lewin, K. (1935). *A dynamic theory of personality.* New York: McGraw-Hill.

Lin, C.-Y. C., & Fu, V. R. (1990). A comparison of child-rearing practices among

Chinese, immigrant Chinese, and Causcasian-American parents. *Child De-velopment, 61,* 429–433.

Miller, P. J., & Mehler, R. A. (1994). The power of personal storytelling in families and kindergartens. In A. H. Dyson & C. Genishi (Eds.), *The need for story* (pp. 38–54). Urbana, IL: National Council of Teachers of English.

Moll, L. C. (1998). Turning to the world: Bilingual schooling, literacy, and the cultural mediation of thinking. *National Reading Conference Yearbook, 47,* 59–75.

Sameroff, A. J. (1997, April). *Developmental contributions to the study of psychopa-thology.* Washington, DC: Society for Research on Child Development.

———. (1989). Models of developmental regulation: The environtype. In D. Ci-chetti (Ed.), *The emergence of a discipline. (Rochester symposium on develop-mental psychopathology,* Vol. I, pp. 41–68). Hillsdale, NJ: Erlbaum.

Sameroff, A. J., & Chandler, M. J. (1975). Reproductive risk and the continuum of caretaking casualty. In F. D. Horowitz (Ed.), *Review of child development research,* Vol. 4 (pp. 187–244). Chicago: University of Chicago Press.

Stevenson, H. W., Chen, C., & Uttal, D. H. (1990). Beliefs and achievement: A study of black, white, and Hispanic children. *Child Development, 61,* 508–523.

6

Facing the Terror Within: Exploring the Personal in Multicultural Education

Peter Taubman

> It has always been much easier (because it has always seemed much easier) to give a name to the evil without than to locate the terror within. And yet, the terror within is far truer and far more powerful than any of our labels: the labels change, the terror is constant. And this terror has something to do with the irreducible gap between the self one invents—the self one takes oneself as being, which is, however, and by definition a provisional self—and the undiscoverable self, which always has the power to blow the provisional self to bits. It is perfectly possible . . . to discover . . . the self one has sewn together with such effort . . . is gone: and out of what raw material will one build a self again? The lives of men . . . to an extent literally unimaginable, depend on how vividly this question lives in the mind. It is a question which can paralyze the mind, of course; but if the question does NOT live in the mind, then one is simply condemned to eternal youth, which is a synonym for corruption.
>
> —James Baldwin (1985, p. 383)

The quote that opens this chapter appears in an essay James Baldwin wrote in 1964 titled, with no small irony, "Nothing Personal." In that essay Baldwin argued that Americans are trapped between a romanticized past and a denied present. Unable to face *who* they are, Americans lie to themselves about *what* they are and find themselves in an identity crisis. "And in such a crisis," he wrote, "it becomes absolutely indispensable to discover, or invent . . . the stranger [and] the barbarian, who [are] responsible for our confusion and our pain" (p. 386). More than thirty years later, we are still inventing barbarians and strangers, and, I would add, many of us who write about multicultural and antiracist education continue, at our peril, to ignore the "personal,"[1] where, according to Patricia Williams (1991, p. 93), "our most idealistic and our deadliest politics are lodged, and are revealed."

Several years ago, in my capacity as head of the English department at an urban prep school,[2] I was observing, Jane, a white[3] woman, teaching Richard Wright's *Native Son* to a class of racially mixed high school juniors and seniors. An experienced and sophisticated teacher, Jane was willing to "contain" (Kahn, 1993) the ambiguity and anxiety of her students, and she allowed the discussion on race to emerge and grow in intensity. A white senior, John, firmly stated that he didn't see color, he saw individuals. A black junior, Simone, fired back that that was racist, that John would never understand because he was white. The boy, increasingly agitated, argued that she was being racist, because she was basing everything on color. At that point, Jane intervened by asking the boy what was wrong with seeing someone's race as part of who they are. The white boy couldn't really respond, mumbled something about prejudice and was pretty silent for the remainder of the class. Jane went on to give some definitions of race and racism and to discuss how whiteness is invisible and how hard it is for Whites to see themselves as being affected by their race. She backed this up by pointing out how the white kids had had trouble responding in their essays to the question of how race had affected them, just as earlier in the semester boys had had more difficulty than girls writing about how gender had affected them.

After class I asked Jane about the incident. She worried she hadn't done enough to make clear that "white/European culture often masquerades as universal," and she expressed concern that John hadn't really "gotten it." But she also said that he was angry about affirmative action policies, that he often complained the class was reading too many books by Blacks, and that he was probably racist. I remember thinking that she was too hard on John, turning him, as Simone had done, into a "stranger" (Baldwin, 1985 [1964], p. 383); then I worried that I had probably identified with him because we were both white males, and so I quickly dropped the question that I probably should have asked, which was, "Is there any way John, you, and Simone could have furthered the dialogue?"

We talked a bit more, and I asked her why she was doing this kind of antiracist work, why she did multicultural education.[4] Jane gave several reasons having to do with a commitment to racial justice, with witnessing racist violence firsthand at demonstrations, with having politically radical parents, with her being a woman, and with her own hatred of all prejudice.

I told her that I often wondered why I, as a white male, was so involved in multicultural education, that I shared many of the reasons she had for doing the work, but that I also thought my involvement had to do with my own psychic structures—the dynamics of familial relationships, my ambivalence about my own identities, and a good many fears I had. Jane gave me a jaundiced look and reiterated that she did the work because she always had been and was committed to fighting racism. I felt a bit stupid, as if I had inappropriately introduced material from the analysand's couch into a conversation about morality and racial justice. I was anxious that while her "ideals" were revealed, perhaps my "deadliest politics" were creeping to the surface. We quickly reestablished comfort by moving to a strong condemnation of the defensiveness and the resistance on the part of the school's administrators and some teachers to our efforts to make the school more inclusive.

I have often thought about that exchange and many more like it. Over the years I have come to believe that many approaches to multicultural education are shot through with defenses against examining our own investments in multicultural education, as well as against facing the provisionality and contingency of all identities. Baldwin was right; it appears easier to name the "evil without" than confront the "terror within." It seems easier to avoid the personal and our own complicity in the disorder we denounce in the world, than to explore the messiness and complexity of our motives for doing this work and our feelings and thoughts about race. And in the face of unremitting discrimination, it seems safer to armor ourselves in cultural or racial identities that we can claim as our own, than to stay open to the provisionality of those identities and to the "undiscoverable self." But we pay a price for such evasion. The price may well be that, while we enjoy our apparent moral rightness and the knowledge that we are making schools better places, we are sabotaging the goals we long to accomplish.

In general, multicultural education has consciously rejected the personal for a few reasons. First, the personal, like the self, has often been used as a kind of Trojan Horse, out of which, under cover of the darkness of universality, slides some dominant group, usually heterosexual white men or women, whose members want to believe the personal is neutral and wind up defending the status quo. Second, to look at the personal, to begin to face the provisionality and contingency of identity, is to surrender the security of stable identities, identities that are often necessary if one is not to be worn down by the daily grind of living in a racist society. Third, we have yet to develop a public language to describe the personal that does not dissipate into psychologisms or unexamined narratives, or reduce our experience to some sociopolitical script.

This chapter offers one way to explore the personal in multicultural education. While acknowledging the conscious reasons for its absence in the work, I want to focus on the unconscious reasons for the resistance to the personal and the consequences of that resistance. What follows is an attempt to work through,[5] in the psychoanalytic sense, the defenses that run through many approaches to multicultural education, the defenses against the "evil without" and the "terror within." Such a working through, which in part involves mourning the loss of familiar identities, requires us to expose in multicultural discourses on education the contradictions, double binds and paradoxes that result from and signal the existence of these defenses. It also requires some attempt to perform an analysis of the personal.

In the next section of this chapter, I sketch some of the double binds, contradictions, and paradoxes that regularly appear in our efforts at multicultural education and analyze how these are symptomatic of various defenses.

DOUBLE BINDS, CONTRADICTIONS, PARADOXES AND DEFENSES

> The first thing you do is forget that I'm Black. Second, you must never forget that I'm Black. (Pat Pardee quoted in Pellegrini, 1997, p. 83)

> I'm going to fix up everything, just the way it was before. (Fitzgerald, 1980 [1925], 111)

> The white kid from Shaker Heights says blandly, "I don't know why we can't just all be human," and the colored kid from Andover snaps back, "That just means you want us all to be white." (Appiah, 1997, p. 35)

> The same physical features of a person's body may be read as "black" in England, "white" in Haiti, "colored" in South Africa and "mulatto" in Brazil. (Phelan, 1993, p. 8)

> [P]art of the price of the black ticket is involved fatally with the dream of becoming white. This is not possible because white people are not white: part of the price of the white ticket is to delude themselves into believing that they are. (Baldwin, 1985 [1964], p. xiv)

Those of us involved in multicultural education are all too familiar with the double binds, contradictions, and paradoxes that are part of this country's racial matrix and that disproportionately affect people of color but that also damage Whites. The double binds placed on Blacks[6] in this society are both notorious and well documented. Howard Winant (1997), who referred to the "Du Boisian idea that in a racist society the 'color line' fractures the self, that it imposes a sort of schizophrenia on the bearers of racialized identities, which forces them to see themselves simultaneously from within and without" (p. 40), was alluding to the profound strain placed on American Blacks by the double binds of the race system. That double bind has contributed to, among other horrors, Blacks dying younger than Whites in this country and the higher rates of physical ailments among Blacks (Cose 1995; Marable, 1983; West, 1993).[7]

There is an enormous body of literature (e.g., Fanon, 1967; Kovel, 1984; McCarthy and Crichlow, 1993; Pinar, 1993; Williams, 1991) that describes the savage toll on our souls that these contradictions, paradoxes, and double binds have taken and that suggests that these binds, paradoxes, and contradictions result from defenses against death, loss of self, and terror at one's perceived failings and impotence. The fact is that these defenses that constitute this country's racial matrix quite literally drive us all crazy.

What has not received so much attention is that various approaches to and discourses on multicultural education are also filled with double binds, contradictions, and paradoxes and that these are also symptoms of the defenses that structure these approaches and discourses. I want to turn now to some examples of these double binds, paradoxes, and contradictions.

Using the work of Gregory Bateson, who conceptualized the double bind as a lose/lose situation that is repressed and leads to schizophrenia, Liz Ellsworth (1997) pointed out what she called "the double binds" of whiteness as it emerges in multicultural discourses and approaches. One of the binds she described is that whites are often positioned in multicultural discourses as either "guilty perpetrator[s]" or "unimplicated bystander[s]" (p. 263). This "replace[s] writer and reader in no-win relations to whiteness" (p. 264). This double bind, a result of collapsing the personal into the social, forecloses any possibility of elaborating on the different ways each of us has constructed because of and been constructed by race and thus blocks any real exploration of the personal.

Another bind is what she called the "definitional bind." In offering definitions, in positioning ourselves as the ones who know about diversity, white academics "assume yet again the position within knowledge that has historically been reserved for [us]" (p. 265). These double binds place white academics in a position where if they write about the meaning of race or diversity, they reinscribe privilege and the dominant organization of race. These double binds make it very hard to find any "outside" to race. For example, as a White writing this paper, I may experience whiteness in multiple ways and at times may not experience it at all, but the fact that anything I do experience, think, or write may be determined by race is incontestable given the hegemony of the racial matrix. Thus, to even say what I am saying may be in part a performance of privilege accruing in part to my whiteness. The leisure time to reflect on these issues and the apparent academic disinterestedness of tone that is present, the impulse to offer an original or inclusive analysis, the attempt to have the last word and offer definitions—all these result from, perpetuate, and reinforce particular privileged positions that I am familiar with and at times occupy. The style and content of this chapter, the attitudes expressed herein, the experiences relied on, the forum in which it appears, the immediate social time of its writing that resonates in it, and the unconscious and conscious audience it addresses have all been shaped within the racial matrix, such that there is no way for me to talk about race from outside race. There appears to be no "outside" to the system of racial organization, yet I am forced by the professional demands of my position to offer some analysis that, ipso facto, colludes with "white" structures of privilege and power.

Another bind concerns the contradiction between treating race as mobile, fabricated, shifting, contextual, and never the same in any situation and the fact that oppression and its resistance require stable, repeated identities. Here the bind exists between the contingent and fluid and the socially fixed. Opt for the former and we evaporate into a Heraclitean flux of differences. Opt for the latter and we disappear into socially determined subject positions.

The contradictions and paradoxes that haunt multicultural education are perhaps most evident when we look at the "culture" in multicultural. Many educators, in their approach to multiculturalism, assume that culture is stable, homogeneous, monolithic, bounded, and somehow either possessed by individuals or in some way determinant of their actions, intentions, and motivations. Diane Hoffman (1996) criticizes this multicultural education that "sees culture as a recipe for social behavior" (p. 550) because it maintains "the established categories and relations of power that thrive on simplification, reductionism and universalism" (p. 555). She writes: "Anthropologists have criticized the way the concept of culture has been simplified and reified to fit multiculturalist discourses that support visions of personal, ethnic or national cultural identity that are fixed, essentialized, stereotyped and normatized. The underlying theme is that culture has some kind of existential autonomy that 'does things' to people" (p. 549).

On the other hand, proponents of multicultural approaches that anchor themselves in racial cultures, respond to the anthropological and poststructural critiques by suggesting these critiques preserve the hegemony of dominant groups (Collins, 1991; Harstock, 1983). In other words, they argue that just as subordinated groups are beginning to give voice to their cultures and cultural identities, academics announce that culture, itself, does not exist. One hears here paradox enunciated in the quote from Pat Pardee at the opening of this section: You must forget my racial/cultural identity and never forget my racial/cultural identity.

Another criticism leveled at those multicultural approaches founded on cultural essentialism comes from sociologists and historians influenced by poststructuralist critiques. One of the projects of these multicultural approaches to education is to provide a sense of a culture's history, so that the culture may assume a more stable present. A sense of "I was" is, according to David Lowenthal (1985, p. 183), "a necessary component of the sureness of 'I am,' " and this applies to cultures as well as personal identity. Lowethal, in his classic *The Past Is a Foreign Country*, reminds the reader that Americans have always been ambivalent about the past, not knowing whether to sweep tradition away and claim a permanent position of youth in history and immunity from decline and decay or feel toward it nostalgia, reverence, and filial piety. According to Lowenthal, Americans deal with the ambivalence by *inventing* traditions, histories, and the past, again and again, "cobbled together" as Kathleen Conzen (1989, p. 47) writes, referring to the invention of German American rituals and traditions "from the remnants of village, guild, ecclesiastical and courtly customs."

Few popular approaches to multicultural education historicize their own project, nor do they explore how and why groups develop or manufacture their histories and identities. Rather, ethnic, national, and racial cultural identities assume the givenness of their histories. In the case of national and ethnic cultures, these histories and traditions are presented as *identity kits*, essentialized yet treated as equal and exchangeable within a liberal democratic universe, de-politicized yet seen as deserving of the same political rights, and de-historicized, yet accompanied by invented historical narratives.[8] In the case of racial cultures, these histories are often homogenized and reified as a way to contest the hegemony of the dominant history that, of course, is also homogenized, reified, and just as invented.

Furthermore, there is some evidence that moves to affirm cultural identities among recent immigrants or among descendants of white immigrants are compensatory fictions for the imagined loss of older cultural traditions and reflect both a dissatisfaction with the cultural standardization in America and a nostalgia for what, in fact, may never have been (Appiah, 1997). In other words, the very culture longed for and appropriated with pride was never as homogeneous or as tied to the country of origin as imagined. It was always complicated by class, region, religious differences, and, if one goes back far enough, by the lack of unity only recently imposed by the modern nation-state.

The fabricated or fictional quality of cultural identity leads to some interesting paradoxes. If culture, as defined and employed in those multicultural approaches that focus on national or ethnic groups, is descriptive of customs, practices, accomplishments, and languages, aside from country of birth, and this becomes the United States with the second generation, how can we determine who is a legitimate member of this culture? Who is entitled to bear particular cultural identities? Are cultural identities self-defined? Can anyone choose the culture of their preference? Can an Irish American choose a Latino cultural identity? Can a youth raised as Chinese American choose a Palestinian cultural identity? Does American culture synthesize or stand alongside other cultures? What criteria are used for assigning cultures? Is someone whose only connection to Italy is one Italian great-grandfather entitled to consider him or herself Italian? If a parent or Other names or calls the child by or to a particular culture, does that interpellate[9] the child permanently within that culture? If culture as defined in these approaches to multiculturalism consists of customs, practices, and values, can anyone claim that culture by following or holding these? If, as Werner Sollors (1989) argues, ethnicity is invented, who is entitled to claim it and what function does it have? The paradox is evident, for example, in the Irish American community whose Irishness is perceived by Irish visitors as more Irish than the Irishness found in Ireland. Witness the fact that gays were not allowed to march in the New York St. Patrick's Day Parade but marched in the significantly less celebrated St. Patrick's Day parades in Dublin and Cork, or the strong support of the Irish Republican Army (I.R.A.) among many Irish living in the United States as compared to the significantly more complicated views of the I.R.A. held in southern Ireland. Or to take another example, one finds second-generation Italians in New York proclaiming an Italianness that is, given Italy's relatively recent unification, less than 150 years old. As Sollors, Anthony Appiah, and Lowenthal point out, second-generation immigrants are more likely than their parents even to want to celebrate their culture, for the very reason that it is already gone.

Appiah has perhaps done more than anyone to point out the way race is discursively constructed. For some time, biologists have dispensed with the category of race, recognizing that it cannot be useful in determining anything other than some gross anatomical differences or variations in skin pigmentation and that, even here, variations are so great that any racial categorization seems superfluous. As Appiah (1996, p. 69) writes: " 'Race' then, as a biological concept, picks out, at best, among humans, classes of people who share certain easily observable physical characteristics, most notably skin color and a few visible features of the face and head."

However, as Appiah and Amy Gutman (1996, p. 74) point out, because these criteria are so loose, they do not correspond to the social groups we call "races" in America. For example, Peggy Phelan (1993) notes that the referent of "black" shifts, depending on what country one is in, be it Brazil, England, South Africa, or Haiti, and we are well aware that in this country the referent for "black" has continually slipped and

shifted, suggesting that the referent itself is constructed by its significa-
tion.

Multicultural approaches that introduce race into the definition of culture appear to preserve a logocentrism or binary logic that anchors in
essentialisms the very system they are trying to revise. These approaches,
issuing from a desire to alter the dominant culture, name, re-articulate,
problematize, and often denigrate the dominant culture, for example, as
Eurocentric, white, repressed, and racist. At the same time, these
approaches appropriate for historically dominated groups their own
"culture" and reverse the negative values the dominant culture, whose
anchoring in race is now visible, has ascribed to these racial cultures.
Thus Black English, or Afrocentrism, or African American learning styles
are affirmed. The problem is the circular logic and essentializing implicit
in these approaches. The logic is circular because it anchors the culture
to race and then assigns race based on culture.[10] Thus we can hear par-
adoxical comments such as "Colin Powell isn't really black."

Another paradox that arises when multicultural approaches focus only
on "cultures" and their histories became apparent at Prep and concerns
the implementation of global history, often seen as a goal of multicultural
education and a way to build "tolerance" of other cultures and races. In
1989 Prep moved toward replacing its tenth grade European history with
global history in ninth and tenth grades. Students now would learn, for
example, not only about the unification of Italy but also about Nubia,
about Mussolini's bombing of Ethiopia as well as the presence of sub-
Saharan Africans in Sicily. In 1989 Yussef Hawkins was murdered in
Bensonhurst. As the rise and fall of nations and national cultures un-
folded in global history classes, the murder was constructed by the media only in terms of race. As students learned that Europe's was not the
only history, they were also learning on TV that Blacks shouldn't venture
into an all white neighborhood. As the press spoke only of race, history
teachers spoke only of nations and national cultures. Between the two
fell the ways working and middle-class Italians in Brooklyn's Bensonhurst constructed their identity, the gender and sexual dynamics of the
killing, the history of black and Italian relations and the lived experiences
of the students as they tried to come to grips with a traumatic event.
Global history, the epitome of multiculturalism that is tied to state,
nations, and countries failed to address history as it was taking place.

One could argue that the lack of attention to the Hawkins murder
could have occurred if European history were being taught or that it
could have been given attention had a teacher been willing, no matter
what formal history was being taught, to discuss the murder. The paradox is that the course itself was initiated, in part, as a response to racism
in the society, as a way to increase "tolerance," yet, by focusing on the

"larger world," it worked to hide one form of racism as it was mani-
festing itself in the here and now. Global history itself both represses
race and is informed by it. Thus it represses it as it keeps it always
visible. The same could be said too of those history texts that introduce
Blacks during the Civil War, Reconstruction and the civil rights era but
ignore them the rest of the time, or those teachers who talk about race
and racism in history but neglect it in their classrooms or in their students' lives or for that matter in their own lives.

Having mentioned some of the paradoxes, contradictions, and double
binds that arise within approaches to multicultural education, I want to
turn to how these are, in fact, symptoms formed by particular defense
mechanisms that partially structure and constitute multicultural approaches.

Over the course of his life Sigmund Freud elaborated different kinds
of defense mechanisms by which we defend against, reject and render
unconscious either internal impulses or external stimuli experienced as
painful, traumatic, or unacceptable to the ego. These defense mechanisms
in turn can create symptoms, in this case paradoxes, double binds and
contradictions, some of which I have mentioned. According to Roy
Schafer (1992, p. 37), "Freud laid out what he considered to be the four
major danger situations of early childhood: loss of the love object, loss
of the object's love, castration and the superego condemnation and punishment." These dangers are what give rise to the defenses. According
to Anna Freud (1966) there are ten defense mechanisms, each of which
works positively to protect the ego and negatively in symptom formation. Those mechanisms are "regression, repression, reaction formation,
isolation, undoing, projection, introjection, turning against the self and
reversal [to which] we must add a tenth . . . sublimation or displacement
of instinctual aims" (quoted in Schafer, 1992, p. 44). Denial is often included in this list, although at times it is combined with repression. In
what follows I shall point to only a few defense mechanisms structuring
some approaches to multicultural education, but I think it might be useful, at some point, to analyze how all these defense mechanisms work
in multicultural approaches as well as the discursive and nondiscursive
practices they challenge.

Sigmund Freud (1959 [1915]) defined reaction formation as the turning
of one feeling into its opposite in order to avoid the guilt or trauma
induced by carrying the former. I would suggest that multicultural approaches that focus only on national, ethnic, or religious identities are
themselves reaction formations that have repressed the trauma of racial
difference and fear of difference into the apparent love of cultural differences. The reaction formation keeps race out of sight while making it
present.[11] Clearly, on the political level, this is nothing new. Cameron
McCarthy (1990) has argued that multiculturalism and even the creation

of ethnic studies departments in universities were attempts to coopt and domesticate the political activism that focused on economic and political justice rather than intellectual equity in the academy. I am suggesting that teachers who rush to celebrate "diversity" in their classes, who encourage all students to take pride in their heritage, and who infuse into their curriculum cultural pluralism are, when they deny the salience of race and racism, defending against the trauma of race in America and repressing their own fears and feelings and fantasies about Blacks, Whites, and/or the racial system in this country. What is ultimately being defended against, I believe, is the loss of the object's love, that is, the loss of the love of Blacks or Whites. I am suggesting that white and black teachers who practice this kind of "celebratory" multiculturalism do so as a way to defend against their own fears of difference, of separation, and of facing the trauma of racism.

Let me give an example. When I was head of the English department at Prep, I remember observing a sixth-grade class taught by a warm and loving and very popular teacher who was Greek. She had worked hard to infuse contemporary Greek culture into her classes. Proud of her multicultural efforts and always encouraging students to share histories of and information about their own ethnic backgrounds, she was that day doing a lesson on a Norse tale in which one of the villains is called Black Sven.[12] One of the kids, no doubt curious about the presence of black people in a Viking story, asked why the character was called Black Sven. Ms. K. put the word *black* on the board and asked the kids what they associated with the word. The negative denotations given in any western dictionary came up, and she dutifully wrote them on the board, concluding with the summation that now kids could see why, since he was a villain, he would have the epithet *black* with his name.

Afterward, I spoke with her and questioned her reasoning behind such a troubling lesson. She argued, first, that she was not racist—I had not mentioned racism at all—and second, that she was giving them a lesson in Norse culture and that she was just providing in her explanation the common associations with the word "black." It took a good deal of explaining and finally some suggestions that she might want to show how other cultures look at the color black and how these connotations are produced, before she somewhat understood the bias in her lesson. For all her cultural sensitivity, she had never taken into account the ground on which specific cultures emerged. Her definition of culture was that of many mainstream approaches to multicultural education—that is, a definition pinned overtly to nationality, but covertly to race. No doubt, had she done a lesson on African or African American culture, she would have approached it in much the same way—through some folk tales and introducing costumes and food of African or black culture—but the salience of race and racism would have been just as invisible. Of course, like all defenses, and the paradoxes or double binds they generate, the behaviors that result can be troublesome.

There was a young black girl in that class who put her head down on the desk during the board work. Ms. K. later told me, during our conversation and as evidence of her lack of prejudice, that she was giving the kid "special attention." When I asked her why, she told me, she thought it was hard to be one of the few black kids in an all white class and she really wanted the kid to feel comfortable. I would say she wanted her love. And I would say that a good many white teachers whose defense against losing the love of Blacks is the reaction formation of a watered down multiculturalism, which says that under all our superficial differences we are really the same, are terrified of their own feelings about Blacks but are also unwilling to surrender the innocence of a multiculturalism that celebrates diversity at the expense of discovering who we really are.

I also want to suggest that multicultural approaches anchored in essentialist notions of identity defend against the personal and the terror that all identity is provisional and illusionary, and such approaches unconsciously wind up sustaining the racial system they oppose, thus placing both Whites and Blacks in double binds. In the case of Whites, multicultural approaches often form or are constituted by defense mechanisms that Freud (1959) called "turning against the self." "The turning round of an instinct upon the subject is suggested to us by the reflection that masochism is actually sadism turned round upon the subject's own ego. . . . So the essence of the process is the change of the object, while the aim remains unchanged" (p. 70).

Thus we can encounter in multicultural classes an enormous amount of guilt among Whites that can quickly revert to rage or resentment directed against either Blacks or other Whites. How is it that the rage is not directed against specific systems of white privilege or practices that disproportionately affect Blacks? The answer may be found in the very way these multicultural approaches are organized around the poles of victim/victimizer or oppressed/oppressor. As Henry Giroux (1997) points out, neither students nor, I would argue, teachers want to see themselves as evil. The problem is that once identities are introduced as uncomplicated scripts, white students and teachers are stranded in positions of villainy. More complex explorations of one's own complicity in oppression are foreclosed, because the scripts mandate complicity in particular forms. In other words, the guilt that Whites experience is a defense against rage at Blacks. The rage, I want to argue, is not a result of racism but of the trauma of racism, which leads them to fear that those who have been done badly unto will do badly unto them. Thus, fear of revenge turns to anger, which, in a reaction formation, is then experienced as guilt and emerges in multicultural education for Whites as an exploration of white privilege, the "turn against the self." This exploration, in turn, evokes guilt and rage and continues the entire process.

Some approaches to multicultural education may defend against the personal and the fear of the contingency or fluidity of identity and produce impossible double binds for some black students. Josie was a black Panamanian at Prep. Extremely bright but also overweight and shy, she formed friendships only with the school's "geeks," who, except for one pale black boy, were white Jewish boys who had been ostracized by their classmates. According to her, the most painful event during her ninth-grade year was the Martin Luther King Chapel, which that year consisted of guerrilla theater, scenes from a video by Public Enemy, and some speeches that were unusually militant for the school. Josie recounted to me how she wanted to die, to disappear as she sat next to her white friends and felt, she said, "their eyes on [her] as they moved psychically away." Later, in an English class where the assembly was being discussed, the teacher, defending the program against the critiques of some white students and assuming black solidarity among the black students, called on Josie to explain the "militant" speeches. "It was devastating," she said. Josie went on to embrace her identity as a black woman, but in recent conversations she told me she could easily have turned into what she referred to as a "Dinesh D'Souza type"—that is, someone who elevated the individual above race and argued that institutional racism had ended. I want to suggest that such a valorization is the return of the repressed with virulence. It is no coincidence that one can hear from some "successful" members of subordinated groups that blaming racism or sexism for one's failures is an excuse. What such a statement encodes is the return of the repressed personal as an individualism severed from connection to others. This return results from the initial repression of the personal in those approaches anchored in racial/cultural essentialist identities.

Perhaps nowhere are the double binds of many multicultural approaches more apparent than in the experiences of bi- or multiracial students. Biracialism and multiracialism, like the presence of, for example, gay Blacks or Jewish Blacks, reveals the complexity, provisionality, and contingency of identities. Those approaches to multicultural education that are anchored in black culture or racial/cultural identity often repress the fluidity of identity, because to admit such fluidity and contingency would expose the suturing of difference by and within these approaches. I want to suggest that the repression of the provisional quality of identity, of its fictionality, is a defense against fear of death, detention, disappearance. On one level this is obvious. For Blacks not to appropriate their identity and resignify it as positive is to risk devastation by racists and racisms. Thus, the protests against police brutality *may* speak about such brutality in general but *must speak* about it in particular as it affects communities of color.[13] In the face of white/European cultural hegemony in the schools, black culture must be articulated and positioned as counterhegemonic. The fears of death, detention, and disappearance are legitimate given the precariousness of black life; the fragmentation, invisibility, and voicelessness of the black poor; and the large numbers of black men who are under the supervision of the prison system and have been reduced to numbers, rap sheets, and, in the white "Imaginary" (Lacan, 1977), demons.

Nevertheless, although as Anna Freud (1966) pointed out, defenses are often necessary, they still take their toll. In schools, the repression of the fluidity of identity, of its fictionality, results in double binds for biracial and multiracial kids, who are forced to choose racial allegiances *now*, by those who oppose the very system that reduces them to and marks them as a particular race, but one which these biracial and multiracial students would feel confident challenging if they did not feel forced to choose sides. The repressed returns in an interesting way. It returns, I want to argue, on a metaphorical level as death, dispersion, and disappearance. In other words, what dies when the argument is made that a White is white in any situation and a Black is black in any situation is the possibility of opening a space where one is not condemned to one color or one identity. What disappears is the chance for what Jacques Lacan (1977) called full speech—that is, speech that is not alienated in the Other, in this case in an imposed fiction. What is detained or arrested is change itself, for the very possibility of ways of being that multiracial or biracial identities offer is arrested, held in check, subjected to supervision.[14]

Perhaps nowhere are defenses clearer than in those approaches to multicultural education that are rooted in notions of a universal human. In these approaches, both liberal and neoconservative, one encounters the variations on the theme of universal brotherhood: a common humanity, commonalty uniting difference, and individual responsibility. The paradoxes that emerge in these approaches, some of which I have mentioned, are symptoms of a denial, a negation that defends against fear of castration. Race is literally not seen in this register. Let us look at the work of neoconservative educators like Diane Ravitch (1990) and Chester Finn (1990), who argue that multicultural education is special interest politics and will lead to "Balkanization." The arguments decry particularism and what is seen as ethnic chauvinism. Ravitch and Finn complain that Whites and Europeans are massed together as oppressors and that history, written by a multicultural committee as opposed to disinterested scholars, is distorted into a false celebration of various ethnic groups. Referring to the research that shows no correlation between membership in a particular ethnic or racial group and particular learning styles

(Dunn, 1997) or positive self-regard, they also decry the emphasis on self-esteem building through ethnic and racial pride as denying the individual and the transcendent humanity of the subject.

What is denied, in their view, is that curriculum has always been ethnocentric, particularistic, and politicized.[15] If the center is particularized, it threatens the very ego of such educators, the very core of being of those who hold such views. When they complain of an attack on a common culture, they reveal their inability to see that culture as already particularized. What is apparent in all the references to Balkanization and its overtones of violence and civil war is a paranoia that, I would argue, results from projections of the "evil within" onto those without. That "evil within" is the desire to kill the father, and because the individualism that these educators applaud is a competitive one, one where the "best" comes out on top, it results in the fear of castration, the fear that in fact they will be rendered powerless, are already powerless, will be devoured by the Other and will be punished for their desire to kill the father. I would argue that such competitive individualism evokes tremendous fears of punishment and castration anxiety. It is not surprising that these same educators talk so glowingly of their intellectual forebearers, the fathers in the canon. They, following T. S. Eliot's (1972 [1920]) advice, desire to replace them while still talking to them, and they defend against that desire by making these canonized authors and canonized versions of history untouchable.

On the other hand, those liberals who so often appeal to liberal democratic ideals, wind up with just as much anxiety about difference as the neoconservatives, anxiety that shows itself in the paradoxes in certain mainstream multicultural approaches. That terror of difference is indeed the terror of the mother's castration and eventuates in the denial of difference and one might even speculate, following Freud and Lacan, the fetishization of knowledge and, more particularly, scopophilia or the valorization of what John Dewey (1929) called the "spectator theory of knowledge." Such a theory of knowledge is, according to Dewey, "modeled after what was supposed to take place in the act of vision. The object refracts light and is seen; it makes a difference to the eye and to the person having an optical apparatus but none to the thing seen. The real object is the object so fixed in its regal aloofness that it is a king to any beholding mind that may gaze upon it. A spectator theory of knowledge is the inevitable outcome" (p. 23).

I would speculate that that terror of difference stems from the loss of the mother country so long ago, and the clear loss of power in the British Empire, a loss that Americans contributed to but at the same time deny. It is not surprising that so many liberal multiculturalists are, for all their attempts to bring in other cultures, set on making England the center of history and literature.

When a black teacher in my department at Prep wanted to use only non-Western literature for his tenth-grade English course, those who were most upset were not the conservative teachers, who saw Mr. Hall as simply confirming what they thought the Other would do, but the liberal teachers, one of whom was an expert on Arabic literature. They couldn't bear the fact that no Shakespeare or English literature would be taught for a whole year. Thus, such approaches to multicultural education produce and are constituted by defenses that, I would argue, defend against difference and against the fear of castration. Difference itself is displaced onto the Other. As Ann Pellegrini (1997, p. 70) puts it, "[T]he colonizer generates the fiction of his self-identity by displacing difference elsewhere, onto the colonized, who become the placeholder of absolute difference."

I have suggested that structuring approaches to multiculturalism are defenses against the "evil without" and the "terrors within." These defenses against confronting the personal, against accepting the provisionality of identity, and against coming to grips with the trauma of America's racial systems, or to put it another way, defenses against fears of losing love, of losing the loved one, and fears about castration and death need to be worked through because they produce many of the paradoxes and contradictions that trouble multicultural education. Such a working through, which in part involves mourning the loss of familiar identities, requires us to expose in multicultural discourses on education and in the dominant organizations they challenge, the contradictions and paradoxes that result from these defenses and signal their existence.

I want to suggest that one way to work through these defenses is to examine our own psychic investments in this work, to closely listen to those who resist our work, and to identify with the very terrors that motivate that resistance. I want to offer, in the final part of this chapter, an example of how such work might proceed.

THE PERSONAL

> [I]f I am not what I've been told I am, then it means that you're not what you thought *you* were *either*! And that is the crisis. (Baldwin, 1985, p. 329)

> The individual, and the groupings of people, have to learn that they cannot reform society in reality, nor deal with others as reasonable people, unless the individual has learned to locate and allow for the various patterns of coercive institutions, formal and also informal, which rule him. No matter what his reason says, he will always relapse into obedience to the coercive agency while its pattern is with him. (Indries Shah, quoted in Lessing, 1997, p. 1)

I have been told, over the course of my life, that I am many things. Each time I was called to some identity, it registered on my skin, worked its way into my feelings, and inaugurated or crystallized, subtly or not so subtly, gradually or not so gradually, ways of thinking about myself and others. Of course, I do not remember all the "callings"[16] to an identity, although they may well be buried in my body and unconscious, but I can remember many of them. Familial callings that changed as I aged: "Pumpkin," "my little gentleman," "a good boy," "the weasel," "an idiot," "the eccentric," "the quitter," "handsome," "irresponsible," "selfish," and all those other nouns and adjectives, repeated or said once by my parents or grandmother, that structured the envelope of my being and helped shape the other, less foundational egos I have taken for myself. And there were the callings over the years made by peers: "bony maroney," "skinny," "weird looking," "gorgeous," "cute," "buddy," so many of which marked me in terms of inclusion or exclusion, acceptance or ostracism, but only when I wanted to be included or was. And teachers' or other adults' callings: "shy boy," "sweet boy," "smart boy," "leader," "lazy," "sour," "dependent," "natural athlete," "sensitive," "born teacher," "not serious enough." Or those made by strangers on the street: "queer," "white boy," "Jew."

These callings were not simply words neutrally uttered; they often had an emotional charge that I heard and resonated to, and they named not me as much as a series of affective states surrounding me, ways of seeing and modes of treating me, and constellations of images and fantasies projected onto me. Through repetition or because they suddenly crystallized latent but inarticulate feelings and thoughts that were ready to crystallize, they came into my being and gave it form. And even if I did not identify with the labels or identities, I emotionally answered in some way to what Louis Althusser (1994) named interpellation. For example, I did not identify myself as a Jew even though my father was Jewish, but I answered, in some emotional way, to the way it was hurled as a slur one day by a group of kids, and I felt wounded and marked by the wound. In the same way, I was on my way back from my girlfriend's house when, at age fourteen, I was called "queer" by some kids on a park bench. I ran from them in fear, in my mind confirming their accusation, and I felt marked in a way that crystallized latent feelings or ideas without making me identify with being homosexual or "queer." It was also when I was a teen that while standing on a subway platform, I was called "white boy" by a group of black girls. I walked quickly away, again feeling frightened and humiliated. It was not until I was a senior in high school that I began to assume a vague identity as white and simultaneously began to question and challenge the unfairness of both the racial system in general and the advantages I got because I was white. And it was much later that I began to understand how constellations of feelings and thoughts, unconscious and conscious, were continually being crystallized in and on my body as whiteness and how white could both identify and come into being along with particular attitudes, feelings, or more generally the constitution of my psyche. And it has only been recently that I have begun to think about how race— that is, my whiteness—offered some of the very conditions of my possibility and psychic formation by providing me with certain notions of agency.

I have been called to identities in less overt ways, too. The silent callings that make themselves felt through expectations, privileges, treatment given me by representatives of bureaucracies and institutions, and through images and printed materials that called out to me and told me what I was—these too formed how I came to see myself and how others came to see me. And gradually, these callings and whatever in me made me answer them, came to form the self I became and the selves and egos that came to constitute me. Thus, how I have come to form as white, has resulted from not only interpellation by family, peers, familiar adults and strangers, not only from what in me made me answer these callings but also from the treatment accorded Whites and, in general, non-Whites and representations of Whites and non-Whites.

Of course, we are all called to social identities. Some we answer to and others we don't. Some we have no choice about. Some we re-articulate or resignify. Some we aren't even conscious of. But we are all called, and in that calling and answering we come to form.

But of course it's not that simple; it never is. How I came and come to form in particular identities, or respond to others' identities, seems at times just a mystery, a strange journey, over-determined by family and the journey itself. At other times, it seems a little clearer, and I find some ways to talk about it. For sure it is not just a question of being labeled. Identity formation, as Jacques Lacan (1977), Daniel Stern (1985), and Louis Althusser (1994) have argued, starts before birth as a place, and is given form in the family discourse, imaginary and unconscious. Its origins are positional, waiting in the social grids that sort us or in what Lacan, giving these grids a linguistic turn, called the "symbolic." That symbolic is not as homogeneous as Lacan seemed to have believed, nor as unidimensional as Foucault argued. It consists, rather, of multiple discourses, whose anterior space remains a space for re-articulation and therefore an area of contestation that affects those discourses layering it and shaping it.

I don't remember being called to whiteness, although, through a variety of discursive and material practices, there were somatic sensations, emotions, images, and ideation forming around and as a result of my insertion as white in the northern urban racial system. The first black person I ever knew was a grocery delivery boy named Spahn. In 1957, when I was ten, he helped us move down the block from a tiny apartment, where I shared a room with my grandmother, to a spacious one, where I had my own room. Spahn smelled of mint jelly, and I liked him. I remember him as gentle. (Was he polite out of caution? manners? kindness?) When I heard, probably around that time, from one of my friend's parents who drove us to school, that Negroes smelled differently than "we" did, I wondered if they all smelled of mint jelly. Except for the flickering images on television of the civil rights movement and occasional visits to my father's hospital in Bedford Stuyvesant, the world was completely white, which meant I had no idea of whiteness. I did, however, always feel uncomfortable in my own skin and remember often longing for some lost other, some lost love, some lost body that would hold me or make me feel more at home in my skin.

I look back on my history and find there a good deal of nostalgia and melancholia. I know from an early age that I liked making myself sad by projecting myself into the future and looking back at my life from such a perspective, and I know I always liked flashbacks in films. Analysis suggests that such melancholia resulted from the loss of my grandmother or from an earlier Oedipal loss, the loss of my mother's undivided love. Perhaps there were other losses that resonated in and layered these early ones.

Judith Butler (1997) argues, following Sigmund Freud, first, that our egos are formed in part by introjected images of lost others; second, that we refuse knowledge of such introjection and therefore repress the too painful loss of the loved object; and third, that heightened conscience and self-beratement are "one sign of melancholia." She writes:

The foreclosure of certain forms of love suggests that the melancholia that grounds the subject (and hence always threatens to unsettle and disrupt that ground) signals an incomplete and irresolvable grief. Unowned and incomplete, melancholia is the limit to the subject's sense of pouvoir, its sense of what it can accomplish and, in that sense, its power. Melancholia rifts the subject, marking a limit to what it can accommodate. Because the subject does not, cannot, reflect on that loss, that loss marks the limit of reflexivity, that which exceeds (and conditions) its circuitry. (p. 23).

The idea here is that we take in parts of others whom we figuratively or literally have lost and incorporate these into our egos. In doing this we also direct toward ourselves, our egos, the feelings we had to those lost others, particularly anger at their abandonment of us. The anger becomes the punitive self-denigration, and the guilt that so often accompanies melancholia is a secondary result of that anger and works to preserve the lost love. According to Butler: "Guilt serves the function of preserving the object of love and, hence, of preserving love itself. What might it mean to understand guilt, then, as a way in which love preserves the object it might otherwise destroy? As a stopgap against a sadistic destruction, guilt signals less the psychic presence of an originally social and external norm than a countervailing desire to continue the object one wishes dead" (p. 25). She continues: "Is there not a longing to grieve—and equivalently an inability to grieve—that which one never was able to love, a love that falls short of the 'conditions of existence'? This is a loss . . . of love's own possibility: the loss of the ability to love" (p. 24).

I always felt guilty about the underdog and identified with that position. I always had an overdeveloped sense that somehow if I wasn't responsible for the rotten condition of someone else's life, than at least I was responsible for rescuing that someone. Guilt and melancholia. On one level I longed for lost familial loves, but on another level, to follow Butler, I longed for lost loves that were forbidden and whose loss I also unconsciously mourned and felt guilty about. Certainly I was ripe for what Paulo Freire (1968) called malefic generosity.

Never allowed to love men and certainly never allowed to love black men—the taboo was all the more powerful for never being articulated—my melancholia and guilt coalesced around the presence of racism in this society. Surely it fueled my desire to identify with the oppressed in society. My first roommate in college was black. We met in the lounge at New York University and talked about having had dreams about sleeping with our mothers. I think we loved each other, but we never spoke of it, although I have a recollection of us lying next to one another, and there was something in the air. Reggie later died of a drug overdose. By college I was heavily involved with protesting racism in the college and everywhere. Racism compelled my attention more than the war in Vietnam. Was it because of melancholia? Guilt? Did Spahn return through Reggie? And was there a sadistic impulse to hurt both, as there surely was to tear my parents and grandmother to shreds?

The first year I taught, in 1969, I taught Harper Lee's *To Kill a Mockingbird* (1960) to eighth graders in a prep school. I taught the novel as a liberal tract that soothed the fears of Whites by offering a paternalistic white hero, by condemning militancy in the character of Lulu, and by suggesting the only really bad whites were "white trash." I don't think any of the students knew what I was talking about. It was basically a political monologue that I was trying to pull out of their mouths and the book. I wanted to rescue my students from their ignorance, and I wanted my rage at injustice to burn into their hearts. That year I put up around the school posters celebrating the Black Panthers and advertising their newspaper, "The Militant." I have no recollection of what effect my teaching or sermonizing had on the two black students in the class or for that matter what effect it had on the white students.

Until I was fourteen I looked in the mirror and saw ugliness and awkwardness and found solace in the coziness of my home. It's still easy for me to evoke the smells and sensations of sitting in the kitchen watching my grandmother peel potatoes or my mother do the ironing. The domestic, assigned to women, was comforting and sensually appealing. I liked the feel of wet sheets strung across the kitchen to dry. I have in ways tried to re-create that atmosphere in my classes, filling my classrooms with old couches bought at the Salvation Army, with book cases and books, with old carpets, with kitchen sensuality. It's harder at the urban college where I now work, because the rooms are sterile—the public sector is always aesthetically impoverished as well as impoverished in other ways. Maybe, I am just trying to feel not so "different." I want differences to melt a little in the classroom. I don't want to bring into class, except as objects of study, the sirens, screams, shattering despair in the air outside. I don't have to, of course, because I hear these only as objects of study. The screams, sirens, and despair I have heard come back to me from the lingering deaths of parents and shattered relationships not from physical and psychic wounds inflicted on my body because of its race.

I have walked, over the years, into classes and seen before me students who come from a variety of countries, who speak a variety of languages, who worship various gods, who appear in variegated dress, who return to homes filled with smells of various foods, with the rhythms of different nationalities, and with the heaviness or lightness of American dreams. I have taught students who come from different class backgrounds, who are male and female, who are slotted into or have chosen one of the three sexualities imposed on us, who define themselves and are defined in racial terms, who struggle with various "disabilities" and who bring with them all the problematics of their lives. They have called me "Peter," or "Taubman" or "Doc" or "Doc T." and now they call me "Professor."

They used to call me all those names, except Professor, when I taught high school. Whichever school I taught at, black students would ask me to help them organize dances or clubs or anti-bias coalitions. I liked that. I felt singled out, the way I would if I received best teacher award from the students. I felt honored. It was like being an honorary member. I wasn't like those other Whites, the ones who would have made me feel bad anyway. I was in with the out-crowd, who for me were the in-crowd. I remember one dance, run by the black student union I was advising in 1974, in Philadelphia, where the kids were predominantly black. Everyone was dancing. I suddenly noticed one boy, whom I knew and who'd asked me to help organize the dance, standing alone, looking shy. I felt sorry for him. I impulsively asked him to dance. More surprisingly, he accepted. Who was I dancing with at that moment? My mother? My grandmother? Spahn? Reggie? Or was it myself, awkward and alone in dancing school? Or maybe I was just trying to be hip and provocative. I suppose I try to provoke in my classes too—the provocative professor.

I respond to the calling I hear of Professor, but I invite a name, first or last. The anonymity of Professor is too impersonal, in some ways too ordinary. I have always resisted being ordinary. I fear it. Maybe I liked my "difference," and when I did reach fourteen I found girls liked me and I became popular. White girls were all I knew in high school. I never again wanted to be ordinary in a girl's eyes; I had been for too long. One way not to be ordinary is to be a hero, to rescue. In the classroom and in my writing I dread being ordinary. I want to be special. I want to come up with *the* answer to the race problem. I am a good, white academic caught in the impossible double binds Liz Ellsworth (1997) has described, but I bring to mine the familiarity with an earlier set of binds. If I am the best, than I will be special and loved, but if I am just ordinary, I shall be abandoned. On the other hand, if I get too big for my boots, get too independent, I shall lose out too, because I shall also be abandoned for separating and for being "selfish." Be ordinary, don't be ordinary. How horrible to be ordinary! Will anyone love you if you're not? Will anyone love you if you are?

So classes must be brilliant. It's a lot of pressure. The pressure seeps into this chapter, too. And so I enter classes, get to know the names of everyone in the class the first day, and we begin to address questions of identity. Sooner or later, whether or not it is the formal subject of the course, race and identity come up. How could they not, unless one is living in a dream? If the class is predominantly white with a few black students, the introduction of race creates a palpable tension. I get scared some times, worried that I shall screw up, that everyone will wind up hating one another and hating me. If the class is predominantly black, there isn't that same tension. I feel safe. I am for the moment in some sense in the minority. I like it there. I often have, but I suspect only when I know, secretly or not so secretly, I have power. That power races and races through my body.

That power arises from the positions offered me and that, given various identities I assume, it also permeates my psyche. As Michel Foucault said: "My problem is essentially the definition of the implicit system in which we find ourselves prisoners; what I would like to grasp is the system of limits and exclusions which we practice without knowing it; I would like to make the cultural unconscious apparent" (cited in Butler, 1997, p. 83).

And so I try to be as honest as possible in class. What does that mean?

I trust sometimes to a free association, but that association depends in part on what Shoshanna Felman (1982), following Freud and Lacan, called "transference" and "countertransference" in the classroom. That is, it depends on the flickering presence of the Other I impose or find in the class or on how I answer the callings that emanate from students. It depends on my intentions or desires as a teacher (Taubman, 1993). It depends on the racial constitution of the class and how those identities are mobilized. And it depends on how the *cultural unconscious* or *political unconscious* is resisting consciousness. It depends on the defenses I have discussed. It depends too on how potent I am feeling.

When I was seeing a Nigerian woman, Jan, who was biracial and bisexual, I sometimes found myself feeling more potent than when I would go out with a white woman. I suspect, now, that my sense of power had to do with this cultural unconscious. It may have resulted from a sense of "having" the black man's woman, the sexuality of both black men and black women being exaggerated in the white Imaginary. It may have been the sense of power that arises from a "safe" identification with those at the bottom of the social hierarchy, black bi sexual women are one step up from black lesbians, as Audre Lourde often pointed out. It may have been, as Franz Fanon (1967) would have said, an unconscious displacement onto Jan of desire for the taboo black male body. It may have been from a sense of personal liberation—I was breaking taboos. It may have been that Jan, in her own ways, simply made me feel better about myself. It may have been that I could rescue someone who socially as well as psychically seemed to need rescuing. It may have been that the sense of power came from the absence of a threat of any real intimacy. It may have come from all of these. However, there is no way we can avoid exploring the ways that the cultural unconscious operates in us.

But such exploration requires time, the ability to sit and think, the privilege of having a chapter to write, the privilege of sitting in a class and discussing these topics with some disinterest, knowing that outside the classroom death and violence are not waiting to claim my white body.

The psyche that comes to form as white in America's racial matrix is denied power through the exhaustive energy required to maintain its defenses and repress the cultural unconscious. It comes to power in part through the conditions provided by its whiteness. By turning Blacks into the contemptible or pitiable Other, it insures its sense of agency. The very agency claimed by Whites results in part from its dependence on whiteness, but the repression of that whiteness also saps energy.

Some days I go to teach and I think that I can change the world; other days I go and I fear I have no effect at all. In both cases, I assume for myself the power to do something. I assume I not only can effect change but also *must* do so. I feel entitled and compelled to voice my views, to influence students. I believe I can make a difference. Are those feelings informed by whiteness? Are they produced within the American racial matrix? I think so, and we teachers need to figure out how to explore this question in class and in our lives. But they are also produced by teacher identities that insist on *doing* something.

I have tried so many ways to approach these issues of identity and race. I have at times asked students to create masks of the various racial identities they "wear," I have asked them to write letters to an imaginary person of an other race, placing that person as the god of their faith or imagination, I have asked students to imagine worlds populated with only their race or worlds where racisms do not exist. We have watched countless films about race and identity, read texts by authors of all identities, listened to music and looked at art work composed by all races, listened to speakers who offered different views. We have role-played and fantasized. We have talked about dialects, done research on languages, designed affirmative action programs, debated issues, danced together, made fools of ourselves together, and fought. And at times I have felt it has all been for naught. I have, also, at times been furious, often at white educators, often at white students, and often at Whites involved in multicultural education. There is no attack as vitriolic as the attack of one white multicultural educator on another for some insensitivity, grandiosity, or racism. Why? I suspect it's a defense against ones own insecurity about doing this work. I, as *a white male*, will never be able to speak from the experience of social oppression, and my experience may always be a result of privilege. As Diana Fuss (1989) argues, experience is the trump card if one is black, as long as the game is among liberal or radical Whites. So what is so important about having the trump card? Well, it's having the last word, isn't it? How nice to have the last word. It actually gives one the illusion of being in control, as if one ever really is. I know in this raced country the world around me assumes I am in control, and in some ways it is right; nevertheless I am sometimes frightened.

I suppose I am terrified that I have really understood very little, that I am ordinary, that there really is no way out of our racial horrors. I fear growing old and dying. I fear the loss of innocence, and in that sense I am indeed a child of this country. For we are a country bent on staying young.

For a long time I did not understand the last sentence of the quote by Baldwin that begins this chapter. I understood that the attempt to work in the gap between provisional selves or identities and undiscovered ones could paralyze us. The fear of losing the steady convictions of communal identities if one tries to honor the flux of everyday experience coupled with the fear of losing *who* one is to *what* one is can immobilize us. Only recently have I come to understand that if we don't work in the gap between our invented identities and our undiscoverable selves, if we don't face the "terror within," we will be "condemned to eternal youth." If we continue to believe that hope lies in polishing the armor of our identities or in pretending it doesn't exist, then we will indeed remain forever young and, like Dorian Gray, grow corrupt. It is, after all, the fear of aging, of death, and of powerlessness that leads us to resist change and to deny the provisionality of our existence. And perhaps the only surety we can have, the only safety we can find is in the faith that somehow, if we keep showing up, naming "the evil without" and not hiding from "the terror within," if we embrace the fact that nothing stays the same, that everything passes, there is hope for us and those we teach. As James Baldwin (1985) wrote years ago:

For nothing is fixed, forever and forever and forever it is not fixed; the earth is always shifting, the light is always changing, the sea does not cease to grind down rock. Generations do not cease to be born, and we are responsible to them because we are the only witness they have. The sea rises, the light fails, lovers cling to each other, and children cling to us. The moment we cease to hold each other, the moment we break faith with one another, the sea engulfs us and the light goes out. (p. 393)

NOTES

1. The notion of the personal is complicated. Thirty years ago it was juxtaposed with the political in the slogan "the personal is political" to suggest the hegemony of patriarchy and the way patriarchal ideology and structures inform and affect every aspect of our lives, including those aspects long deemed inappropriate to discuss. Today, with the fusion of the public and private, and with the acceptance of autobiographical writing as a way to understand the world, it would seem that the personal has triumphed. I would argue, following Williams, that there is a difference between the private and the personal. For me the personal suggests not the private and not the purely autobiographical, but that space where the interconnectedness of the psychic and the social can be explored—the "gap" Baldwin refers to in the quote that begins the chapter.

Notice that Baldwin says "undiscoverable self," suggesting that we can never fully or finally know that self which is not provisional. I would argue though that there are approaches and methods that can help us work in the "gap" and that keep us from continually reifying the *selves* or *identities* we find. I have elaborated on this *space* in a paper presented at the American Educational Research Association (AERA) meeting in March, 1997, titled "Autobiography Without the Self: Identity and Aesthetic Education."

Frederic Jameson's (1981) concept of the political unconscious or Foucault's (1973) notion of the cultural unconscious allows us to keep the influence of the social and political in mind, and Jacques Lacan's (1977), Gilles Deleuze's (1994), and Elizabeth Grosz's (1995) elaboration of free associative methods allows us to explore the psychic dimensions of our being without reducing them to the political or social. In curriculum theory, certainly the work of William Pinar (1994) and Madeleine Grumet (1988) has moved in the directions I am talking about.

2. I have used examples from my experiences teaching at an urban prep school, hereafter called Prep. Prep, standing on several acres of beautiful grounds in New York City, is a country day school that goes from grades five through twelve. Approximately 670 students attend. Twenty-seven percent of the students are students of color. Twelve percent of the faculty are teachers of color. There is an extensive program to make the school an inclusive community, but the administration remains white and predominantly male, and there was, while I was there, intense resistance to making the school truly inclusive.

I have changed the names of all Prep students and teachers referred to in this chapter.

3. I realize there is great debate over the correct usage of terms such as *black* and *white* to designate races. I have in my teaching and writing tried to follow the lead of those who have the right to name themselves and to have those names respected. I have capitalized *Black* and *White* in this chapter when these are used as nouns to designate the two racial groups. I have used lower case when using the terms as adjectives. I am sympathetic to Elizabeth Minnich's (1990) argument that *white* should never be capitalized whereas *black* should because they are not parallel terms and those belonging to the white race have not been oppressed because of their whiteness. On the other hand, as will become clear, I am less sure than Minnich of how these groups are defined and of their stability.

I have also chosen *Black* and *White* over *African American* and *European American* to preserve the racial implications of these terms and because so many of my students who are of West Indian origin have identified in these ways.

4. There are differences between anti-bias, antiracist, and multicultural education, and even within each of these there are different emphases and assumptions. For a discussion of differences within and between these approaches, see McCarthy (1990), McLaren (1995), and Pinar, Reynolds, Slattery, and Taubman (1995). In this chapter I have chosen to use *multicultural* to name the approaches to education that (1) seek to create an inclusive community in schools; (2) challenge various racisms and the dominant systems of racial production and organization in schools in the United States; (3) focus on broadening the curriculum to include cultures other than white/European culture; (4) work to oppose discrimination against "people of color" in schools, and/or (5) specifically address issues of race in the school curriculum, culture, extracurricular activities, and institutional structures. I have also used *multicultural* because it is more convenient, and I would have had to use *antiracist, anti-bias,* or *diversity work* every time I spoke about efforts to change prevailing discourses and nondiscursive practices that produce, sustain, and shape our identities in schools.

5. In my use of the term "working through" I refer to the definition given in *A Critical Dictionary of Psychoanalysis,* edited by Charles Rycroft (1968), where it is as defined as the process by which, through analysis, we "can discover the full implications of some interpretation or insight. Hence, by extension, the process of getting used to a new state of affairs or of getting over a loss or painful experience. In this extended sense, mourning is an example of working through, since it involves the piecemeal recognition that the lost object is no longer avail-

able in a host of contexts in which it was previously a familiar figure" (p. 199–200).

I have also used *working through* in the sense Lacan (1977) meant it when he referred to the psychoanalytic process of free association as a way to dissolve the armor of the ego, which he saw as constituted by defenses. I am taking this notion of ego as defense and applying it to identity. In other words, we need our identities to move in the world, but we need to work through these ego-identities because if we take them as fixed, reified, we become estranged from ourselves and others.

6. In this chapter I have focused primarily on the experiences of Blacks and Whites. Although the equation of multicultural education, diversity studies and antiracist work with black/white issues constitutes a serious problem, because it ignores the concerns of other races and ethnicities and often neglects issues of sexuality, gender, class, physicality, and religion, the centrality of black/white issues in the formation of the United States and in multicultural education leads me to focus on it. It was also impossible for me to deal with all the other issues that multicultural education should be addressing and often does address.

7. The double binds, paradoxes, and contradictions that American's racial system produces have both tragic and absurd results. Several writers (Fordham, 1988; Ladson-Billings, 1995; Powell, 1997) have described how black students are placed in double binds, where they are positioned as white if they assimilate the discourses of the academy or speak standard English or if they veer too far from what is normed as black culture. One might ask whether black and white students who succeed in school are "whiter" than those who do not, and whether white students who do not succeed are "blacker" than those Whites and Blacks who do?

Just as Whites are confronted with the double bind that whatever they do or say may be a result of privilege and may, in fact, reinscribe that privilege, so for Blacks there is the possibility that whatever they say or do including resistance, may reveal only the face of an internalized oppressor. As Freire (1968, p. 32) wrote, "[The oppressed] are at one and the same time themselves and the oppressor whose consciousness they have internalized."

There is also the double bind of being too aware of race and never aware enough. For example, for Whites the question arises whether or not to mention the race of an absent someone being talked about. If one doesn't say to a white auditor, for example, "a 'black' student," even if the topic is not ostensibly about race, then one might be allowing the auditor to assume a white student is being spoken about, which may not be true. Therefore one mentions race to interrupt assumed sameness. On the other hand, if one does not always specify race when discussing an absent person, by mentioning "black" one highlights race-as-black against an assumed but invisible field of whiteness. Or finally one can always mention the race of the absent party, which in turn reinforces a system of racial organization.

To be reminded of the absurd contradictions generated by the U.S. racial system, one need only recall the "one drop rule," whereby a white person was considered and may, in certain parts of the country, still be considered black, because he or she was or is related by "blood" to a person who, based on skin color, was or is considered black. On the other hand, a black person is not considered white if she or he has "one drop" of white blood. Or one might consider an incident at Prep where an issue of the school newspaper came out carrying a photo of the first black student to have attended, forty years earlier, the previously all white male prep school. The editor, a black woman, thought that publishing the photo would be one of many ways to celebrate Black History Month. The photo appeared. Only later was it discovered that the printed photo was of a Jewish student who had graduated with the first black student and who looked more "black" than the black student.

8. One of the paradoxes emerging within those multicultural approaches anchored in essentialist notions of culture that become kinds of "identity kits" is that the celebration of difference, of cultures, and of one's roots, promoted as the goal of some multicultural approaches, may in fact do little more than broaden students' appreciation of "different" cultures, as these are made palatable and thus marketable. If culture is viewed as stable, homogeneous, and portable/exportable, it is easily commodified. The question must be raised whether mainstream approaches to multicultural education aren't opening up niche markets within global capitalism. Fredric Jameson (1994), talking about architecture, puts it this way:

[P]ost-Fordism puts the new computerized technology to work by custom-designing its products for individual markets. This has indeed been called postmodern marketing, and it can be thought to "respect" the values and cultures of the local population by adapting its various goods to suit those vernacular languages and practices. Unfortunately, this inserts the corporations into the very heart of local and regional culture, about which it becomes difficult to decide whether it is authentic any longer . . . [N]ow the regional as such becomes the business of global American Disneyland-related corporations, who will redo your own native architecture for you more exactly than you can do it yourself. Is global Difference the same today as global Identity? (pp. 204–205)

9. *Interpellation* is the term Louis Althusser (1994) used in his famous essay "Ideology and Ideological State Apparatuses (Notes towards an Investigation)" to theorize how the individual comes to be a subject or comes to assume social identities or how social identities are produced. He used as an example, a person being hailed by a police officer and that person responding to the hailing. This hailing or interpellation is the way, according to Althusser, that ideology creates subjects, subjects being the abstract position occupied within ideology by individuals. What Althusser didn't address was the psychic dimension or why someone turns to the hailing.

10. Walter Ben Michaels nicely captures the circular logic.

For insofar as our culture remains nothing more than what we do and believe, it is impotently descriptive. . . . It is only if we think that our culture is not whatever beliefs and practices we actually happen to have but is instead the beliefs and practices that should properly go with the sort of people we happen to be that the fact of something belonging to our culture can count as a reason for doing it. But to think this is to appeal to something that must be beyond culture and that cannot be derived from culture precisely because our sense of which culture is properly ours must be derived from it. This has been the function of race. . . . Our sense of culture is characteristically meant to displace race, but . . . culture has turned out to be a way of continuing rather than repudiating racial thought. It is only the appeal to race that makes culture an object of affect and that gives notions like losing our culture, preserving it, stealing someone else's culture, restoring people's culture to them, and so on, their pathos. . . . Race transforms people who learn to do what we do into the thieves of our culture and people who teach us to do what they do into the destroyers of our culture; it makes assimilation into a kind of betrayal and the refusal to assimilate into a kind of heroism (quoted in Zizek, 1997, p. 26).

The inherent idealism of multicultural approaches that organize their programs around racial cultures standardizes all the variations among individuals within the respective racial cultures that are measured against or seen as expressive of the racial cultural noumena. Furthermore, such approaches often foreclose other possible explanations of behaviors. For example, the elaborated codes that Lisa Delpit (1995) attributes to white culture, Basil Bernstein (1971) reads as anchored in class and Deborah Tannen (1990) attributes to gender differences.

Often such multicultural approaches provide particular racial cultural scripts (Appiah, 1997) with which and through which members of that race/culture come into being. In other words, because white culture is seen as homogeneous and the ground for experience, those white teachers and students who write personal narratives about how whiteness has affected them wind up reciting guilt narratives, conversion narratives, accounts of coming to terms with the Other in themselves, reactionary narratives of how their whiteness has victimized them, or racial development narratives, all of which offer specific subject positions or positions from which one may speak that are a priori determined. These teachers and students become white or, following Judith Butler's (1990) analysis of identity, *perform* their identity as they write these, and that whiteness is already determined by a priori narratives anchored in what is often articulated as a homogeneous white culture.

But just as black culture and African American culture are not homogeneous, white culture, too, would appear far less homogeneous than many approaches to multicultural education would have us believe. For example, Whites may all benefit from structures of white privilege but do so asymmetrically, depending on their other identities, what specific situations and contexts are being addressed, and how such privileges are interpreted. One could also argue, that there are several white cultures in the United States, ranging from "white trash" culture to New England Yankee white culture to suburban white culture, and there is the problematic of European culture. Cultures essentialized as or anchored to race tend to provide only one script to articulate these differences. Conversely, black teachers and students, for example, who give personal accounts of their experience of race produce much more nuanced and complex narratives, but often and understandably recount the injuries of racism or the riches of black or African American cultures. West Indian students I have taught consider themselves West Indian and black but not African American, and the local cultures of Caribbean islanders and West Indians differ from African American cultures, although dark skinned West Indians and African Americans are color coded as black and suffer the consequences of the racial matrix in the United States. When black culture or African American culture provides the only script to illuminate experience, then ethnic, national, and religious variations, for example, and individual idiosyncrasies are either flattened or seen as anomalies. One can also argue, as Elizabeth Ellsworth (1997) does, that whiteness and blackness are not only complicated by other identities but also are never the same. Ellsworth points out how "[w]hiteness, like racism, is always more than one thing, and it's never the same thing twice" (p. 266).

It would seem problematic to talk of specific cultures that are anchored in race that is then determined by culture. It is also problematic that so many of the attempts to enrich schools and the curriculum do so through essentialist notions of racial cultural identity. By pinning culture to essentialist racial identities, the very binary logic associated with European regimes of logic (Pinar, 1997) is sustained. Difference is promoted in such multiculturalism as equality of equal differences—a kind of racial/cultural relativism—but actually emerges as frozen. Just as the smiling faces of various racial groups appear frozen in posters in schools, so these approaches to multiculturalism eventuate in varied courses and languages, approaches all anchored in supposedly stable racial cultures. Would this be an improvement over the current situation? Of course! But it would also miseducate our students, because it would not allow for an investigation of how these racial cultures were produced, organized, or sustained or what psychic needs their maintenance served.

11. A good example of a reaction formation found in popular culture is the multiethnic, multiracial, multisexual, and multiclass advertisement—the multiculturalism of Bennetton or Nike ads, for example—that reflects a certain loosening of older prejudices but also subtly renders critiques of racism and sexism out of date and unhip and represses the more recent permutations of racism, homophobia, and sexism. It's not a big step from these commercial reaction formations, where one feeling is disguised by its opposite, to today's latest racial violence.

12. I have changed the name of the character.

13. We see in the recent Abner Louima police torture case, a white cop, with an African American fiancée, sodomizing with a toilet bowl plunger a black Haitian male, and the Police Commissioner, Howard Safir, quoted as saying that "I don't think there's a race factor here" (quoted in Hentoff, 1997, p. 20). When Safir can make this kind of comment, then clearly, although police brutality affects all of us, special attention must be paid to the outrages perpetrated specifically against Blacks and people of color in general.

14. In many of the discourses on multicultural education, biracialism and multiracialism are seen the way androgyny was conceptualized in the 1970s before feminism made the linguistic turn and/or was queered and became feminisms. Androgeny was conceptualized as consisting of male and female sides (Bem, 1970). In the same way, biracialism and multiracialism are conceptualized as consisting of, for example, white and black or a synthesis of the two rather than as a disruption or interruption of the very system that creates such dualisms or racial classifications, and therefore as possibly allowing us to "leave the field of the double bind" (Ellsworth, 1997). We see this in an article titled "The White Girl in Me, the Colored Girl in You and the Lesbian in Us: Crossing Boundaries," where Connolly and Nonmair discover their own and the other's communal or racial/cultural identities in one another and discuss their experiences of these without disrupting the homogeneity or unity of these identities.

15. Neoconservatives and liberals tend to see the world through a kind of nictitating membrane that, one could argue, is constituted by whiteness, but they

are incapable of seeing the membrane. All other races or cultures or ethnicities—that is all communal identities other than white—emerge against the ground of whiteness, as different and particular. Or to put it another way, around the silent center of whiteness, they emerge as strident, marginal differences.

16. By *callings* I am trying to suggest something that combines Althusser's interpellation with the fact that someone answers that "hailing," and therefore that there is a psychic dimension that allows for the turn to that "hailing."

REFERENCES

Althusser, L. (1994). Ideology and ideological state apparatuses (Notes towards an Investigation). In S. Zizek (Ed.), *Mapping ideology*. New York: Verso Press.

Appiah, K. A. (1997). The multicultural misunderstanding. In *The New York Review of Books, 44* (15), 30–36.

Appiah, K. A., & Gutman, A. (1996). *Color conscious: The political morality of race.* Princeton, NJ: University of Princeton Press.

Baldwin, J. (1985). *The price of the ticket: Collected nonfiction 1948–1985.* New York: St. Martin's Press.

Bem, D. (1970). *Beliefs, attitudes, and human affairs.* Belmont, CA: Brooks/Cole.

Bernstein, B. (1971). *Class, codes and control.* London: Routledge and Kegan Paul.

Butler, J. (1990). *Gender trouble: Feminism and the subversion of identity.* New York: Routledge.

Butler, J. (1997). *The psychic life of power.* Stanford, CA: Stanford University Press.

Collins, P. H. (1991). *Black feminist thought.* New York: Routledge.

Conzen, K. N. (1989). Ethnicity as festive culture. In W. Sollors (Ed.), *The invention of ethnicity.* Oxford: Oxford University Press.

Cose, E. (1995). *The rage of the privileged class.* New York: HarperCollins.

Deleuze, G. (1994). *What is philosophy?* New York: Columbia University Press.

Delpit, L. (1995). *Other people's children: Cultural conflict in the classroom.* New York: New Press.

Dewey, J. (1929). *The quest for certainty.* New York: Minton, Balch.

Dunn, R. (1997). The goals and track record of multicultural education. *Educational Leadership, 54* (7), 74–77.

Eliot, T. S. (1972). *The sacred wood: Essays on poetry and criticism.* London: Methuen. (Original work published in 1920.)

Ellsworth, E. (1997). Double binds of whiteness. In M. Fine et al. (Eds.), *Off white: Readings on race, power and society.* New York: Routledge.

Fanon, F. 1967. *Black skin, white masks.* New York: Grove Press.

Felman, S. (1982). Psychoanalysis and education: Teaching terminable and interminable. In B. Johnson (Ed.), *The pedagogical imperative: Teaching as a literary genre.* New Haven, CT: Yale University Press.

Finn, C. (1990). Narcissus goes to school. *Commentary, 89* (6), 40–45.

Fitzgerald, F. S. (1980/1925). *The great gatsby.* New York: Collier Books. (Original work published in 1925.)

Fordham, S. (1988). Racelessness as a factor in black students' school success: Pragmatic strategy or pyrrhic victory? *Harvard Educational Review, 58* (1), 54–84.

Foucault, M. (1973). *The order of things*. New York: Vintage Books.

Freire, P. (1968). *Pedagogy of the oppressed*. New York: Seabury Press.

Freud, A. (1966). *The ego and the mechanisms of defense*. New York: International Universities Press.

Freud, S. (1959). Instincts and their vicissitudes. *Collected Papers*, Vol. 4. New York: Basic Books. (Original work published in 1915.)

Fuss, D. (1989). *Essentially speaking: Feminism, nature and difference*. New York: Routledge.

Giroux, H. (1997). Rewriting the discourse of racial identity: Towards a pedagogy and politics of whiteness. *Harvard Educational Review, 67* (2), 285–320.

Grosz, E. (1995). *Space, time and perversion: Essays on the politics of bodies*. New York: Routledge.

Grumet, M. (1988). *Bitter milk: Women and teaching*. Amherst: University of Massachusetts Press.

Harstock, N. (1983). Rethinking modernism: Minority vs. majority theories. *Cultural Critique 7*, 187–206.

Hentoff, N. (1997, September 23). Jim Crow in blue. *The Village Voice*, 20.

Hoffman, D. (1996). Culture and self in multicultural education: Reflections on discourse, text, and practice. *American Educational Research Journal, 33*(3), 545–569.

Jameson, F. (1994). *The seeds of time*. New York: Columbia University Press.

———. (1981). *The political unconscious: Narrative as symbolic act*. Ithaca, NY: Cornell University Press.

Kahn, W. (1993). Facilitating and undermining organizational change: A case study. *Journal of Applied Behavioral Science, 29* (1): 33–34.

Kovel, J. (1984). *White racism: A psychohistory*. New York: Columbia University Press.

Lacan, J. (1977). *Ecrits: A Selection*. Alan Sheriden (trans.). New York: W. W. Norton.

Lee, H. (1960). *To kill a mockingbird*. Philadelphia: Lippincott.

Ladson-Billings, G. (1995). Toward a theory of culturally relevant pedagogy. *American Educational Research Journal 32* (3), 465–492.

Lessing, D. (1997). *Walking in the shade: Volume two of my autobiography, 1949–1962*. New York: HarperCollins.

Lowenthal, D. (1985). *The past is a foreign country*. Cambridge: Cambridge University Press.

Marable, M. (1983). *How capitalism underdeveloped black America*. Boston Southend Press.

McCarthy, C. (1990). *Race and Curriculum*. London: Falmer Press.

———. (1988). Rethinking liberal and radical perspectives on racial inequality in schooling: Making the case for nonsynchrony. *Harvard Educational Review, 58* (3) 265–279.

McCarthy, C., & Crichlow, W. (Eds.). (1993). *Race, identity and representation in education*. New York: Routledge.

McLaren, P. (1995). Critical pedagogy and predatory culture: Oppositional politics in a postmodern age. New York: Routledge.

Minnich, E. K. (1990). *Transforming knowledge*. Philadelphia: Temple University Press.

Pellegrini, A. (1997). *Performance anxieties: Staging psychoanalysis, staging race.* New York: Routledge.

Phelan, P. (1993). *Unmarked: The politics of performance.* New York: Routledge.

Pinar, W. (1997). Regimes of reason and the male narrative voice. In W. Tierney and Y. Lincoln (Eds.), *Representation and the text: Re-framing the narrative voice.* Albany: State University of New York Press.

————. (1994). *Autobiography, Politics and Sexuality: Essays in Curriculum 1972–1992.* New York: Peter Lang.

————. (1993). Notes on understanding curriculum as racial text. In C. McCarthy and W. Crichlow (Eds.), *Race, identity and representation in education.* New York: Routledge.

Pinar, W. F., Reynolds, W. M., Slattery, P., & Taubman, P. M. (1995). *Understanding Curriculum: An Introduction to Historical and Contemporary Curriculum Discourses.* New York: Peter Lang.

Powell, L (1997). The achievement (k)not: Whiteness and "black underachievement." In M. Fine et al. (Eds.), *Off white: Readings on race, power and society.* New York: Routledge.

Ravitch, D. (1990). Diversity and democracy: Multicultural education in America. *American Educator, 14* (1), 16–20, 46–48.

Rycroft, C. (1968). *A critical dictionary of psychoanalysis.* New York: Basic Books.

Schafer, R. (1992). *Retelling a life: Narration and dialogue in psychoanalysis.* New York: Basic Books.

Sollors, W. (Ed.). (1989). *The invention of ethnicity.* Oxford: Oxford University Press.

Stern, D. (1985). *The interpersonal world of the infant: A view from psychoanalysis and developmental psychology.* New York: Basic Books.

Taubman, P. (1993). Separate identities, separate lives: Diversity in the curriculum. In L. Castenell & W. Pinar (Eds.). *Understanding curriculum as racial text: Representations of identity and difference in Education.* Albany: State University of New York Press.

West, C. (1993). *Race matters.* Boston: Beacon Press.

Williams, P. (1991). *The Alchemy of race and rights: Diary of a law professor.* Cambridge, MA: Harvard University Press.

Winant, H. (1997). Behind blue eyes: Whiteness and contemporary U.S. racial politics. In M. Fine, et al. (Eds.), *Off white: Readings on race, power and society.* New York: Routledge.

Wright, R. (1940). *Native son.* New York: Modern Library.

Zizek, S. (1997). *The abyss of freedom/ages of the world.* Ann Arbor: University of Michigan Press.

7

Transforming the Deficit Narrative: Race, Class, and Social Capital in Parent-School Relations

Hollyce C. Giles

It is 8:45 A.M. I, a white psychologist for a school-based mental health team, am sitting near a guard desk strategically placed in the lobby at the entrance of an elementary school, waiting for a parent with whom I have an appointment. Most children have made their way to their morning class line-up. A few stragglers and their parents approach the security guard, hoping to be able to come in the front door and go to their classes by the shortest route. Enforcing school policy, the guard sends the parents and children back out the front door of the school to the rear cafeteria entrance. Even though this policy has been in place for more than a year, parents resist. Some parents grumble loudly, but comply. The policy bars admission of children and parents through the front door in the early morning as part of an effort to protect the occupants of the school from "intruders." Teachers and other staff move freely past the desk, rushing to meet their classes for the morning line-up.

One parent's insistence on entering through the front door antagonizes the African American guard, who comes out from behind the desk and tells the parent, in a hostile tone, that she must calm down or leave. The parent, an African American woman with two children at her side, argues loudly with the guard and demands to see the principal. The guard replies that the principal is unavailable. The parent takes her children's hands and moves toward the front door, proclaiming her unfavorable opinion of the guard, the school, its policies, and the principal on her way out. It was not clear whether she was, in fact, going to the cafeteria entrance to the school or taking her children back home.

INTRODUCTION

The guard desk at the entrance represents the closely watched boundary between this urban school and the community that surrounds it. This scene is a metaphor for educators' power to control and channel parents' access and participation in the school and parents' anger about the way in which the school has taken up its power. While the school's entrance policy is intended to keep out the dangers of the surrounding community, the policy also reflects ambivalence about what the parents, African Americans and Puerto Ricans with few financial resources, might have to offer to the school. The entrance policy suggests that the school cannot distinguish parents from intruders.

A prominent theme in the most recent wave of school reform has been the importance of collaboration among schools, parents, and communities to educate children (Cochran and Dean, 1991; Cortes, 1996; Epstein, 1993; Giles, 1998; Hamburg, 1993). The rationale for such collaboration is that the social capital—that is, trust, information channels, and norms and obligations—that develops from relationships will contribute to a more effective educational process (Coleman, 1990; Stone & Wehlage, 1994). This results in improved student academic performance (Henderson, 1987), increased feelings of parental competence (Winters, 1994), and the empowerment of parents to advocate for public and private support of school reform (Cortes, 1996).

Surprisingly little attention has been given, however, to how to build these relations and social capital across the racial, class, and role boundaries that separate parents and teachers in urban schools in neighborhoods of concentrated poverty (Lareau & Shumar, 1997). The limited nature of this key part of the discourse around parent involvement has resulted in efforts to enhance relations among parents, schools, and communities that simply reproduce the hierarchical and often oppressive structure of relations among classes and races in our society. This inequitable structure stands in the way of engaging parents and motivating educators to collaborate with each other in an authentic, effective manner (Delpit, 1995; Fine, 1993; Lareau, 1987, 1989; Lightfoot, 1978; Seeley, Niemever, & Greenspan, 1991; Winters, 1994).

Central to this structure of relations is an entrenched deficit model that informs the attitudes of many middle-class educators toward parents of color from lower socioeconomic groups. This model compares parents of color and those from the lower and working classes with a white middle-class standard and finds these parents to be deprived, deviant, or "at-risk" (Carter & Goodwin, 1994; Laosa, 1983; Swadener, 1995). Educators working with this model tend to have low expectations for parents of color and to implicitly and explicitly devalue their participation in the educational process. Such deficit-based attitudes do not foster a desire for collaboration from parents or educators.

In this chapter, I describe a process that occurred at the urban elementary school—the school referred to in the opening vignette—in which African American and Puerto Rican parents with low-incomes transformed workshops designed to train them to become better parents into a vibrant parents' group with its own agenda. I consider the ways that the roles, racial identities, and classes of the educators, parents, and community members helped to shape a group process in which parents eventually rejected the deficit-based attitudes of educators and representatives of community agencies. This process ignited the interest of educators and representatives of community agencies to work *with* the parents and to stop treating them as "denigrated others" (Skolnick & Green, 1993) and start treating them as human beings with whose needs and strivings they could identify. I also include my reflections on the influence of my own racial and class identity on the group process in my position as the white psychologist who was first the "trainer" and then a "facilitator" of the parents' group.

My method can best be characterized as participant observation. The sources of evidence I draw upon in my analysis of this process of parent involvement come primarily from my own case notes and observations of myself and of the other participants. The study, then, is essentially my narrative of what occurred among parents, educators, and community members in this school. I recount parents' and teachers' verbalizations and nonverbal behaviors as I recorded and perceived them. A limitation of this method is that the observations are filtered through my lens, without the benefit of the points of view and reflections on their experience of the other participants. Because of this limitation, I generate questions and hypotheses from the data to be explored further in future research that will draw more upon the multiple perspectives of participants.

In this study, I bring together three bodies of theory—racial identity, group relations, and social capital theory—to reflect upon the evolution of the structure of relations among parents, educators, and community members in this process. Racial identity theory (Helms, 1990, 1994, 1995) helps to formulate questions about the relation between the educators' and the parents' racial self-concepts and the ways in which they related to each other in the school setting. Group relations theory (Wells, 1990) offers a framework for considering how different levels and components of group process influenced the evolution of the parents' group, given members' classes and hypothesized racial identities. Social capital theory (Coleman, 1990; Couto, 1995; Stone & Wehlage, 1994) offers a rationale and strategy for creating bonds among parents, educators, and members of the community as a means for improving children's education.

The purpose of this analysis is to derive lessons that can be used by educators, parents, and communities in building relations across race and class boundaries. The following sections briefly review these theories.

The Influence of Race and Class on Relations Among Educators, Parents, and Communities: The Contribution of Racial Identity Theory

Despite our discomfort with this reality, race and class continue to have a strong influence on our relations with each other in the United States. Societal attitudes and tensions around these issues are imported into groups in organizations and institutions, including schools. Racial identity theory offers a framework for understanding how educators', parents', and community members' attitudes about and behaviors in dealing with race influence the nature and outcome of the process of parent involvement.

Racial identity is a person's racial self-concept, including one's beliefs, attitudes, and values about oneself relative to people from other racial groups (Helms, 1990). Race and racial identity are not synonymous; within each racial group exist several different racial identity statuses, or ways of relating to one's race. Janet Helms' theory assumes that individuals from all socioracial groups experience a racial identity development process in which they evolve through different racial identity statuses. Helms defines these statuses as "the dynamic cognitive, emotional and behavioral processes that govern a person's interpretation of racial information in her or his interpersonal environments" (Helms, 1995, p. 194). Helms has developed separate racial identity theories for Whites and people of color, given our different racial socialization processes in this country.

Each racial identity status correlates with particular attitudes, beliefs, and strategies for processing information related to race (Helms, 1995). White racial identity theory assumes that Whites generally are socialized to protect the entitlements and privileges accorded to our race in this society and, therefore, develop attitudes and beliefs and process information in a way that preserves these entitlements. Helms (1995) identifies the developmental issue for Whites as the relinquishment of entitlements.

One information processing strategy is to deny or to remain oblivious to racial information and racism, thus preserving the status quo of advantage for Whites (the contact status). Another strategy is to reshape racial data to conform to a liberal worldview in which people of color are viewed as deficient when compared with a white middle-class standard (the pseudo-independent status). Both ways of processing information lead to the conclusion that the failure of people of color results from their own inherent deficits, often in spite of the concerted efforts of white institutions and professionals to assist them (Delpit, 1995; Skutnabb-Kangas, 1984).

People of color racial identity theory (Helms, 1995) conceptualizes the developmental process through which people of color become aware of and overcome the psychic consequences of internalized racism. The theory hypothesizes that individuals of color have various attitudes toward their race and that of others, from rejecting or denying that part of themselves to valuing themselves and people of other races according to characteristics other than race (Helms, 1990). A positive racial identity is characterized by rejection of racism and oppression and an ability to evaluate Whites and white culture based on their strengths and weaknesses.

Racial Identity in Context: The Reciprocal Influence of Social and Organizational Processes and Racial Identity Statuses

Racial identity was first conceptualized as a variable of individual differences with a focus on internal psychological processes. In subsequent iterations of her theory of racial identity, Helms (1990, 1995) articulated more fully the influence of environment on individuals' expressions of their racial identity statuses and on the ways in which individuals' racial identities and relative amounts of social power influence the nature and quality of interpersonal and group interactions. She suggests that a person develops new racial identity statuses and draws from his or her existing repertoire of statuses to respond to personally meaningful racial material in the environment in a way that protects his or her self-esteem and sense of well-being (Helms, 1995).

The process of parent involvement described in this chapter suggests the need for a way to connect two theories—racial identity theory and group relations theory—to develop more complex hypotheses about the power of the dynamic social and organizational context on the expression of individuals' racial identities and, in turn, the ways participants' racial identities influence the process. Consideration of the influence of the racial identities of those with social power on the ways in which resources—financial, social, and emotional—are distributed to others, represents a step in the direction of joining racial identity theory with group relations theory. For example, it can be hypothesized that when Whites or Blacks with the greatest social power in a setting operate from a deficit perspective, individuals with less social power may risk losing access to available resources if they behave in a way that challenges the status quo of a worldview that sees low-income people of color as deprived or deficient.

bell hooks (1994) offers an example of the impact of the interaction of social power and racial identity. She identifies the desire to maintain class power as a motive that sometimes leads intellectuals, including black intellectuals, to assimilate into white middle-class culture and betray the concerns for change of Blacks who are not in privileged locations. A similar process occurs with some white educators and educators of color in their relations with parents. Christine Sleeter (1993) notes that some educators of color who have become part of the middle class accept aspects of the class structure that ought to be challenged. One aspect of the class structure that contributes to its reproduction is the assumption that people with fewer financial resources or in lower socioeconomic classes have inherent deficits rather than being the bearers of the deleterious impact of such social barriers as racism.

The above analysis suggests that the desire for class power or, stated differently, the desire for access to important resources may play a strong role in the development and expression of racial identity statuses for both Whites and people of color. Group relations theory, described in the following section, offers a framework for understanding the ways in which individuals' racial and class identities and desire for power, resources and belonging are negotiated in groups.

Group Relations Theory: The Negotiation of Needs for Power and Belonging Across Racial and Class Boundaries

Systemic socioanalytic theory of group relations (Wells, 1990) identifies different levels of process that occur simultaneously in groups. The intrapersonal, group, intergroup, and interorganizational levels are particularly relevant here. The intrapersonal level concerns the internal life of an individual, including his/her racial identity and other personality characteristics. The group level involves the behavior of members as participants in a social system and is the level at which such processes as scapegoating occur. At this level, members act on behalf of the group as well as on their own behalf. The intergroup level covers how individuals relate to each other as members of subgroups defined by one or more aspects of the group memberships they carry with them into groups, such as race, class, organizational role (e.g., parent or educator), and gender. Finally, the interorganizational level refers to the influence that a group/organization and its context have on each other. An example of this would be the impact on a school of a mandate from its district office to increase parent involvement.

Two key phenomena that occur at the group level of process and are particularly relevant for the processes described in this chapter are splitting and projective identification (Wells, 1990). Splitting occurs when individuals or groups disown or split off parts of themselves that are undesirable, such as their feelings of incompetence. Projective identification is a psychological process in which individuals or groups disown a part of themselves and act as if another person or group has that part or quality—that is, a particular quality or characteristic that a person or group does not want to acknowledge is denied in them and located in another person or group.

Splitting and projective identification tend to occur in organizations and groups where individuals are experiencing a high level of anxiety or ambivalence in the course of their social relations. Often, all of the "good" qualities in an organization will be located in one subgroup, while the "bad" qualities are located in another group. In this way, groups subconsciously "protect" the good qualities from contamination by the bad. The price paid for this way of coping is that the subgroups remain isolated from each other, and the higher quality of information that would be yielded from each group integrating its own good and bad parts and engaging in dialogue with the other group(s) is lost. These group conditions are not conductive to the production of social capital.

The following section describes one means of generating social capital in schools in which the positive and negative attributes of individuals and subgroups are integrated and conditions are created in which group members feel free to bring themselves fully and authentically to the group.

Free Spaces

Robert Putnam (1993) and R. A. Couto (1995) propose that mediating structures such as schools, churches and civic associations can create the conditions for the generation of social capital. One strategy for creating such conditions is the development of a free space, an "environment in which people are able to learn a new self-respect, a deeper and more assertive group identity, public skills, and values of cooperation and civic virtue" (Couto, 1995, p. 17). In these spaces, a group such as parents can create or reveal narratives "that provide alternative understanding of their condition, pride in their group's accomplishments, and precedents and examples of resistance" (p. 18).

Drawing on Alastair MacIntyre (1981), Couto (1995, p. 19) notes that "without their own narratives within their own free space, marginal groups become the virtueless groups of the dominant culture." Parents of color with low incomes have been marginalized in many schools. Through a process of projective identification, they have also been constructed as virtueless.

Free spaces offer opportunities for marginalized groups to reclaim their virtue. A school or other organization creates the conditions for parents to build relationships with each other as they construct an alternative narrative about their lives based on their strengths and the identification of the barriers to opportunity that they have all faced. One key condition for the successful creation of a free space where these relationships can develop is that the racial and class identities of educators must be such that they are able to facilitate parents to speak frankly about their experiences of raising their children from a perspective of competence rather than a deficit perspective and avoid defensiveness when parents claim the right to speak frankly, and perhaps critically, about the school.

THE EVOLUTION OF A PROCESS OF PARENT INVOLVEMENT AT AN URBAN ELEMENTARY SCHOOL

In this section, I describe a process in which parents led the way in creating a free space that generated social capital for the education of their children. The description offers some evidence for the hypothesis that the racial identities and classes of the educators, parents, and members of the community influenced the evolution of the group process that led to the development of a free space.

The public elementary school where this process occurred, was founded in the late 1800s as a school for children of African descent. In this narrative we call the school the Freedom School and designate its locations as the Brooklyn Hills neighborhood. The majority of children currently enrolled are African American, but there are also a large number of Latino children. Ninety-eight percent of the children in the school are eligible for free lunch (New York City Board of Education, 1997). All of the children who attend the school live in the surrounding New York City housing projects. A positive sense of community is evident in several older women who "watch over things" in the housing projects from their windows and plant and tend gardens in communal spaces. At the same time, a significant amount of drug dealing and related violence occur in the Brooklyn Hills projects. Children have been injured by cross fire and parents often express concern about the danger of stray bullets, even inside their own apartments.

My role in the school was that of a psychologist with a pilot project jointly sponsored by a large community mental health agency and the New York City Board of Education. We provided supportive services to keep children who had been identified by their teachers and the guidance counselor as having emotional or behavioral problems in mainstream classes.

A significant portion of the school staff is black, the same race as the majority of people in the community. The other staff members are white and black Latinos and white European Americans. The principal, in her position for the second year, is Latina.

The salience of race in the thoughts and feelings of students at the school and, by extension, their parents is reflected in the vignette below. It is evident that the strength of the negative associations the children had to whiteness created cognitive dissonance when they tried to reconcile these associations with their relationship with me, a white person. One week during my semester-long work on conflict resolution with a fourth-grade class, the children demanded to know why I had missed the previous week's session. When I asked what the previous Monday had been, they recalled that it had been Martin Luther King's birthday. When I asked the children who King was, the first child who spoke said, "He was killed by Whites." Other children began describing in great detail how much Whites hate Blacks and how mean Whites are, referring at times to stories their parents had told them. When I asked whether anyone had noticed that I was white, one child immediately said, "No, you're not." After some further discussion about my race, another child raised her hand to say (as if she had come up with a solution to a dilemma), "I know, you're white on the outside and black inside."

Although the differences in the races and classes of parents, children, and educators at this school played an important role in their relations, the adults in the school remained largely silent about these topics. The children were more forthcoming than their parents or the school staff, not having been socialized fully into the taboo against talking about race with people outside one's own racial group.

The silence of administrators, teachers, and mental health professionals (referred to as "educators" in this chapter) about race and class belied the strong influence these characteristics had in their work with parents. In numerous ways, school staff communicated their criticisms that students and parents who were of different races than themselves did not talk, act, or dress in the way that they should, which might be characterized as a stereotypically white middle-class way (e.g., use standard English, behave and dress calmly and unflamboyantly, make polite requests to discipline children, etc.). Interventions to help parents began with the assumption that these parents had inherent deficits and aimed to train them to hew to what school officials saw as a standard of ideal parenthood. These interventions engaged very few parents.

The literature suggests that this school is not alone in its silence about race and class (Cohen, 1993) or its deficit approach to work with parents (Cochran & Dean, 1991; Delpit, 1995; Harry, 1992; Laosa, 1983; Rioux & Beria, 1993; Torres-Guzman, 1991; Winters, 1994). Researchers note that few schools explicitly consider or address the influence of the race or class of parents, children, and educators on the educational process (Cohen, 1993), even though these factors are hypothesized to significantly influence the interactions of participants in the school (Carter & Goodwin, 1994; Sleeter, 1993).

A social class difference exists between parents and teachers in the Freedom School; parents generally do not have as many years of education and have lower incomes than the teachers (as noted earlier, most families qualify for free lunches for their children; teachers' average salary is $45,000 in New York City). Many times, I overheard teachers and pupil services personnel of different races make critical comments about how poorly parents cared for their children. An African American teacher once remarked to me and another African American teacher, "You can tell by their shoes how well the parents take care of their children—the children with Adidas and Nikes have parents who take good care of them." The implication was that even parents with very little income could find the money to buy status sneakers for their children if they were good parents.

The lack of participation of most parents in their children's education surfaced and resurfaced as a dominant theme in the school. Teachers and mental health professionals expressed frustration over the parents' absence from school functions and from scheduled appointments. The school's formal efforts to involve parents—a newsletter, open school nights, and the inclusion of a parent on the new School-Based Management Team—seemed to be driven by regulations from above rather than by a desire to engage parents. Often, I heard members of the school staff express variations of "the district office says we have to do this." A sense of mistrust and lack of communication between school staff and parents belied the outward compliance with these mandates and limited the effectiveness of activities geared toward increased parent involvement. While a handful of parents had made a place for themselves at the school in the Parent-Teacher Association (PTA) and as volunteers, the great majority of parents were not drawn in to participate.

Phase One: Getting Started

The intervention at the center of this narrative was born of a confluence of events at this particular school. My colleagues in the pilot project and I were eager to expand our work to include primary prevention aimed at achieving systemic change. The recently organized School Based Management Team, composed of the guidance counselor, teachers, parents, and the principal, was seeking to implement the Board of Education mandate for greater parent participation in schools with a series of parent training workshops. The guidance counselor, as the chair of the team, asked me to lead a series of three workshops on topics that she and the team had chosen: "Handling Stress and Overload,"

"Discipline: The Ins and Outs of Parent Control," and "Saying No and Meaning It."

In the first three workshops, I left narrow, defined spaces for parents' voices: written responses to a questionnaire on their levels of stress, ideas for examples of the topic I was discussing, and questions during brief question and answer periods at the end of workshops. I followed the topics designated by the school fairly closely, using an outline that I had developed from generic materials on parenting that made no reference to the contexts in which parents raise their children.

A core group of parents asked to continue and to expand the workshops in the spring.

Phase Two: The Incidental Creation of a Free Space

School staff and parents planned for six workshops that I would lead in the spring on topics related to parenting. Several stakeholders in the school lent their support in developing the workshops. A large room on the ground floor of the school, shared by both the PTA and the pre-kindergarten (Pre-K) program, was offered by both groups as the site for the workshops.

From the Generic to the Specific: Bringing in Race and Class. During the fall workshops, the pervasive influence of the parents' neighborhood on the particular ways in which they raised their children laced through every discussion. Learning from this experience, we anchored the spring workshops to parenting in their specific community, rather than presenting the workshops as generic parenting workshops. We named the workshops "Being a Parent in Brooklyn Hills."

Participants in the first spring workshop included the parents, three African American paraprofessional women, and myself. We began by introducing ourselves to each other, telling the ages of our children and what we hoped to get out of the workshops. As part of my introduction, I noted that I had grown up and was raising my son in a different neighborhood from that in which they were raising their children. I identified my childhood neighborhood as being in a white suburb in Texas and my current neighborhood in Manhattan. I also noted the obvious: that I was white and they were African American and Puerto Rican. I added that because of these differences, there were things about their lives that I would not know and wrong assumptions that I might make, and I invited them to point out my lack of adequate information and erroneous ideas. The parents listened intently and silently. Talking about race had felt risky, like I was walking a fine line, and I worried about saying something that would alienate parents.

The parents spent much of the first spring workshop talking about the stresses in their lives, including crowded housing and the dangers their children face going to and from school and even in their own apartments—stray bullets, drug dealers, and various forms of violence. At times it was difficult for me to listen to the stories they were telling. I stifled an impulse to move the discussion to a more hopeful topic. I was afraid that parents would leave the workshop depressed and despairing. I was also uncomfortable with my awareness, and I assumed theirs, of my more comfortable economic circumstances and the unjustness of the difference in our lives.

After a period, I asked the parents how they managed, given these problems. They suggested resourceful solutions for changing the stressful situations they faced and for managing the stress of living with the painful situations that they could not change. Parents also talked about their desire to become more involved in the school and their perceptions that the administration did not listen to them or make them feel welcome.

I had mixed feelings about this first session. I was concerned that I had covered little of the curriculum I had prepared. At the same time, I was excited by the extent to which the parents were engaged in the discussion.

In the next workshop, two weeks later, I planned to focus on helping the parents to develop listening skills with their children. I began the session by asking parents to share a problem with discipline that they experienced with their children. The parents became very involved in talking about discipline problems and then expanded to the problems of violence and drug dealing in the neighborhood and other problems in daily living that interfered with their ability to raise their children.

Though I was still somewhat reluctant, we decided to leave the topic of "Listening to Your Children" and give the whole session over to a discussion of some of the problems in raising children in their neighborhood. The parents' hunger for connection with each other was very powerful. During this workshop, I observed a growing level of trust and a greater openness among participants.

Toward the end of this session, I asked parents about the impact of racism on their ability to raise their children. In this context, having talked together for several sessions about personal topics in which I shared information about myself at times, a few parents appeared to trust me enough to talk about racism. They mentioned specific instances where racism had prevented them from getting jobs and taking advantage of other opportunities. A few parents said that racism had not had a big impact on them because they simply were not around Whites very much. Most parents listened and did not participate verbally.

A Shift in the Role of the Principal. A critical incident occurred halfway through the second spring workshop, which marked the beginning of a shift in the relationship between this group of parents and the school's principal. The principal came into the session at the midpoint and listened quietly to parents' concerns for a while. She then offered to invite the housing police, the precinct police, and representatives from the tenants' association to meetings with the parents in which parents could raise their concerns. The parents accepted her offer.

I had frequently heard parents and staff members describe the principal as preoccupied with impressing her supervisors at the district office by producing improved attendance figures, higher test scores, and beautiful bulletin boards to comply with mandates. Her participation in this meeting clearly impressed the parents. She had listened to them and appeared to be taking on more of an advocacy role.

From Parent Workshops to a Parents Group. At this point in the series of workshops, I became more and more aware of a tension between following the mandate given to me by the School-Based Management Team to conduct parent training—to teach parents (in my role as "expert") how to listen to and discipline their children—and following the parents where they wanted to go. Parents clearly wanted to use the workshops to talk with each other about their experiences raising their children in this neighborhood rather than to be trained to be better parents.

At the end of the second workshop, I negotiated a compromise. I would present the planned curriculum, "Listening Skills," for half of the next session, and they would talk with each other about topics important to them for the other half of the session.

An important shift occurred in the third workshop. I communicated to the parents my impression that the workshops had become more and more theirs as they had begun to define the group's task. Given this shift, I reframed my role from that of leader to that of consultant. The parents responded by taking on a larger share of the leadership in a relatively seamless and cohesive fashion. I finally put away the school's curriculum, whose objective was to train the parents. The parents decided that they wanted to address conditions in their community that had an impact on their ability to raise their children. Toward this goal, the parents helped set up a series of dialogues with representatives of various school, community, and city Housing Authority groups.

Based on their strong interest in these dialogues, I hypothesized that the parents were beginning to view themselves as authorized to speak about their housing concerns and their children's education and to consider the possibility that people with authority might listen. The following section shows, however, that the stance taken by those entering into dialogue with the parents did not support their sense that they had a right to speak.

The Dialogues: Parents Find Their Voices. During the series of dialogues the parents met, first, with a representative group of teachers;

next, with the captain and two lieutenants from the local police precinct; then with members of the New York City Housing Authority social services department and Housing Authority police officers; and finally, with the local managers of the Housing Authority, who are responsible for the physical plant of the Brooklyn Hills Projects. With only one exception—an African American community police officer with the Housing Authority Police—the representatives from these different groups approached the parents in the stance of experts whose job it was to educate and inform them; often they spoke to the parents in condescending and patronizing tones.

For the first meeting in this series of dialogues, the principal provided release time from their classes to four teachers so that they could meet with the parents. This act in itself reflected the principal's commitment to the meetings, given her usual reluctance to take teachers away from their academic work with students. An assistant principal carefully selected four sensitive, dedicated teachers, all women—three African Americans and one white Italian American—to attend the meetings. We had described the meeting as an opportunity to talk about *ways* to improve the collaboration between parents and teachers at the school in order to better educate their children.

My notes from this meeting suggest an underlying assumption by the teachers that the parents approached the task of educating their children with several handicaps, most prominently, their own lack of education. This assumption was reflected in the teachers' opening remarks to parents: "You can ask us to explain the homework if you don't understand it," and "The important thing is to be sure your kids spend a block of time doing their homework every night. You don't have to understand the homework to do that." The parents, however, had not raised a concern about understanding the work.

The parents listened quietly and were generally receptive to the teachers' suggestions. One parent remarked that not all teachers were so open as this group, suggesting that the problems resided in certain other teachers but not in these. I intervened, unsuccessfully, several times to encourage parents to share with the teachers more of the hopes and frustrations that they had shared earlier.

After the teachers returned to their classes, parents reviewed the meeting with each other. Toward the end of the meeting, the parents engaged in a heated discussion in which they harshly criticized other parents at the school, whom they viewed as irresponsible about their children's education. Thus, the parents at this meeting were the "good" parents talking with the "good" teachers. The "bad" had been split off and located among "other" parents and teachers.

After the group's discussion, the principal came in and handed out and explained curriculum sheets to help parents prepare their children for the upcoming reading tests. The guidance counselor announced a workshop he would be giving the following week to suggest questions parents could ask teachers on open school night. It was clear that the parents group was offering important information channels (social capital) that educators were beginning to use to give parents information about how to improve their children's education.

The captain of the local police precinct attended the next meeting. The number of participants at the workshop increased to approximately a hundred, more than triple the number at previous meetings. Members of the community, who did not currently have children at the school, including leaders of various community organizations, attended the meeting. At this meeting, I met community leaders (for example, the director of a local community center working with youth) who later proved to be valuable resources in my work with children, another instance of social capital being created.

The captain and his two lieutenants, all three white, arrived and proceeded to lecture the parents and residents about what they needed to do to reduce crime in their community. He addressed the parents as "you people" and spoke about how residents of the projects made the job of the police more difficult by protecting drug dealers. Parents listened, and it seemed that the meeting could continue as it was, with the captain lecturing to a tense, quiet group, or that it could explode.

I eventually challenged the captain's statement, "If you people don't call and tell us where the drug deals are, we can't protect you. I'm not going to send my officers in blind to that kind of dangerous situation." I asked whether there wasn't a way to get information about drug deals that didn't endanger residents who would be identified when they called. This exchange with the captain seemed to open the door to an intense debate between parents and other participants about the relations between the police and residents in the projects around the issue of safety. Some residents focused on ridding the projects of drug dealing, while others voiced the concern that some of those involved with drugs were youth from the community—their children—and that residents needed to address underlying problems. The debate was not resolved, but parents and other community residents shifted their stance toward the police and each other by directly voicing their thoughts and feelings about this controversial issue.

At the third in the series of dialogues, two weeks later, parents and community residents met with senior representatives of the social services department of the New York City Housing Authority. Most of the representatives were people of color. A discrepancy between parents' interests and the mission of the social services staff surfaced early in the meeting. The staff was prepared to present information about the availability of social services to address the social and emotional problems of the community residents, while the residents were focused on improving the living conditions related to the physical plant of the projects. These conditions included chronic lack of heat and hot water in the winter, broken intercoms, and unlocked doors at the entrances of buildings. In contrast to the earlier meeting with teachers, at this meeting parents immediately asserted their interests and needs. The social services staff acknowledged the problems raised by the parents and said that their colleagues in management were the people to speak with and that they would talk with them about attending the next parents' meeting.

At the fourth meeting, officials from the management arm of the Housing Authority and representatives from the tenant councils met with the parents. A member of the Housing Police also attended. The managers of the houses in which the residents lived and two levels of the Housing Authority hierarchy above them attended the meeting. Parents were impressed and pleased to meet directly with these individuals who had significant power over their lives, and they clearly felt authorized to voice their grievances about their housing and related concerns. The representatives of management—who included men and women of color and a white man—took an expert stance (condescending, know-it-all, distant) with the parents. They generally deflected parents' concerns as inaccurate and uninformed or took the position that they were unable to respond to the problem raised because it was out of their hands.

A defining moment occurred in the meeting when a Latina parent, who had been one of the more silent members of the group, raised a concern about plaster failing off the walls in her apartment, pointing out that the management had not responded to her complaint to them even though she had young children who might try to eat the paint and plaster chips. The deputy director of management, rather than acknowledging the concern, responded in a patronizing tone that "The problem's not the plaster; it's the pipes leaking behind the wall." The resident retorted, "Well, then I want the pipes fixed." Other parents discussed this moment with some pride after the meeting.

Parents also discussed safety issues at the meeting, specifically people shooting up drugs in the elevators and shooting guns in and around the buildings. Parents and housing officials discussed various strategies for reducing the level of violence, most related to greater involvement by the tenants in existing councils and patrols. The presidents of the tenants councils invited parents to participate and identified meeting times, locations, and current projects. A community police officer discussed with parents ways in which they could organize to take action on a particular issue. Parents expressed interest in working together to get the Housing Authority to repair their intercoms, given the danger of buzzing in people without knowing their identities.

During the course of the workshops and the series of dialogues, my role shifted from that of trainer to that of facilitator. Parents took charge of the meetings.

Transition: Deciding on Future Directions

The last meeting of the parents group of which I was a part was a transition meeting, focused on reviewing past meetings and deciding on future directions the group would take—both how the group would be structured and what its purpose would be. I would be moving to a position at another location in the community agency and so would no longer facilitate the group. A community police officer and other paraprofessionals who had attended previous meetings were present to help facilitate the meeting.

Parents viewed their group as the nucleus of a network of organizations that could function to generate interest in parent training and other activities at the school and in the community—the PTA, tenants' organizations, etc.—a place where people could develop relationships of trust that would encourage them to become involved in a variety of activities, including organizing to take action on a problem of common interest to them. They were eager to move from talking to action. With the encouragement and advice of the Housing Police community officer, parents decided that their first project would be to organize a survey of residents in the projects to determine interest in having working intercoms installed. The Board of Education had also initiated a parent-training program in which parents taught other parents skills in workshops at schools. Parents felt ready to participate in such training and to continue their social action efforts as well. A group of the parents went to the state capital as part of a larger educational advocacy effort and another group visited a school in another city to observe and study its innovative parent involvement program.

The decision about the model of leadership the group would use proved to be difficult. Although I had reduced my involvement significantly, parents felt uncertain about taking on more of the leadership when I left. They were not sure that they had the skills to lead the group themselves. Ultimately, a small group of parents and staff met after this meeting as a planning committee to decide how to facilitate the group in the future.

Afterward

The parents' group continued the following year, facilitated by my successor, an African American psychologist, and a core group of parents and paraprofessionals. According to a paraprofessional who helped to facilitate the parents' group, parents initially viewed the psychologist as condescending and distant. As I had in the beginning, she approached them as an expert, ready to impart her knowledge to them. After receiving feedback about parents' feelings about her approach, the psychologist changed her stance and parents responded with greater openness toward her.

Discussion

This process of parent involvement began with the intention of offering economically poor parents of color training in skills that would help them to raise and educate their children. While such training is valuable in theory, few parents initially were drawn to attend the workshops, severely limiting their impact and their value. Parents transformed the nature of the workshops by talking about issues central to their lives and to their ability to raise their children. The bonds they developed with each other in these conversations created a web of support that enabled them to challenge the deficit-based attitudes and behaviors they encountered from public officials.

This section offers my reflections and some hypotheses about the social processes that contributed to the evolution of the relations among the parents, educators, and representatives of community agencies. The purpose of this discussion is to draw lessons from the experience that can inform future efforts to build relations among parents, educators and communities across racial and class differences.

The Interorganizational Context. Locating this school in its larger context helps to identify the societal attitudes that may have been imported into the school and that constituted the interorganizational level (Wells, 1990) of the process that influenced the relations among parents, educators and the community. The school's social location is near the bottom of the American socioeconomic hierarchy—the children and families who live in the housing projects surrounding the school are considered among the least fit in the "survival of the fittest" paradigm. Largely for this reason, many educators view the school as an undesirable assignment for teaching. Several times, I heard new teachers talk about transferring to other schools in "better neighborhoods" as soon as they could.

Projective identification occurs on a societal level, in that white middle-class members of society split off negative attributes and associate them with the economically poor children and families of color in communities such as the one surrounding this school. Toni Morrison (1992) alludes to the racial component of this phenomenon in her book *Playing in the Dark: Whiteness and the Literary Imagination.* She writes, "Africanism is the vehicle by which the American self knows itself as not enslaved, but free; not repulsive, but desirable; not helpless, but licensed and powerful; not history-less, but historical; not damned, but innocent; not a blind accident of evolution, but a progressive fulfillment of destiny" (p. 52). By locating undesirable traits in particular races and classes, Whites and those from other classes can compare themselves favorably and justify the advantages they have as fairly earned and well deserved. They can also locate blame for the ills of society.

My hypothesis is that the importation of such attitudes into the school, attitudes in which parents and teachers at this particular school are viewed as having undesirable traits, fostered a sense of ambivalence and anxiety among educators about working in this school. Discomfort with such societal attitudes toward the school, combined with the serious academic and social problems experienced by many of the children, may have led teachers, administrators, and mental health professionals to seek someone to blame for these problems. Parents were the easy and obvious choice. The parents were the incompetent, neglectful others who offered a useful contrast to the competence and dedication of school staff members to the well-being of their children. Teachers' frequent negative comments about parents' lack of concern for their children's education contrasted with teachers' remarks about their own unrecognized hard work to help their students offer support for this hypothesis.

I suggest that this process of projective identification contributed to a climate of isolation and alienation among the educators and the parents. The white middle-class worldview (Helms, 1995) that appeared to prevail in the school resulted in educators and parents acting as if race and class differences did not exist among parents and teachers and that these differences did not matter in their relations with each other or in the life chances of the children they were educating. The school climate did not support educators or parents speaking honestly and openly about their thoughts or feelings. It was in this climate that the parent training workshops were conceived.

A mandate from an external organization that had a strong impact on the school, the Board of Education, provided the initial impetus for the workshops. The authority of the Board of Education to provide rewards to educators in the school for complying with its initiatives contributed to educators' motivation to hold workshops for parents.

Another organization in the school's orbit, the community mental health agency for which I worked, also influenced the process of parent involvement. Since the agency did not place pressure on its staff members to increase children's grades or their test scores and we were not directly evaluated by the Board of Education, we approached our work with parents from a location different from that of teachers and administrators. Our location can be best characterized as on the boundary between the teachers and administrators and the parents. Being on the boundary, we had access to the perspectives of both groups and could function as a facilitator of their relations with each other. One of our staff members, an African American paraprofessional, was also a parent of children who had attended school in this community, which helped us to understand the parents' perspectives.

The Deficit Narrative and Factors That Supported Its Dominance. The expectations of ignorance, incompetence, and neglectfulness that educators and community representatives had of parents and that parents, on occasion, had of each other were manifested repeatedly in their interactions. This section identifies some of these interactions and considers how the racial identities of participants and the desire for "class power" contributed to a group process of splitting and projective identification that interfered with the development of more empowering and productive relations.

The school's initial approach to parents grew out of a deficit model: the school invited the parents to be trained in generic parenting skills at workshops given by a white middle-class psychologist, leaving little room for parents to offer their narratives of the strengths and challenges of their particular context. I believed that my professional success—one route to class power—hinged on presenting myself to parents as an expert on how to raise their children.

In the meeting between parents and teachers, both white and African American teachers clearly communicated their low expectations of parents through their comments and their condescending and paternalistic tone. The dominant strategies for processing race-related information in the school—denying racial and class differences, and viewing parents from a deficit perspective—appeared to strongly influence the attitudes of teachers toward the parents. In this interaction, paradigmatic of teacher-parent interactions in the school, the teachers' identifications with their roles appeared to be stronger than their identifications with their races, in that the African American and white teachers were joined across the racial boundary in their deficit approach to parents. The African American teachers did not differentiate themselves from their white colleague to cross the role boundary to join with the African American parents by relating to the parents in a more respectful, strength-oriented manner.

One way to view the white teacher's deficit-based approach to parents is that it served to protect a structure of white advantage: Viewing and responding to parents of color as if they had little to offer supports the belief that Whites generally deserve the advantages that they have. The African American teachers, on the other hand, may have been hesitant to cross the role boundary to form a greater connection or alliance with the parents of color out of concern that they might threaten their white colleague by their racial solidarity or engage in a behavior that is dissonant with the school's racial climate. Threatening white colleagues or departing from the school norm by forming closer relations with parents of the same race could conceivably detract from the stability of their professional role and, thus, their class power. Also, in a climate where parents of color are treated as the "other" and negative traits are loaded into them, teachers of color may resist tendencies to identify more closely with them.

Parents at the meeting avoided direct conflict with the teachers by identifying these teachers as the "good" teachers, splitting off the "bad" treatment they had complained about from teachers in earlier meetings and locating it in the other, "bad" teachers who weren't at the meeting. Parents also disowned any negative parenting in themselves and located it in the "bad" parents who were not at the meeting and had not been active in the school.

Thus, these parents and teachers, on behalf of the other parents and teachers in the school, preserved superficially harmonious relations but did not address or resolve underlying conflict-laden issues that served as barriers to fuller and more productive relations among parents and teachers. Neither parents nor teachers brought their whole selves—their good and bad parts, their racial selves, their classed selves—into the dialogue. My sense is that the climate did not feel safe enough; the teachers' greater social power, combined with what I hypothesized to be their contact and conformity racial identity statuses (Helms, 1995), did not invite challenge or criticism by the parents whose roles carried less social power in that particular context. The parents, many of whom had developed insider status as members of the PTA or as volunteers at the school, may have been reluctant to disrupt generally positive relations with individuals who had such a great influence on their children's lives.

The "bad" parents, those outside the school, may have been too angry and too critical to be tolerated inside the school, again cutting off an important source of information about parents' experience. The scene between the security guard and the parent who challenged the school's entrance policy graphically illustrates the school's response to angry, challenging parents. I also recall the voice of a challenging parent who came "in" to the school via the parents' group during the dialogue with the police. In later meetings, she challenged me and other parents quite directly. She raised difficult issues, such as whether parents could trust each other, given the drug dealing in the neighborhood and parents' loss of control over their children as they grew older. She questioned the usefulness of the group in light of the enormity of the problems it faced. Although her questions were difficult, they brought important realities into the meetings that we needed to address if the meetings were to be relevant to parents' lives.

Another instance of deficit-driven behavior occurred when the Housing Authority sent social services personnel to the meeting to address parents' social needs (i.e., deficits), rather than management personnel who could be held accountable for the serious state of disrepair of the parents' apartments and buildings. An exchange in which the social services personnel could respond to the needs of "disadvantaged" parents placed Housing Authority personnel in a more powerful position than one in which Housing Authority managers are confronted by parents as consumers who want to hold them accountable for a product. It is to the credit of the Housing Authority that they did send the managers when parents made the request.

In summary, deficit-based attitudes about race imported into the school from its context, the contact and conformity racial identity statuses (Helms, 1995), and a desire for access to the resources of educators, parents, and community representatives contributed to a process of splitting and projective identification, which allowed the deficit narrative to remain dominant in this school. The splitting and projective identification, in turn, isolated individuals of different roles and races from each other and prevented more open, genuine communication among the stakeholders in this community.

The Transformation of the Deficit Narrative and the Creation of a Free Space. This section describes the factors that contributed to the creation of a free space in the school through which parents began to transform the deficit narrative. It analyzes the group process through which parents previously isolated from each other developed sufficient cohesion as a group to challenge the deficit attitudes of educators and representatives of the community. In this process, parents were able to reintegrate "bad" and "good" parts of themselves and their community and engage in a richer and more productive dialogue about factors interfering with their ability to raise and educate their children.

Parents' persistence in expressing and acting on their desire to talk with each other about raising their children was the catalyst for altering their course from deficit-based workshops to the creation of a free space in which they developed a cohesive parents' group. Framing the spring workshops in terms of parenting in their specific community, a neighborhood of African American and Puerto Rican residents, also proved to be a key factor in defining a space where parents could talk more about their "real lives." These workshops also became a space where the lives of all of the participants—parents, school staff, and community residents and workers—were raced and classed, implicitly if not explicitly. Acknowledging that racism and classism constitute barriers to opportunity in our society helped to counter the assumption that failure is the result solely of individual deficits.

Thus, the context and climate for discussions about race appear to have been altered in this particular space in the school. Parents' freedom to speak more fully about their lives facilitated the development of their relationships. Hearing that other parents had similar problems may have raised the possibility that they, individually, were not to blame for their difficulties in child rearing, that they were all facing similar economic and social barriers that made it difficult for them to raise their children. Such an environment is hypothesized to be more conducive to the expression of positive racial identity statuses within the wider school environment that generally did not acknowledge racial and class differences or associated people of color and those with limited financial resources with deficits.

This environment eventually reduced the level of anxiety among parents in the group, since there was less pressure to act as if racial and class differences did not exist and as if the parents were in some way more deficient or less deserving than whites or people with greater financial resources. Since the deficit narrative was not as salient in this space, there was not as much pressure to disown bad parts and locate them elsewhere. Parents were freer to bring their whole selves—good and bad parts—to their discussions, which made it easier for them to develop relationships with each other. These relationships strengthened their collective voice, which enabled them to challenge the deficit attitudes and behaviors they encountered in their debate with the police captain and the Housing Authority social services staff and to confront the Housing Authority manager's effort to discredit a Latina mother and her concerns by alluding to her ignorance about construction.

The integration of positive and negative disowned parts and the consequent benefits are exemplified in the parents' debate with the police. One subgroup of parents expressed the view that the youths selling drugs in the projects were dangerous and should be arrested and imprisoned. Another subgroup eventually gave voice to the reality that many of the youths selling drugs were children of their community. Parents were able to integrate the two realities in their discussion and come to the conclusion that they wanted to eliminate the danger that comes with drug dealing, but that they needed to find a solution that addressed the underlying causes of youths turning to drug dealing, rather than simply locking up their young people. By integrating two polarized points of view, parents arrived at a potential solution that was more likely to be effective than locating the danger in the drug dealing youths and putting all of their efforts into locking them up.

As educators at the school witnessed this process in which parents strengthened their collective voice, offered support for each other, reintegrated disowned parts, and challenged deficit-based attitudes and behaviors directed at them, their views of the parents and their relation to them appeared to shift. The principal and other school staff seemed to be better able to see parents as people rather than as denigrated others. They assumed the role of advocates for parents vis-à-vis the representatives of community agencies with whom the parents were engaging in dialogues. The school staff actually seemed excited and energized by the parents' newfound strength and voice, at least when that strength was directed at institutions other than the school.

Limitations of the Process. The school was the one institution that parents did not challenge directly. Their exchange with the teachers was the first in the series of dialogues, and parents built up their collective voice gradually to challenge representatives from the police and the Housing Authority. However, I believe that other factors also were at play in parents' reluctance to challenge the school.

In analogous processes, the school as an organization and I as an individual dissuaded parents from challenging us directly. In our roles as advocates for the parents, we encouraged the parents to give voice to their criticisms and concerns regarding other institutions, but in subtle and not so subtle ways, we discouraged their criticism of us.

My discomfort with the parents' challenging me led me to avoid saying things that might arouse their anger at me, thus limiting the range of feedback I gave them. By avoiding challenging parents, I lessened the likelihood that they would question or criticize me. If the parents had been able to challenge me more, they might have felt more comfortable about taking up the leadership of the group when I left. In reflecting on my experience, I realized that my discomfort with the parents challenging me stemmed in part from my need to have them validate my nonracist status. They could criticize other Whites and I would support them, but I was not ready for them to challenge me. This off-limits sign constrained parents from fully expressing their thoughts, opinions, and resistance.

In her essay "Choosing the Margin as a Space of Radical Openness," bell hooks (1990) captures my voice and that of other white liberals "helping" people of color from a similar stance in this passage: "[S]peak, tell me your story. Only do not speak in a voice of resistance. Only speak from that space in the margin that is a sign of deprivation, a wound, an unfilled longing. Only speak your pain" (p. 152). I felt more comfortable when parents talked about their struggles. Yet I also felt comfortable encouraging them to criticize *other* Whites. This criticism located racism in other Whites and not in me. Like the parents in the meeting with the teachers splitting off their incompetence and locating it in the parents outside the school, I split off my racism and located it in other Whites.

Similarly, the principal of the school helped to foster conditions in which parents were able to articulate their concerns and criticisms of other agencies and institutions, but not to challenge the school or the educational process itself. Because of a strong general tendency of schools to avoid hearing and responding to criticism by parents, some educational advocates (Domanico, 1995) recommend that structures to generate social capital among parents should not be located in schools but in other institutions in the community, such as churches and community centers. The social capital or community power (Domanico, 1995) that parents build in churches and community groups then can be marshaled to challenge and change problematic educational policies and practices from outside the schools. This approach assumes that schools in which educators derive greater power than parents from their roles, races, and classes will not be motivated sufficiently to create conditions for parents to develop a powerful voice in their children's education.

The process described in this chapter exemplifies the advantages and disadvantages of trying to develop schools as mediating structures. When viable free spaces are created in schools, middle-class educators participating in this process develop relationships with economically poor parents of color and, through these relationships, may transform their deficit-based views and behaviors toward parents. It is harder to view as denigrated others parents whose joys and struggles one has come to know and identify with more intimately.

The question remains, however, whether white middle-class educators and middle-class educators of color will be sufficiently motivated to change their deficit-based attitudes and behaviors toward parents of color with low incomes. Christine Sleeter (1993) concludes from her research that white educators are unlikely to modify their racist perspectives. She hypothesizes that white educators' reluctance to change these perspectives stems from their unwillingness to give up the advantages that come from being white. On the other hand, the success of a few schools where educators and parents have worked together across racial and class differences to improve educational outcomes of students suggests that some white middle-class educators and middle-class educators of color have indeed changed their deficit-based attitudes and behaviors (Giles, 1998; Murnane & Levy, 1996).

Assuming that a consequence of altering one's deficit-based attitudes and behaviors toward parents of color eventually will involve relinquishing privileges, including economic privileges, and some measure of power and control, what is the motivation for making such changes, particularly in American society, where individual economic self-interest is a guiding value? I know of no easy answer to that question. Fragments of an answer come to mind: the satisfaction that comes from living by other values important in the American heritage—equity, fair play, justice, pursuit of the common good—and the deep pleasure of "I-Thou" relationships (Buber, 1970) in which we form bonds with others as subjects relating to subjects rather than as the dehumanizing exchange of subjects relating to objects. Finally, the world we create is the world in which we must live, and allowing individual economic self-interest to grossly overshadow our concern for the common good will be reflected in the quality of our public institutions, including schools.

Lessons for Practice and Research. The primary lessons for practice that I derived center on the need for educators and parents to work to create free spaces in schools and in other mediating structures, such as churches and community centers. Until we know more about the conditions that facilitate and impede the creation of free spaces, it is preferable to try to develop such spaces both inside and outside of schools. These free spaces should provide ways to include "split off parts," such as the angry and critical parents who have not been able to find a place in the school, and the angry and the critical parts of those parents who have been in the school but have not experienced sufficient safety to express their anger and criticism. In these spaces, parents can identify issues pertaining to raising and educating their children that they care about.

To accomplish the above, attention must be given to the racial identities of educators and parents. One approach would be to create parallel free spaces for educators and parents in an initial phase of an effort to develop social capital among parents and educators across the role boundary. In their respective groups, educators and parents could explore their visions for the education of children in the school and the ways in which the school climate, and educators' and parents' racial identities, ethnicities, and classes influence the realization of their visions. Some schools have developed advisory or family groups (Powell, 1994) for educators that could serve as free spaces. Once educators and parents have achieved some cohesion and understanding of their different perspectives within their group, they could then come together to engage in dialogues with each other across the parent-teacher role boundary.

One organization, the Industrial Areas Foundation (IAF), a national nonprofit coalition of churches, synagogues, mosques, unions, schools, as well as civic, environmental, housing and health groups, has successfully created social capital by developing mediating structures in their member institutions (Cortes, 1996; Giles, 1998; Murnane & Levy, 1996). IAF has channeled this social capital into significant improvements in the educational outcomes of schools. IAF's equivalents of free spaces are their individual meetings and house meetings. In individual meetings, an organizer or parent leader meets with a parent to get to know her (or him) and to hear what issues are important to her in raising and educating her children. In a house meeting, a small group of parents identifies issues of common concern in their school and community that they want to address and to take action on. As a consequence of IAF's approach of creating cross-racial alliances to address issues of public concern, discussions about race are not central to their work. However, I have observed that IAF organizers of various races are able and willing to give airtime in their meetings to concerns about the racial inequity manifested in many of the issues they are addressing.

The primary lesson for research is that we need to develop a much better understanding of the social and organizational processes that influence relations among parents, educators, and communities, specifically, the ways in which the racial identities and classes of parents and educators influence and are influenced by the different levels and phenomena of group and organizational processes. Leroy Wells' (1990) systemic socioanalytic framework is useful as a heuristic for exploring the reciprocal influence of group processes and the racial identities and classes of educators and parents.

One question which such research may help to answer is: What are the conditions that indicate that a school is likely to be a successful mediating structure of social capital and what are the conditions that suggest that the school cannot accommodate such a process? In cases where the school appears not to offer the appropriate conditions, parents and advocacy groups working with parents may be advised to look primarily to structures outside of the school, such as religious congregations and community centers, to develop free spaces.

CONCLUSION

This chapter examines the evolution of a series of parent workshops that was based on a deficit model of training parents of color to be more like white middle-class parents into a parents group in which the participants identified problems that interfered with raising their children, made contact with service providers in their community, and began taking actions to change their lives. This process highlights the potential and the barriers involved in a school becoming a free space in which parents can meet to create a narrative about their lives that is oriented to their strengths rather than their deficits. By pursuing this approach, the school can create the conditions for the development of social capital (Couto, 1995)—trust, information channels and norms and obligations—that can improve the collective efforts of parents and educators from different races and classes to educate children.

For such an approach to work, educators' racial identities must be such that the educators are able to facilitate a competence-based approach that acknowledges the races and classes of all participants. Avoiding or denying the races and classes of parents and teachers perpetuates a deficit perspective, fosters group processes, such as splitting and projective identification, that contribute to parents' and educators' isolation from each other, and keeps parents from full partnership in the schools and their children's education. An approach to parent involvement geared to creating social capital offers the possibility of engendering the genuine and vibrant participation of parents, educators, and community members from diverse racial and class backgrounds in creating an environment that can respond to the unique needs of the children in their community.

REFERENCES

Buber, M. (1970). *I and thou*. New York: Scribner.

Carter, R. T., & Goodwin, A. L. (1994). Racial identity and education. In L. Darling-Hammond (Ed.), *Review of Research, 20*, 291–336. Washington, D.C.: AERA.

Cochran, M., & Dean, C. (1991). Home-school relations and the empowerment process. *The Elementary School Journal, 91* (3), 261–269.

Cohen, J. (1993). Constructing race at an urban high school: In their minds, their mouths, their hearts. In L. Weis & M. Fine (Eds.), *Beyond silenced voices: Class, race and gender in American schools* (pp. 289–308). Albany: State University of New York Press.

Coleman, J. S. (1990). Social capital. In J. S. Coleman (Ed.), *Foundations of social theory* (pp. 300–321). Cambridge, MA: Belknap Press of Harvard University.

Cortes, E. (1996). Organizing communities and constituents for change. In S. L. Kagan & N. E. Cohen (Eds.), *Reinventing early care and education: A vision for a quality system* (pp. 247–266).

Couto, R. A. (1995, May). *Social capital and transforming leadership*. Paper presented at the Twelfth Scientific Meeting of the A. K. Rice Institute: Leadership as Legacy: Transformation at the Turn of the Millennium. Washington, DC.

Delpit, L. (1995). *Other people's children: Cultural conflict in the classroom*. New York: New Press.

Domanico, R. (1995). Discussant. In S. Opotow (Chair), *Individual and organizational challenges and resilience*. Paper presented at the American Psychological Association Convention, New York City.

Epstein, J. L. (1993). A response (to [Ap]parent involvement: Reflections on parents, power and urban schools. *Teachers College Record, 94* (4), 711–717.

Fine, M. (1993). [Ap]parent involvement: Reflections on parents, power and urban schools, *Teachers College Record, 94* (4), 682–710.

Giles, H. C. (1998). *ERIC Digest: Parent engagement as a reform strategy*. New York: ERIC Clearinghouse on Urban Education.

Hamburg, B. (1993). President's report: New futures for "the forgotten half": Realizing unused potential for learning and productivity. *Annual report, William T. Grant foundation*. New York: William T. Grant.

Harry, B. (1992). *Cultural diversity, families and the special education system: Communication and empowerment*. New York: Teachers College Press.

Helms, J. E. (1995). An update of Helms' white and people of color racial identity models. In J. G. Pontoretto, J. M. Casas, L. A. Suzuki and C. M. Alexander (Ed.), *Handbook of multicultural counseling* (pp. 181–198). Thousand Oaks, CA: Sage.

——. (1994). Racial identity in the school environment. In P. Pedersen & J. Carey (Eds.), *Multicultural counseling in schools* (pp. 19–37). Boston: Allyn & Bacon.

————. (Ed.). (1990). *Black and white racial identity: Theory, research, and practice.* Westport, CT: Praeger.

Henderson, A. (1987). *The evidence continues to grow: Parent involvement improves student achievement.* Columbia, MD: National Committee for Citizens in Education.

hooks, b. (1994). *Teaching to transgress: Education as the practice of freedom.* New York: Routledge.

————. (1990). *Yearning: Race, gender and cultural politics.* Boston: South End Press.

Laosa, L. M. (1983). Parent education, cultural pluralism and public policy: The uncertain connection. In R. Haskins & D. Adams (Eds.), *Parent education and public policy* (pp. 331–345). Norwood, NJ: Ablex.

Lareau, A. (1989). *Home advantage: Social class and parental intervention in elementary education.* London: Falmer Press.

————. (1987). Social class differences in family-school relationships: The importance of cultural capital. *Sociology of Education, 60,* 73–85.

Lareau, A., & Shumar, W. (1997). The problem of individualism in family-school policies. *Sociology of Education,* 24–39.

Lightfoot, S. L. (1978). Worlds apart: Relations among families and schools. New York: Basic Books.

MacIntyre, A. C. (1981). *After virtue: A study in moral theory.* Notre Dame, IN: University of Notre Dame Press.

Morrison, T. (1992). *Playing in the dark: Whiteness and the literary imagination.* Cambridge, MA: Harvard University Press.

Murnane, R. J., and Levy, F. (1996). The first principle: Agree on the problem. In R. J. Murnane and F. Levy, *Teaching the new basic skills: Principles for educating children to thrive in a changing economy* (pp. 80–108). New York: Martin Kessler Books/Free Press.

New York City Board of Education (1997). *Annual school reports.* New York: Board of Education.

Powell. L. (1994). Interpreting social defenses: Family groups in an urban setting. In M. Fine (Ed.), *Chartering urban school reform: Reflections on public high schools in the midst of change* (pp. 112–121). New York: Teachers College Press.

Putnam, R. D. (1993). *Making democracy work: Civic traditions in modern Italy.* Princeton: Princeton University Press.

Rioux, J. W., & Beria, N. (1993). *Innovations in parent and family involvement.* Princeton Junction, NJ: Eye on Education.

Seeley, D. S., Niemever, J. H., & Greenspan, R. (1991, July). *Principals speak report #2: Improving inner-city elementary schools, report on interviews with 25 New York City principals.* New York: Research Foundation of the City University of New York.

Skolnick, M., & Green, Z. (1993). Diversity, group relations and the denigrated other. In S. Cytrnbaum & S. Lee (Eds.), *Transformations in global and organizational systems: Changing boundaries in the 90's.* Jupiter, FL: A. K. Rice Institute.

Skutnabb-Kangas, T. (1984), *Bilingualism or not: The education of minorities.* Clevedon, England: Multicultural Matters.

Sleeter, C. E. (1993). *How white teachers construct race.* In C. McCarthy & W. Crichlow (Eds.), *Race identity and representation in education* (pp. 157–171). New York: Routledge.

Stone, C., & Wehlage, G. (1994). Social capital, community collaboration and the restructuring of schools. In F. Rivera-Batiz (Ed.), *Reinventing urban education: Multiculturalism and the social context* (pp. 103–134). New York: IUME Press, Teacher's College, Columbia University.

Swadener, B. B. (1995). *Children and families "at promise": Deconstructing the discourse of risk.* Albany: State University of New York Press.

Torres-Guzman, M. (1991). Recreating frames: Latino parent involvement. In M. McGroarty & C. Faltis (Eds.), *Languages in school and society: Polity and pedagogy* (pp. 528–552). Berlin: Mouton de Gruyter.

Wells, L. (1990). The group as a whole: A systemic socioanalytic perspective on interpersonal and group relations. In J. Gillette & M. McCollom (Eds.), *Groups in context: A new perspective in group dynamics* (pp. 49–85). New York: Addison-Wesley.

Winters, W. G. (1994). *African American mothers and urban schools: The power of participation.* New York: Lexington Books.

8

The Path to Academic Disability: Javier's School Experience

Alberto Bursztyn

Multicultural education, James Banks (1996) tells us, involves bringing about changes in the total school environment in order to create equal learning opportunities for all students. This view, shared by most writers in multicultural education, advocates a model of schooling that is more just and equitable by virtue of its inclusive purpose and democratic ideals. Banks emphasizes that multicultural education is not a mere add-on or co-curricular set of activities to increase cultural awareness, but rather a way of redefining school culture itself to embrace a multicultural ethos. School culture, however, does not change easily; a time traveler visiting from the 1920s would find few surprises visiting public schools around the country today, despite eight decades of school reform.

Multicultural education is taking root in schools not so much because of substantial ideological and policy shifts, but rather because school children and teachers have become increasingly more culturally diverse. Public schools historically have shown particular adeptness at responding to public demands for change with half-measures, changing just enough to satisfy the public, while retaining entrenched practices almost intact. Schools typically add programs, where specific populations of children are undeserved, while sustaining "mainstream" practices unchanged. Over the years, schools have created a panoply of programs for children with physical disabilities, for bilingual children, children "at risk," pregnant teens, gifted students, learning disabled, emotionally handicapped, and others who were deemed significantly different on a given parameter. Even more pronounced and indefensible has been segregation by race, which is echoed in the present through de facto geographic separation by income and unjust inequities in public school funding (Kozol, 1993).

In spite of demographic changes in school populations and teacher ranks, multicultural initiatives are, in fact, losing the spotlight to highly politicized arguments about school choice and centralized regulation of curriculum through implementation of state-mandated learning standards. Multicultural education, disparaged in conservative circles, stands in danger of becoming one of the many issues advocated in the noisy arena of school politics, fighting for attention and resources claimed by new teaching and testing programs, instructional technologies, and other perennial interests, such as creationism and school prayer.

Paradoxically, the marginalization of multicultural curriculum may close a door to broader examination of how minority-culture children fare in public schools. This question, still inadequately addressed by policy makers, will continue to puzzle those who look at schooling from the vantage point of the superintendent's desk or test publisher's office. Performance on academic tasks tends to be assessed with little regard to context and quality of instruction, yet answers to early academic difficulties that portend failure may best be explored in the complex environment of the classroom and its immediate surrounds (Trueba, 1993). Nevertheless, large-scale studies on enrollment patterns in special education are informative; they continue to document disproportionate identification and placement of culturally and linguistically diverse (CLD) children in categories of mild learning disability (Artiles & Zamora-Duran, 1997, Coleman & Gallagher, 1995; Markowitz, 1996). Subsequent placement of these children in progressively more restrictive settings is associated with high rates of failure and drop out (Markowitz, 1996). The persistent inequities of referral practices raise fundamental questions about the treatment of CLD children in public schools. These concerns were taken up by the U.S. Office of Special Education (OSEP) and the U.S. Office of Civil Rights (OCR), who argued that placement practices may (1) deprive children of services or provide services that are inadequate for their needs; (2) inappropriately label and stigmatize children; and (3) result in placement of CLD children in special education and that this may be a form of discrimination (Burnette, 1998). Understanding the resilience of this referral and placement pattern requires careful study and intense observation in the field (Harry, 1994). Since the major criteria for identification of mild learning problems are scores on tests of achievement and cognition, themselves often critiqued for inconsistency and arbitrariness (Coles, 1987; Sleeter, 1986; Skrtic, 1991a), research needs to focus attention on where those decisions are made—in schools.

The attempt to curtail inappropriate placement of CLD children in special education settings has brought teacher roles and responsibilities into question (Watson & Kramer, 1995). Yet educators are often challenged by the difficulties that CLD children present in the classroom and, consequently, feel that they would be better served elsewhere. The scarcity of guidance and rules for referral not only places CLD children at risk, but also leaves teachers feeling uncertain and alone with these problems. The referral may, in fact, be understood as a teacher's call for help (Bursztyn, 1999). Unfortunately, placement in special education in resource-poor schools is generally equivalent to a sentence of restrictive education with few opportunities for appeal, escape, or parole. Once a child is labeled as disabled, expectations about the child are dramatically lowered; and perhaps more significant, once the child crosses the system's boundary, bureaucratic and mechanistic notions about "services" develop into a regulations-driven embrace from which few children are set free. The momentum generated by the initial referral casts a long shadow into future decisions and may obscure the evolving needs of the student (Ferguson, 1987; Mercer, 1973).

Contemporary writers who are critical of regular and special education practices (Apple, 1993; Freire & Macedo, 1995; Robinson-Zanartu, 1996, Skrtic, 1991b, 1995; Sleeter, 1986; Tomlinson, 1995) have called into question some basic assumptions about school organization and curricular practices that result in student labeling and tracking. Skrtic (1995) in particular has sought to apply tools of critical analysis to elucidate the often costly and generally ineffective approaches to the education of children who experience school difficulties. In the following pages, I will present Skrtic's conceptual thesis and illustrate its usefulness as an analytical frame in the case study that follows.

Thomas Skrtic (1991b, 1995) advances a well-reasoned critique of special education practices, drawing on poststructural and postmodern theories. He describes a system that now serves over twelve percent of America's children, but that falls short in its promise to return children to regular classrooms upon delivering effective remedial or adaptive education in segregated settings. The massive failure of that approach has been attributed to the development of a separate system with little relation to regular education. This development has led to a call for inclusionary practices and legislation that deters placement of children in separate classes. Skrtic (1995) traces the failures of the special education system to two major cultural and political aspects of education, namely the professionalization of special education and the nature and beliefs that support notions of school failure.

In regard to the problem of professionalization of knowledge, he argues that professions have grown and multiplied as problems have become more complex and that we seek rational and objective means for making decisions. The basic premises on which professions draw their credibility and legitimacy are (1) professionals have access to a body of knowledge not available to the general public, and (2) professionals exercise judgments based on the best interests of clients, serving the common good rather than private gain. This modern view of professionals is premised on a positivist view of knowledge and reality: "Professionalization produces individuals who are certain that they both know and do what is best for their clients because, given the positivistic model of professional knowledge, they assume that the knowledge behind their practices and discourses is cumulative, convergent, and, above all, objective" (Skrtic, 1995, p. 11).

Thomas Kuhn's (1962) influential critique on the nature of knowledge in the natural sciences has had profound resonance in the social sciences and education. Above all, his observation about the nature of scientific discourse reveals the human dimension of the enterprise. Kuhn explained that science is characterized by the emergence of scientific communities that adhere to shared views of reality. When contending paradigms emerge, this shared view of reality is threatened and, ultimately, will be supplanted if the new paradigm can be substantiated through clinical observations. Scientific inquiry is depicted not as an impersonal and rational systematic accumulation and analysis of data, but rather as a struggle for preeminence among communities of scientists proposing incompatible ideas. The process of making science is thus demystified, and described in terms of its social construction. Postmodern scholarship (Lyotard, 1984 [1979]) embraces Kuhn's view of the scientific enterprise and challenges the assumptions that elevate and insulate knowledge and the practices that support contemporary institutions and professions.

Skrtic (1995), a postmodern scholar, describes and questions four assumptions that support the institutional practice of special education in public schools. He argues that these basic assumptions have guided and justified the development of special education as a separate and parallel educational system and contributed to its growth. These assumptions are: (1) Student disability is interpreted by schools as a pathological condition residing in the student; (2) The practice of differential diagnosis is seen as objective and useful; it allows for grouping students according to diagnosis or estimated ability, thereby increasing school efficiency; (3) Special education is a rationally conceived and coordinated system of services that benefits diagnosed students; and (4) Progress in special education (i.e., achieving greater efficiency) is understood as a rational-technical process of incremental improvements in conventional diagnostic and instructional practices. Given the assumptions that support and define special education, Skrtic questions whether a system guided by those assumptions is a rational and just response to the problem of school failure.

Articulating a progressive postmodern perspective, Skrtic deconstructs

the special education system. He sets out to expose the inherent inconsistencies, contradictions, and silences in special education discourse and
practices, with the intention of reconstructing the system along new
forms of emancipatory social knowledge. As other postmodern thinkers
within and outside education, he too assumes an antifoundationalist and
subjectivist view of social and psychological knowledge. Postmodern
writers argue that social knowledge is not the objective and indisputable
reflection of reality, but rather is subjective knowledge based on a particular historically and culturally situated frame of reference. They challenge the preeminent positivist mode of theorizing, which equates
knowledge with truth, and instead propose that nothing in education is
inherently true or correct, that, in fact, practices are derived from theoretical frames or paradigms, which themselves are social constructions.
In postmodern light, most social science and education theories seem to
emanate from cultural and political webs, which their proponents have
been historically unwilling to recognize because such grounding limits
notions of universal applicability (Kincheloe & Steinberg, 1993).

Skrtic's first argument centers on a rarely challenged understanding
of student failure. In the functionalist model of understanding educational practice, schools are rational organizations that are continually improved through scientific research and incremental changes that lead to
greater efficiency. This view of schools yields unintended consequences
for children who fail to meet the expectations of a school; they are identified as pathological. Their school difficulties become reflections of their
inadequacies as learners, when, in effect, they often reflect the school's
inability to teach. Failure to learn is placed squarely on the child in order
to preserve the belief in the scientific progress of education. "The institutional practice of special education is an artifact of the functionalist
quest for rationality, order, and certainty in public education, a quest
that is both intensified and further legitimized by the institutional practice of educational administration. The existence of special education dis-
torts the anomaly of school failure by objectifying it as student disability,
thus eliminating it as an occasion for educators to question their conventional practice (Skrtic, 1995, p. 69).

In practical terms, this system of beliefs leads teachers and clinicians
to look for the etiology of academic difficulty exclusively within the child
and to interpret poor learning outcomes as symptoms of a disorder
(Cummins, 1986). The role that school plays in "failure to teach adequately" does not attract attention, since school administration and curriculum practices are presupposed to be grounded on a scientific,
objective, and rational process.

Once the child is seen as failing to meet the standard and routine
expectations of a school, the educational system transfers the responsibility for educating that child to specialists. Skrtic contends that the pro-

fessionalization and specialization of workers in special education further isolates the identified child from regular education. By virtue of possessing a diagnostic label, the child becomes the subject of therapeutic interventions, which become codified in the Individualized Educational Plan (IEP). Dispensing professional services in a fashion borrowed from the medical field, special educators prescribe remedial therapies to correct the difficulties previously noted while freeing regular educators from the awkward challenge of confronting the limits of accepted instructional practices. Unfortunately, this arrangement stifles problems solving in the regular classroom and inhibits educational innovation.

Skrtic, echoing Schon (1983), states that by its very nature, professionalization complicates and restricts innovation in the education of children identified as disabled. As a result of an inductive training process that relies upon a single paradigm, professionals resort to formulaic ways of problem solving rather than question the epistemological root of that practice. Professionalization produces individuals who believe that their practices benefit clients because those practices are assumed to reflect accumulation of knowledge that is convergent and objective. Skrtic points out that professions are insulated and self-regulated and that their members adhere to a communally accepted definition of valid knowledge. The difficulty in bringing about change in any profession can be traced to the circular relationship between professional autonomy and professional knowledge; the profession is the sole judge of the adequacy of knowledge and skills.

In education and psychometric psychology, professional preparation leads to the development of a finite set of skills and standard practices that are matched with predetermined student needs and characteristics. Professional practice may be understood as a matter of pigeonholing a presumed client need into one of the standard practices in the repertoire. Should the client's need not match the skills and standard practices, professionals tend to force those problems into "old pigeonholes" (Mintzberg, 1979, 1983). Typically, problems presented by learners that are not easily accommodated in the regular curriculum are resolved by turning student characteristics and difficulties into jurisdictional problems. These students are subsequently assigned to different sets of specialists, who design specialized interventions.

In special education, professional prescriptions for remediation typically involve offering a "stronger dose" of the regular curriculum, a practice that calls for the breaking down of learning tasks into smaller and smaller chunks—often leading to drills devoid of meaning. Not uncommonly, special educators will justify their methods by pointing out that their students cannot grasp holistic principles and require more structure than non-identified peers. However, special education methods have yielded disappointing learning outcomes and have spurred a parent-led revolt. Under the banner of inclusion, parents and advocates have demanded that children with special needs remain in the regular classroom rather than being served by specialists in segregated settings. This protest has resulted in significant changes to the Education for All Handicapped Children Act (PL 94–142), the 1975 law that proclaimed the right of equal education for all children, including those with disabilities. The revised law, the Individual with Disabilities Education Act (IDEA), passed in 1990 and reauthorized in 1997, now places a greater burden on schools to prove that the promised benefits of alternative placements to the regular classroom outweigh potential perils (Bursztyn, 1999).

The case presented here documents and analyzes a path constructed by school professionals for children who encounter early academic failure and who, by virtue of linguistic and cultural characteristics, are more vulnerable to labeling. It explores the dynamics of decision making under conditions of uncertainty, exacerbated by a child's learning pattern not easily pigeonholed into readily available diagnostic instructional categories. This case is intended to illuminate the process that results in disproportionate numbers of immigrant and racial minority children being identified as educationally disabled.

CASE PRESENTATION

This case study evolved from a supervised action research project conducted by a graduate student enrolled in my graduate course in research methods. The graduate student, referred to as Ms. Astor, was a new special education/early childhood teacher at a local urban school and a graduate student in special education. Although she lacked proficiency in Spanish, Ms. Astor was assigned several Spanish-speaking students as a result of the district's inability to hire sufficient numbers of bilingual teachers to serve its growing immigrant population. In order to comply with local and federal regulations, the school provided a bilingual paraprofessional to assist in the instruction of these pupils in her class. In the course of collecting data for the project, Ms. Astor kept careful notes of her interactions with a parent of one of the children in her class and with other school personnel who had worked with this child, referred to here as Javier. Ms. Astor generously made her notes and associated documentation available for this case study. I have made some minor changes in the details of this case in order to protect the privacy of child and adult informants.

Javier

Javier was seven and a half years old at the start of this study. He had been placed in an ungraded self-contained class for children with learning disabilities. Ms. Astor described him as "a tall boy with a sweet smile and shy demeanor who loves to play; has a great imagination for play-acting, games, and building. Extremely well behaved, polite . . . a quiet boy." She soon found that Javier had a unique talent that extended beyond making friends easily: he was able to draw the most challenging children into elaborate fantasy play.

Javier was different from my other second graders. One of the most startling differences was obvious when the children had playtime. Most children would get involved in action-type games, playing house (which usually included some tossing of the baby in the air), playing with blocks (which generally culminated with destroying their creations), or some other "rough and tumble" kind of game. Javier rarely joined those games; he would bring a small doll or action figure from home and would take a car or toy horse from the cabinet and head for the dollhouse. He would formulate stories that centered on saving the world or a princess from evildoers. In the process, he would use blocks, bits of paper, and art supplies to build planes, cars, buildings. Soon another child would join him, and they would play in English or Spanish, depending on the child. Others would get absorbed in the game as he did. Javier was an extremely good influence on some of the most difficult children in the class. The most aggressive children calmed down whenever they played with Javier; and he never got into fights or arguments with them.

Clearly Ms. Astor felt great affinity for Javier. He played a constructive role in her class, almost like a co-worker; he could assist her in a class that, in less competent hands, might show a tendency for collective exuberant and unfocused behavior. Academic concerns, though, were evident from the beginning. Except for mathematics, Javier was substantially behind in every area of the curriculum. Rather than label his difficulties a manifestation of disability, Javier's teacher understood his academic delays as due in part to his limited English proficiency and his tendency to drift away from academic tasks. Ms. Astor noted that the engagement and intensity he evidenced in play quickly dissipated when the class was engaged in more formal, structured learning. She wrote:

One of the first things I noticed about Javier was that he did not speak up in class unless he was called on specifically to answer. As the children in my class are encouraged to speak up—I don't require them to raise hands to answer questions—Javier would not speak at all. My first goal was to get him to speak up when he did not understand something. When it comes to academic work he is distractible and tends to daydream. He is an extremely slow moving child. It takes him twice as long as other children to copy his homework, pack his things, and get his coat on. I found Javier distractible when he was not interested in the lesson being taught. When we learned a story or did a project he enjoyed, he had no trouble with attention span. Javier particularly liked stories about animals and silly stories. As the year went on, he developed a sight vocabulary of a few high-frequency words; he was able to read most three-letter words, though he got confused with the vowels sometimes. He began to write, "I love you" and "Happy Birthday" on his own to his friends.

School History

In the effort to understand Javier's trajectory from a healthy infant with no remarkable deviations in development to his present placement in special education, we reviewed his academic record and evaluation file. The teacher discussed its content with pertinent clinicians, educators, and the family to gain information beyond the written record.

Javier began pre-kindergarten (pre-K) at the local public school when he was four years old, soon after his sister was born. His pre-K teacher reported, "He had no problems at all in pre-K." But when pressed for details she admitted that she did not remember him at all. The phantom child phenomenon was repeated in an interview with his kindergarten teacher, Ms. Thomas. A teacher in the school for seventeen years, she could not describe Javier in any meaningful way. Ms. Thomas noted that the class was an English as a second language (ESL) kindergarten, although no ESL services were provided to the children, since she had no training in that field and no itinerant teacher was available. She did not remember Javier at all.

Ms. Sosa, Javier's mother, summarized his experience during that period as follows: "In kindergarten there were no real complaints, just that he was not very cooperative. He was very quiet, isolated from the other children." Javier's tendency to be inwardly directed, capable of engaging in prolonged and involved fantasies while the class was in session, enabled him to pass through the initial phase of formal school virtually "undetected." His behavior was soon to raise concern as he entered the first grade in an "English-only" mainstream class.

Ms. Sosa said that the first-grade teacher, Ms. Winter, soon called her at home. She reported: "It was the first grade, the first or second week of classes. The teacher started giving complaints: he wasn't listening, he wasn't participating, stuff like that. She said that he would just sit in his seat and not answer her, like he was 'spaced out,' not participate at all." Ms. Sosa felt that her son was not understood in class and that the teacher was especially impatient with the children in her class who did not understand English. (Curious to verify whether the parent's statement might be inaccurate, we checked the record and confirmed that all three Limited English Proficiency [LEP] students placed in that class were referred for evaluation early in the year.)

Ms. Sosa was alarmed by the teacher's perception of her child and requested transfer to a class where Spanish was the language of instruction. The principal responded curtly, noting that the bilingual class already had thirty children in it and that there was no room for Javier. Again, organizational constraints dictated Javier's educational trajectory. Moreover, the institutional priority regarding class size was presented as a valid argument for failure to address the learning needs of this student and the services to which he was legally entitled.

At the time, Javier was unable to carry on a conversation in English and was "programmed" to receive ESL services in lieu of a bilingual class; he participated in midmorning pull-out lessons on a daily basis. Upon returning to the mainstream class from ESL instruction, he tended to become even more confused. The hour of instruction away from the mainstream class increased his bewilderment in the English-only class. As the days went on and the year progressed, his daydreaming in class increased.

That fall, Javier was absent for two months. Obliged to attend to her ailing mother, Ms. Sosa traveled with her children for an extended visit to the Dominican Republic. Javier returned to school unable to express himself freely in English or follow instructions; his teacher soon referred him for evaluation.

Initially, Ms. Sosa refused to have Javier evaluated and resisted any suggestion that he might have a disability. She did not trust the teacher and did not agree with her view of her son. In a written statement, Ms. Winter described Javier as follows: "Javier is functioning below grade level. He has difficulty keeping up with classwork. Javier has a very short attention span. Very often he shows signs of not being in touch with class instruction and seems to be somewhat withdrawn." Although wary of special education placement, Ms. Sosa consented to sign a brief note that triggered a formal evaluation for disabilities. The note in the child's record states laconically: "I request that my son Javier be tested by the school based support team. (Signed) Mrs. Sosa."

As the note was not consistent with Ms. Sosa's opposition to special education placement, Ms. Astor sought an explanation:

When I questioned Ms. Sosa about this letter, she blushed, laughed nervously, and said that she did not write it. When I asked why she agreed to sign it, Ms. Sosa seemed embarrassed and hid her face with her hand. She said, "I thought it was for a special program to help him in school itself. Like someone would work with him each day." Ms. Sosa did not understand, nor did she know to ask, that the proposed testing could result in recommendations for more restrictive placement. I asked her if she now regretted having signed. She said she did.

Clearly opposed to special education placement for her child, Ms. Sosa had used a strategy of resisting coercion. The teacher then manipulated her by appealing to the need for Javier to receive "extra help." Rather than an isolated incident, the author believes that such efforts to extract consent for evaluation from parents are widespread. Beth Harry (1992) in her influential study of Puerto Rican families interacting with the special education system documents instances of coercion and miscommunication. Most poignantly, she details the negative consequences of parental powerlessness in relation to highly formalized and legalistic school rules.

Once the parental request for testing was signed, the school proceeded to test Javier for disabilities within the thirty-day period mandated by federal law. The formal evaluation began in May. The reason for testing was indicated as: "Javier is currently in a monolingual first grade class where he is experiencing academic difficulties. As per his teacher, he is functioning below his peers in all areas."

According to the record, Javier was tested in Spanish with the assistance of a translator. Ms. Sosa related that the man who interviewed her spoke Spanish, but that the man assigned to assist her at the time that the school recommended placement spoke very little English and had more difficulty than she in understanding some of the evaluation team's statements.

The evaluation was conducted at a private agency under contract with the local board of education; it took place over a two-week period. The results of the evaluation are described in the order that they appear in the report.

The educational evaluation contains information about the student's behavior and performance. The evaluator noted the Javier "was very reluctant to leave his mother." When she accompanied him to the testing room, he only agreed to stay if his little sister would remain there. The examiner states that "once he settled down, he was very cooperative, and attempted all tasks presented to him." Two lines down, the evaluator contradicts himself; he states that Javier "would not attempt or complete tasks that he felt were too difficult."

The educational tester found that Javier often called upon his knowledge of Spanish to answer questions: "Specially when being questioned about items used in the home, he resorted to Spanish. When he did not know the correct word, he was generally able to describe the object's use or purpose." He found Javier's language to be delayed in both English and Spanish, with Spanish dominant in informal expression, and noted that articulation was "below age expectations." Academically, Javier is described in the report as evidencing delays in mathematics, reading, and writing. Letter reversals in writing were noted. Emphasizing Javier's weak academic and expressive abilities, the evaluator recommends "a full time special education class, with an emphasis on the use of visual clues." (I believe he meant *cues* here.)

The psychological evaluation was very trying for Javier. He had difficulty leaving his mother's side and reluctantly accompanied the non-too-friendly man (the translator), who escorted him to a room where another man (the psychologist) waited. While he was in the testing room, his mother left the clinic to make a phone call. When Javier realized that she was gone, he began to cry inconsolably and could not be drawn back to the test tasks. Upon his mother's return and after much cajoling and reassurance, Javier consented to continue the test. He insisted that his mother sit in the adjoining room where he could see her. Throughout the testing session, Javier's baby sister walked in and out of the room, touching testing materials and distracting Javier on numerous occasions. Testing took an inordinate amount of time; toward the end of the session Javier was exhausted from working and crying for the better part of two hours.

Ms. Sosa corroborated the description of the child's behavior during the session, but took issue with some of the statements written in the report. She disagreed with the assessment of Javier's linguistic proficiency. The report notes

significant expressive and receptive language delays in both languages. . . . Javier has difficulty understanding and following simple directions. He found it difficult to talk about his feelings and what he wanted throughout the session. His mother reports similar difficulties, that Javier often speaks without her being able to understand him, and that he often appears not to understand what she is telling him, even though she repeats it over and over.

Ms. Sosa emphatically denied having made that statement and, to the contrary, believed that Javier had a good grasp of language. The assertion seems to have been inserted to support a hypothesis about Javier's language "disability." To the extent that we see the parent as a reliable informant, we may question the veracity of that comment. Unfortunately for the parent and the child, clinician written statements carry the weight of professional authority and are therefore practically impossible to contest. Carl Milofsky (1989) elucidates the power that school psychologists wield by arriving at decisions through an inaccessible and mysterious evaluative process.

In addressing Javier's intellectual functioning, the school psychologist remarked that Javier is an extremely shy child, has some difficulty with expressive language, and that he had just spent a long time being terrified when his mother left him in the evaluation room. The psychologist stated that verbal scores "could be affected by these factors, as well as second-language acquisition." Although the caveat about verbal scores is appropriate here, a more valid statement would have been that *all* of Javier's test scores were undoubtedly affected by second-language learning issues and by his distressed emotional state (Barrera, 1995).

Javier's performance on the WISC-III (test of intelligence) subtests range from very deficient on a test of abstract verbal reasoning to average on most tests of visual-motor integration, spatial thinking, and nonverbal problem solving. His scores on most of the verbal subtests were in the deficient range, with the exception of a test about social judgement and conventions. On that subtest he scored in the average range. Despite the difficulties in testing and the use of a test that was not developed to assess second-language learners like Javier, the psychological report indicates the following findings as valid for educational placement purposes: "Verbal IQ: Deficient Range; Performance IQ: Low Average Range; Full Scale IQ: Borderline Range." The report explains the findings as follows:

While Javier's overall functioning is in the Borderline Range, it must be noted that there was a significant difference between his performance and verbal IQ scores. These results indicate some significant auditory processing difficulties. In the verbal subtests, Javier received deficient scores in the areas of general information, verbal concept formation, basic arithmetic and computation, basic vocabulary and short-term memory auditory recall.

It is unclear how the evaluation addressed Javier's limited English proficiency. Indeed, this test of intelligence may be better described as a test of English knowledge (Cummins, 1986; Rueda, 1989).

Social-emotional functioning was evaluated through the administration of the House-Tree-Person Test and the Vineland Adaptive Behavior Scale. The school psychologist wrote:

Javier's house was very small, with tiny windows and a door that did not meet the bottom of the house. Since it was at this time that his mother left the testing area, his distress was so great that he could not continue the rest of the test. Overall, Javier presented as a very immature, anxious and withdrawn child. It is possible that all this is the result of difficulties understanding the verbal world around him, and his ability to make his needs and anxieties known through the use of language.

The school psychologist emphasized the language problem in relation to the Vineland scores, suggesting that that the score in the Communication domain was low, while reporting the scores on Socialization and Daily Living Skills were above average for his age. He concluded: "These results seem to support the idea that Javier is experiencing particular difficulties in language based communication skills."

Again, the tester does not mention that the Vineland Scale was normed on English-proficient and nonimmigrant populations, thus rendering the results suspects. Moreover, the report does not address the contradictory view of the child who is seen here as both "above average in Socialization and Daily Living Skills," yet is elsewhere described as immature and withdrawn. Disregarding disconfirming evidence, in this case about social-emotional development, the clinician chooses to elaborate on weaknesses that support his hypothesis and the team's emergent consensus. This approach validates the emerging critique that evaluators seek to confirm the referral statement and selectively emphasize findings that are consistent with it. Test scores that suggest strengths or disconfirm the initial hypothesis are more likely to be disregarded (Bursztyn, 1993). Not surprisingly, the psychological report mentions none of the strengths evident in the protocols, but reiterates the "language deficiency" hypothesis. It states: "The tests showed a large discrepancy between Javier's verbal and performance abilities. Javier appeared to be withdrawn and frightened, not an uncommon presentation for a child with significant difficulty with communication skills at the age of six and a half." This report also concluded with a recommendation for a "small, self-contained special education class," with the emphasis here on "a language rich, nurturing and safe environment."

A bilingual speech and language pathologist conducted the third and last assessment. For this evaluation, Javier was taken out of his classroom during the school day. The speech pathologist wrote: "Javier was alert, well related, and had no difficulty establishing rapport with evaluator. He seemed shy, but participated with minimal prompting. He seemed distractible, and seemed to have a limited attention span. His knowledge of English is very limited." Regarding articulation, the speech examiner found no physical difficulties that would affect speech; his intelligibility, voice, and fluency were described as good and "normal for his age and gender." This statement contradicts the educational evaluator's finding that Javier's articulation was "below age expectations."

The report on formal measures indicates some difficulties:

On the Woodcock Language Proficiency Scale, Javier had moderate deficits in receptive and expressive language. He had trouble labeling pictures, providing synonyms and antonyms, and completing analogies. On the Spanish version, The Bateria Woodcock de Proficiencia en el Idioma, he demonstrated mild vocabulary delays. However he appeared to have difficulty with auditory processing and word retrieval, as demonstrated by his long response time. He had deficits in processing spatial, temporal, and quantitative concepts as well as other attributes despite Spanish translations. Javier had some grammar difficulties as well. He had some difficulty answering "Wh." questions, yet communicative intent was age appropriate.

In the next paragraph we note an important inconsistency; it states: "Javier appeared to have delays in short and long term memory. He had difficulty with word retrieval and lapses in response time, a common pattern among bilingual children." The evaluator focused on slow word retrieval, casting this in a pathological light in one part of the report, while later indicating that this pattern is actually common—in fact, normative (Bursztyn, 1999)—for second-language learners. Basing her decision on a questionable use of an English normed test of language proficiency on a Spanish dominant child and a confusing interpretation of the Spanish equivalent, the assessor recommended that Javier receive "Speech and Language as a related service twice a week in a small group." The recommendation fails to clarify what areas of language proficiency require remediation, but it clearly stated that the service should be provided in Spanish.

Javier began second grade in a self-contained monolingual, English class. Although the Individualized Educational Plan (IEP) called for a bilingual Spanish classroom, as there was no Spanish special education second grade in the building, Javier was placed in Ms. Astor's monolingual class. To conform to the legal requirements of the IEP, a bilingual paraprofessional was assigned to the class. Ms. Rosas, a gentle middle-age Cuban woman with a high school education assisted in the instruction of the five bilingual children placed in Ms. Astor's class. The school faced similar difficulties in providing Javier with Spanish speech services. Since no bilingual therapist was available, Javier was scheduled to participate in English speech services with English-dominant children who had speech impediments.

Ms. Astor noted that Javier had little understanding of English at the beginning of the year, that his class participation was minimal, and that his written work was spotty. She soon found that some of his difficulties with academic work were due to limited English proficiency. For instance, she discovered that on phonics tasks where students have to write the initial letter of illustrations, Javier's difficulties were due to his lack of knowledge of English. Once he learned the English words, he had little trouble identifying initial sounds.

Ms. Astor also wondered how Javier's disposition to do things slowly might have affected his performance on formal assessments. She felt that his way of interacting and moving were more a matter of personal style than the more ominous "auditory processing difficulties." She observed:

Javier took forever to copy his homework, put on his coat, eat his lunch, or pack his bag. I used to joke with my paraprofessional that his mother must "go crazy" getting him dressed in the morning. His mother confirmed this to be true. At one point I suspected that Javier had a mild hearing loss, but that proved to be false. Javier is just a slow moving child in all areas, he can do and understand, but it takes him longer. In an English classroom, this made more problems for him, as he had to hear in English, translate to Spanish, formulate a reply in

Spanish, and translate back to English to say anything to his teacher. The delay was much less pronounced when he spoke in Spanish with Ms. Rosas.

Javier was mainstreamed for mathematics with a first-grade class. Ms. Paterno, the regular education teacher who taught him that subject was found of him. She reported: "Javier is doing very well in math. I was impressed with his abilities. The only problem is that he has trouble following directions. I assigned a peer tutor to review instructions with him in Spanish. The other problem is scheduling. We don't always do math at the same time in first grade."

Scheduling difficulties interfered with Javier's mathematics placement later in the year. The special education students' lunch period was moved to accommodate construction in the building, and Javier was unable to participate in most math lessons in the mainstream class due to conflicting times of instruction. Ms. Astor continued working with him using a regular education math book. He had little trouble with it.

The scheduling problem in mainstreaming serves to highlight one of the problematic assumptions about partial participation in regular education. Based on the notion that a disabled child should participate with nondisabled peers in areas of the curriculum where he is competent, Javier was scheduled to join the regular education class on a daily basis for mathematics instruction. Following this professionalized and compartmentalized system, Javier was to be instructed in mathematics by a nonspecialized teacher and would follow a mainstream curriculum. This approach to education is supported by notions of focused remediation and gradual normalization, but in Javier's case, as in the case of many students, it proved impractical and the arrangement soon fell apart. This model assumes a rigid and routinized classroom schedule and a discipline-based approach to instruction, a pedagogy that is now generally viewed as developmentally inappropriate for the early grades. Newer approaches to learning in the early grades capitalize on interdisciplinary and project-based learning, where inflexible scheduling is discouraged.

In Javier's case, and for most of his partially mainstreamed classmates, the mainstreaming plans were undermined not only by the standard approach to instruction in the regular first- and second-grade classes, which was more flexible than IEP envisioned, but also by a more powerful factor—organizational and contractual priorities. Use of space, class size, and personnel priorities all interfered with the mainstreaming plans for Ms. Astor's "mild to moderately disabled" students.

Ms. Astor was impressed with Javier's progress in her class and felt strongly that he should be placed in a less restrictive setting the following year. She explained: "I wanted to have Javier repeat the second grade in a regular bilingual Spanish class and receive resource room services. I discussed this idea at length with Ms. Sosa, who agreed with my recommendation." There was no need to request a re-evaluation, since all second graders in Ms. Astor's class were "aging out" of the program and were due for another round of evaluations.

The second set of tests proved to be less problematic for Javier. All the evaluators were part of the school staff, people he had seen in the school building interacting with his teacher. Moreover, many of his friends had preceded him and returned to class with shiny stickers. The results of the re-evaluation, this time conducted almost entirely in English, again showed a major discrepancy between verbal and visual-spatial abilities. The summary scores indicated borderline/deficient range in the verbal areas, and high average in performance, with an overall IQ in the low average/average range. Academically, though he was still behind his regular-education peers, he had narrowed the gap; he showed a growth in academic achievement of more than a year.

Although Ms. Astor (and I) interpreted the results as an indication of a potential for average verbal scores (two of five subtests were in fact in the average range) and of scores that were depressed by a nonnormative language-learning process, the School-Based Support Team (SBST) explained to the parent and teacher their belief that Javier had a "probable learning disability." They explained that Javier did not know enough English to be in a regular class and was still nearly a year delayed. Despite the teacher's protest, they recommended a self-contained class for children with mild to moderate disabilities. As a concession to the teacher, they included the following note: "Javier's teacher does not agree with this recommendation and would like Javier to be decertified from special education. Javier's mother agrees with the teacher's recommendations."

Placement decisions were made over the summer; Ms. Astor received a phone call from the district office. Given the opportunity for additional input, Ms. Astor stressed her belief that Javier's difficulties and test scores reflected difficulties associated with learning a second language. The supervisor, at the other end of the line, did not disagree with the teacher's assessment; in fact he told her that Javier's profile was typical of bilingual students. But then he went on: "At this time we have no bilingual second grades in the district. In order to be in a bilingual class, Javier would have to travel quite a distance by bus."

The supervisor closed the conversation by saying that Javier would be placed in an English-only special education class, because "that's the best the school can offer." Disappointed with her lack of success in changing Javier's disability designation, Ms. Astor called Javier's mother to alert her of the district's decision and asked her if she needed an advocate to contest the decision. Ms. Sosa hesitated, telling Ms. Astor, "In the other school [where Javier attended kindergarten and first grade], he didn't learn anything. He learned more in the special education class than in the regular class. I don't think he has a learning problem; he is restless like any other child. His only problem is in school, and he learned more with you."

Although Ms. Astor raised the possibility of busing with Ms. Sosa, she knew that Javier's family was likely to reject that option because they did not own a car, Ms. Sosa was expecting her third child, and Javier's sister was about to begin prekindergarten at the school that Javier was now attending. Ironically, Ms. Astor's effective instruction and advocacy served as the strongest argument to keep Javier in special education. Ms. Sosa hoped that future special education teachers would be as competent and warm. Accepting a label for her child, a diagnosis that she did not support, was a small price to pay for superior instruction.

DISCUSSION AND THEORY REVISITED

It may be impossible to determine conclusively whether Javier has or does not have a learning disability. Young children embedded in a different culture and language often encounter difficulties when they enter the English-dominant American school. These difficulties are a tangle of linguistic, emotional, cultural, and cognitive issues that, more often than not, prove impossible to tease apart.

In this case study, my intent has been to expose the holes in the mesh that purportedly supports children in school. Children become vulnerable to labeling and to being poorly served when the adults in the system fail to recognize and appreciate differences—generally associating difference with deficiency—and when organizational priorities supersede individual needs. Sadly, Javier's case is one that highlights the disjunction between the state of clinical knowledge, professional decision making, and institutional and individual needs. In this case, advocacy and parental education failed to bring about corrective change, and the momentum generated by the referral gained speed and strength, even in the face of conflicting evidence and discrepant perceptions of the child.

In global terms, when we follow Javier's school experience, we discern a disturbing pattern of decision making that may be encapsulated as an intense effort to explain his failures to learn without ever exploring the school's role in the observed difficulties. The dialogic nature of learning is lost as clinicians and administrators construct the child as disabled, invariably disregarding the obvious limitations in the school's ability to teach him appropriately.

We may ask: How did Javier become a disabled child? His initial experiences in school as a monolingual Spanish-speaking child with an introverted disposition suggest a mismatch. The large impersonal and regimented classrooms drove him further into himself as he sought refuge from unempathic teacher demands. Arguably, he would have benefited from a highly interactive and language-rich classroom that valued and engaged his imagination. Unfortunately, he learned to "tune out" early, being present without being engaged, seeking comfort in elaborate fantasies that took him far away from "seat-work" in a noisy classroom. He became a stealth child who made no lasting impression on his teachers. Had he been a nuisance, a child who disturbs instruction and demands attention, then perhaps he might have been identified earlier as a candidate for special attention or special education. But Javier's coping style obscured characteristics that differentiated him from other children in the class. The fact that he understood practically nothing that was said in class did not seem to bother his kindergarten and prekindergarten teachers.

The evaluation process set in motion by his first-grade teacher within the first two weeks of the year became an irreversible engine that ploughed through legal safeguards and diagnostic inconsistencies until he was given not only a label, but also a placement in a restrictive, self-contained class. As stated above, the driving assumption in the educational planning for Javier was that he suffered from a neuro-psychological condition that interfered with his ability to learn. The questionable nature of his prior school experience could not be explored because it was simply not part of the equation.

As Skrtic observed, educational administration science supports the belief that our schools are the most evolved and perfected form of schooling available because they are a product of a rational and positivistic enterprise. Children such as Javier who fail to profit as expected from these ostensibly rational organizations are not considered as possible evidence of the limitations of the school, but rather are constructed as defective students in need of special services to be delivered by specialists. Professional specialists justify their own knowledge domain by emphasizing that their clients' problems are best identified and addressed through their own scientifically derived methods, which lie outside of the knowledge base of regular teachers.

One could argue convincingly, based on learning patterns and test data, that Javier has a learning disability; perhaps just as easily one could make the opposite argument. However, beyond assessment issues, this case may be more profitably explored to highlight the inconsistencies in a decision-making process that reveals little rationality or fairness. Even if we accept as valid the correctness of the vague label he was given ("probable learning disability"), we can still legitimately ask if assignment to an English monolingual, self-contained special education class was the best educational setting for Javier. Indeed, looking carefully at his educational trajectory, we may raise questions about the basic assumption that regular and special education are rationally conceived and coordinated systems that provide services of benefit to its students. More emphatically, we could state that the failures of regular education—the neglect of Javier's linguistic, cultural, intellectual, and emotional needs in his earliest schooling—predisposed him to fail with a teacher who had little sympathy for bilingual learners or tolerance for difference. What followed—coercion, assessments, and placement—revealed that organizational priorities overrode individual needs and justified a model of educational practice where difference was equated with disability.

Skrtic (1995) focused primarily on the assumptions that support special education teaching methods, but a similar critique could be articulated in regard to clinical assessment methods. The cloak of positivistic science that covers the clinical professions obfuscates a much more complex reality in which actual implementation departs substantially from prescribed methods that originate in laboratory environments and is grounded on paradigms that may not fit the client at hand.

Although the diagnostic and evaluation issues raised here may be interpreted as instances of poor training or sloppy practice, concerns about the closed and uncontestable nature of the outcomes warrant further attention. Professional decisions carry great weight in our culture because they are associated with a specialized field of inquiry and with privileged access to pertinent knowledge. Ironically here, the people who understood Javier best, his mother and Ms. Astor, lacked credibility and the power to affect the educational trajectory required by the child as a result of their nonprofessional status. Their knowledge, grounded in extensive interaction and observation, was disregarded because it did not carry the clout of an empirically grounded, scientific discipline. From the process described here, we may conclude that the opinions of teachers and mothers cannot compete with the legally and culturally endorsed judgments of administrators and certified professionals. Everyday knowledge and common sense do not measure up to knowledge enshrined in the guarded and inaccessible workings of the professions.

This concept of disqualified knowledge offers a perspective into the discursive process in education, which fails to acknowledge inconsistencies as well as the potential to oppress the clients it purports to serve. John Dewey (1980 [1916]), concerned with the democratic and moral implications of scientific inquiry, urges the inclusion of the voices and observations of those who are practitioners or subjects of scientific study. In this case study, we observed the ignoring of the protests of a mother and a teacher precisely because they protested the implacable designation of disability. A more constructive path to problem solving—one that was not seeking to validate an a priori expectation of disability—would have amplified, rather than ignored, the voices of the people who knew the child best and who were the most likely to have an impact on his learning capacity.

Revisiting Skrtic's (1991b, 1995) questions regarding the rationality and fairness of special education and, by extension, the process that leads to the classification and placement of children in classes for the disabled, we may conclude that in the case of Javier the process failed on both accounts. The basic assumptions that undergird the educational system are evident in this case. The child's learning problems were identified as *his* pathology; clinicians rushed to diagnose him, believing that a disability designation would lead to appropriate and necessary services. Later, the nature and quality of special education services provided went unquestioned because these were thought to have been rationally conceived and coordinated. In Javier's situation, which greatly resembles that of thousands of language minority children encountering American schools for the first time, the disjunction between cultures and languages attracted less attention than potential neurological dysfunction as an explanation for lack of academic progress. Schools seem hardwired to construct all academic problems as disabilities.

For example, Javier's initial assessment suggested an overall IQ in the borderline range, with verbal skills in the deficient (i.e., retarded) range and visual/spatial ability (capacity to complete timed nonverbal tests) in the low average range. One year later he was reported to be functioning in the borderline range in verbal skills and high average in the visual/ spatial areas, with an overall IQ in the low to average range. If the roots of Javier's problems were solely or primarily neurological, the dramatic jump in IQ would be truly puzzling. Jumps that amount to one or two standard deviations in intelligence in the span of one year are worthy of publication in scientific journals. Yet these increments are not unusual among acculturating children because they reflect increasing familiarity and comfort with the language and expectations of the test. The second testing session was, in fact, conducted entirely in English, which suggests an underestimation of true potential. Despite these counterindicative data, however, clinicians focused almost exclusively on Javier's test profile, which mimics that of a monolingual English, severely language delayed child. Testing conditions, acculturation patterns, second-language acquisition, and emotional state—factors that could have accounted, at least in part, for Javier's initial test scores and dramatic increase upon later evaluation—were ignored as clinicians focused on making the case for neurological disability.

The expectation that a diagnosis, or at least a statement of eligibility for services, will trigger a rational and effective educational plan incorporating an array of appropriate services was not borne out. Javier's educational placements seemed to be driven more by administrative concerns than by his educational needs. Availability, convenience, and ideology played a greater part in his educational trajectory than rational efforts to serve him. The school district's lack of bilingual personnel reflected the ideological bent of its board, which was unsympathetic to bilingual education. Immigrant parents, often lacking documentation or linguistic skill in English, were routinely denied access to bilingual classes. Similarly, there was little indication of a rational process in the way services were delivered. Pull-out classes in ESL and, later, in math created confusion and disruption. Although, in theory, mainstreaming or remediation seems fair and rational, the implementation of these services invariably breaks down because children cannot be "fixed" by adjusting parts, the way automobiles can be fixed by mechanics. The stigma of coming from the "defectives" class or being pulled out of a regular class to receive special support damages children's sense of self-worth. Pull-out also disrupts classroom-based learning because those children who are removed systematically miss substantial instruction in the regular classroom.

Lastly, we could ask: Why object to full-time special education placement? Maybe the reduced class size and individualized attention could be beneficial, even if the child has no disability. Unfortunately the achievement patterns of children placed early in such classes are not encouraging. National figures suggest that few ever return to regular education; local district trends reveal that high school graduation rates of these children are dismal. The atomized approach to instruction and the slow presentation of material virtually guarantees that children in special education will not "catch up" with the regular curriculum, which is increasingly driven by a lock step testing program.

A quarter of a century after the enactment by the federal government of PL94-142, which established a highly regulated and professionalized approach to working with children with disabilities, we need to evaluate its impact. Although advocates for and families of children with severe disabilities primarily championed the law, the system has been hijacked by other priorities. Most students served in special education are not those with severe needs, but rather are children with mild behavior and learning problems who are often difficult to differentiate from those not designated as disabled. Those children who are at greatest risk of misdiagnosis because of linguistic and cultural differences do not need new labeling categories or specialized services; they need caring and competent teachers who are supported within their school communities to address all challenges in the classroom. Under IDEA, PL94-142 was revised to expand services and to correct some of the unintended negative consequences of special education. Unfortunately the legal mechanisms are blunt and will only bring about the intended changes when the culture and organization of schools become responsible for all its students.

NOTE

The author wishes to thank Ms. Sari Alter, a former student in the Graduate Program in Special Education at Brooklyn College, City University of New York, whose work provided the foundation for this chapter.

REFERENCES

Apple, M. W. (1993). *Official knowledge: Democratic education in a conservative age.* New York: Routledge.

Artiles, A., & Zamora-Duran, G. (1997). *Reducing the disproportionate representation of cultually diverse students in special and gifted education.* Reston, VA: Council for Exceptional Children.

Banks, J. A. (1996). *Multicultural education, transformative knowledge, and action: Historical and contemporary perspectives.* New York: Teachers College Press.

Barrera, I. (1995). To refer or not to refer: Untangling the web of diversity, "deficit" and disability in preschool children from culturally diverse populations. *NYSABE Journal, 10,* 54–66.

Burnette, J. (1998). Reducing the disproportionate representation of minority students in special education. (ERIC-OSEP Digest #E566).

Bursztyn, A. M. (1999). Psychological vistas on pre-referral interventions for CLD students. In M. Lupi & G. Rivera (Eds.), *A monograph on prereferral intervention strategies for linguistically and culturally diverse students* (pp. 36–58). New York: Hunter College–CUNY and NYS VESID.

————. (1993). School-based cross-cultural assessment: Science, hunch or stereotype? In S. Johnson & R. T. Carter (Eds.), *Assessing cultural issues in organizational context* (pp. 45–51). New York: Teachers College, Columbia University.

Coleman, M. R., & Gallagher, J. S. (1995, May) State identification policies: Gifted students from special populations. *Roeper Review, 17* (4), 268–275.

Coles, G. (1987). *The learning mystique: A critical look at learning disabilities.* New York: Pantheon Books.

Cummins. J. (1986). Psychological assessment of minority students: Out of context, out of control? *Journal of Reading, Writing and Learning Disabilities International, 2,* 1–8.

Dewey, J. (1980 [1916]). Democracy and education. In J. A. Boydston (Ed.), *John Dewey, Vol. 9: The middle works, 1899–1924* (pp. 1–370). Carbondale, IL: Southern Illinois University Press.

Ferguson, P. M. (1987). The social construction of mental retardation. *Social Policy, 18,* 51–56.

Freire, P., & Macedo D. (1995). A dialogue: Culture, language and race. *Harvard Educational Review, 65,* 377–402.

Harry, B. (1994). *The disproportionate representation of minority students in special education: Theories and recommendations.* Project FORUM. Final Report (ED374637).

————. (1992). *Cultural diversity, families, and the special education system.* New York: Teachers College Press.

Kincheloe, J. L., & Steinberg, S. R. (1993). A tentative description of post-formal thinking: The critical confrontation with cognitive theory. *Harvard Educational Review, 63*, 296–320.

Kozol, J. (1993). *Savage inequalities.* New York: Crown.

Kuhn, T. S. (1962). *The structure of scientific revolutions* (1st ed.). Chicago: University of Chicago Press.

Lyotard, J. F. (1984). *The postmodern condition: A report on knowledge.* Minneapolis: University of Minnesota Press. (Original work published 1979.)

Markowitz, J. (1996). *Disproportionate representation: A critique of state and local strategies.* Project FORUM. Final Report (ED392195).

Mercer, J. (1973). *Labeling the mentally retarded: Clinical and social system perspectives on mental retardation.* Berkeley: University of California Press.

Milofsky, C. (1989). *Testers and testing: The sociology of school psychology.* New Brunswick, NJ: Rutgers University Press.

Mintzberg, H. (1983). *Structure in fives: Designing effective organizations.* Engelwood Cliffs, NJ: Prentice Hall.

———. (1979). *The structuring of organizations: A synthesis of the research.* Englewood Cliffs, NJ: Prentice-Hall.

Robinson-Zanartu, C. (1996). Serving Native American children and families: Considering cultural variables. *Language, Speech and Hearing Services in Schools, 27* (4), 373–384.

Rueda, R. (1989). Defining mild disabilities with language-minority students. *Exceptional Children, 56* (2), 121–128.

Schön, D. A. (1983). *The reflective practitioner: How professionals think in action.* New York: Basic Books.

Skrtic, T. M. (1995). *Disability and democracy: Reconstructing (special) education for postmodernity.* New York: Teachers College Press.

———. (1991a). Students with special educational needs: Artifacts of the traditional curriculum. In M. Aincow (Ed.), *Effective schools for all* (pp. 20–42). London: David Fulton Publishers.

———. (1991b). *Behind special education: A critical analysis of professional culture and school organization.* Denver: Love Publishing.

Sleeter, C. E. (1986). Learning Disabilities: The social construction of a special education category. *Exceptional Children, 53*, 46–54.

Sleeter, C. E., & McLaren, P. L. (1995). *Multicultural education, critical pedagogy, and the politics of difference.* Albany: State University of New York Press.

Trueba, H. T. (1993). Cultural diversity and conflict: The role of educational anthropology in healing multicultural America. In P. Phelan and A. L. Davidson (Eds.), *Renegotiating cultural diversity in American schools* (pp. 195–215). New York: Teachers College Press.

Watson, T. S., & Kramer, J. J. (1995). Teaching problem solving skills to teachers-in-training: An analogue experimental analysis of three methods. *Journal of Behavioral Education, 5*, 281–294.

Conclusion: Reflections on Collective Identities

Alberto Bursztyn

The discourse on cultural diversity in schools continues to be dominated by concerns about the development of an inclusive curriculum, one that reflects the multiple origins that children present in our increasingly crowded urban classrooms. This discourse has promoted greater awareness of cultural issues in teacher preparation programs and compelled school districts to examine their curricula to address inclusion of minority groups. Reflecting the new zeitgeist, most textbook publishers are now sensitive to the new multiracial and multicultural market. Test developers too are more vigilant about test items that may reflect bias or insensitivity to minority group members and continue to expunge insensitive material. These changes have become accepted practice and institutionalized in most urban school districts; although there are occasional skirmishes regarding content and pedagogy, the educational field now explicitly seeks to represent multicultural concerns.

The distance traveled in a generation becomes evident when one reviews texts and curricula published before 1975. Almost without exception, readers and curriculum materials depicted white children enjoying suburban life in traditionally organized nuclear families. Children with disabilities were invisible and were depicted only when the stories dealt specifically with health and disability issues. Similarly, racial minorities seldom appeared in the readings, and when they were included it was as part of a discussion of the struggles and obstacles that specific groups, particularly African Americans, had historically encountered. In contrast, current classrooms reflect a new multicultural ethos; they often call attention to various cultural and linguistic groups with conspicuous posters of prominent minority scientists and inventors and pictures of children representing various racial and ethnic groups on the walls; books and tests are designed to provide academic inspiration for minority children and to promote greater tolerance among their white American peers.

Significant changes in these visible elements of curricula, unfortunately, have not brought the anticipated "gap reduction" in the achievement patterns of children from linguistic minorities and diverse ethnicities and cultures, nor have they eliminated racial and ethnic tensions in schools. Poor, immigrant, migrant, and racial minority students continue to be overrepresented among those who score below grade level in achievement tests, among those who are classified as educationally and/or emotionally disabled, and among those who quit school prematurely. Tinkering with the content of texts, celebrating diversity in classrooms, and eliminating blatant bias in tests have largely failed to reverse the achievement trends that spurred these educational changes. Perhaps, as others have argued (Nieto, 1999), those changes have not been pursued aggressively enough; perhaps they have not been sufficiently inclusive. More likely, the multicultural curriculum has not transformed schools because it occupies a relatively unimportant space within them. The traditional distribution of power in schools, the view of minority children as deficient, and the uninspired pedagogy used to "deliver instruction" to them may be cited as reasons for the scanty impact of a more explicitly inclusive cultural curriculum.

More recently, the pressure to raise test scores has undermined the enactment of a multicultural curriculum and the commitment to its ideals. Academic standards and the benchmarks set by policy makers to evaluate performance are central to the lives of teachers and administrators, who are ever preoccupied with meeting achievement targets. Some have come to regard the multicultural curriculum as a luxury they may not be able to afford as classrooms and schools are asked to emphasize and privilege test-driven curricula.

Although academic standards and a multicultural curriculum are not mutually exclusive, teachers understand and comply with priorities that emphasize measured, evaluative achievement and have clear parameters for accountability. The intangible nature of multiculturalism's overt goals make them easier to ignore or marginalize. If we identify those goals broadly as (1) improved self-concept among children of oppressed groups, (2) better relations among students of different backgrounds, (3) greater respect and appreciation for other cultures, and (4) better relations with community and parents, we sense simultaneously the vital importance of those goals and the difficulty in developing measurable outcomes.

At a teacher education graduate seminar I recently taught, in which all the students had teaching jobs in local schools, the conversation before class centered on classroom décor as February (African American Heritage Month) came to an end and March (Women's History Month) approached. One of the more veteran teachers suggested that it was a good idea to find posters depicting prominent African American women, because those pictures do not need to be replaced in March, when women are celebrated. Most students in that class, a racially diverse group of women, thought that was a great tip. During class I pressed the students on their commitment to multicultural work, alluding to their previous conversation on posters. One third-grade teacher expressed a popular sentiment this way: "My job does not depend on how well kids know each others' holidays; it does depend on whether they make the cut-off for reading on grade." Although my students were sympathetic to the aims of multiculturalism in schools and had embraced aspects of a multicultural curriculum on their own, their commitment to this work was tested by other school priorities.

My students were expressing the same doubts about the utility of multicultural education that Sonia Nieto (1999) alludes to when she poses the rhetorical question: "But can they do math?" Nieto, a prominent proponent of multicultural education, answers the question with a call for comprehensive educational reform that engages social, institutional, personal, and collective priorities and practices. Yet she places her ultimate hope for change with teachers. She states:

[I]f teachers begin by challenging societal inequities that inevitably place some students at a disadvantage over others; if they struggle against institutional policies and practices that are unjust; if they begin with the strengths and talents of students and their families; if they undergo a process of personal transformation based on their own identities and experiences; and finally, if they engage in a collaborative and imaginative encounter to transform their own practices and their schools to achieve equal and high quality education for all students, then the outcome is certain to be a more positive one than is currently the case. (pp. 175–176)

Nieto expresses the hope, shared by many writers in this field, that multicultural education, if done well, will translate into improved academic outcomes. A more inclusive learning environment will unquestionably create learning conditions for improved academic performance, particularly for children who have traditionally been constructed as deficient or inferior. But for that type of educational change to take place, the curriculum and experience of school must be transformative (Banks, 1996), not simply decorative. As Carol Korn noted in the Introduction to this volume, multiculturalism tends to inhabit the hallways instead of the classrooms when it is implemented without understanding or commitment. Eager to promote a more comprehensive adoption of multiculturalism, its advocates enlist a functional argument (i.e., multicultural approaches will lead to higher test scores).

Multicultural scholars are not alone. Some musicians, for example, have sought to capitalize on a study that claims that listening to Mozart results in gains in mathematics scores. In this formulation, music should be used as a vehicle for higher mathematics scores. In a similar vein, reading the *New York Times* is a common prescription for higher verbal SAT scores. It is as if neither Mozart nor the *New York Times* has intrinsic value—their utility is confined to playing a supporting role in test performance. In these distortions of learning, the lives of children in school are reduced to preparation for the next set of tests. Some valuable principles in public education have been lost in the rush to meet new and more regulated learning standards. The idea that schools must change to provide a workforce for an evolving and technology rich economy spurs a school culture that has little use for play, art, enjoyment, socialization, rebellion, and simple daydreaming. Children caught engaging excessively in any of the above are candidates for special education placement. Ironically, some of the most successful innovators in the new economy are questioning the value of formal education.

John Dewey (1938/1963) proposed that schools should not only prepare individuals for life in a democracy, but the schools themselves should reflect democratic processes and ideals. How else to prepare the young if not by lived experience in a democratic institution? Unfortunately, public schools today seem to have all but abandoned that ideal. They not only embrace hierarchical, mechanistic, and bureaucratic approaches to organization, they also reflect lack of tolerance and empathy for those who struggle to meet the rising academic standards bars. Although, ostensibly, schools are preparing the workers of the new century, those workers will carry the scars of a lifetime of close external scrutiny and the mounting anxiety associated with pressure to perform in a hierarchical institution. Is the new economy expected to be based on competitive individuals who are driven to meet productivity standards? Perhaps. However, the current model of schooling appears better suited to achieve the industrial era ideals of producing a docile workforce to "man" the assembly lines in huge factories than to meet the demands of the twenty-first century workplace. Public schools are conservative and, in fact, never abandoned the industrial organization model, which is premised on educating children the way factories assemble products. They begin school as raw material and, after undergoing a standardized and uniform process, exit at graduation with predictable knowledge and capacities. Those who do not conform to specified standards are labeled as "disabled" or become "dropouts"; in industrial lingo, they are the equivalent of "seconds" or "defectives."

Today, however, workers may require a different set of skills. The ability to succeed in the information age workplace, which now literally encompasses the world, may hinge on the capacity to work well with diverse colleagues in a collaborative and rapidly changing information rich environment. What multicultural education may offer all students, not only those defined as cultural minorities, is basic preparation for work in the new economy. Gaining an appreciation and respect for diverse points of view and traditions, capacity to negotiate difference across cultural and historical boundaries, learning other languages and value systems, and becoming more tolerant and conscious of others' past and present oppression are tangible educational benefits for all students.

Although one can make the case for multicultural schooling on economic grounds, that kind of thinking ultimately leads to an instrumental approach, albeit not one directly linked to test performance. It may be more compelling if we explore multiculturalism in relation to the broader purposes of education in a liberal democracy. Recognizing that schools are institutions that both reflect and shape the society they educate, we must grapple with the needs of all individuals for recognition, dignity, and respect and with the needs of groups for preservation and protection of their collective identities. It is this unresolved tension between individual and group demands for recognition that is the root of the debate on multiculturalism.

The democratic society advocated by Immanuel Kant and Jean Jacques Rousseau leaves little room for addressing the interests of groups within the social contract, yet all modern liberal democracies now contend with the presence of various cultural identities in their midst demanding recognition. The cries for and against group rights grow louder, often threatening the integrity of nationhood and the shared notion of communal purpose as minority group agendas move from private beliefs and practices to demands for accommodation, reparations, or special status. The historic pattern of oppression of minority groups and women in self-identified democracies points to the political failure in translating rhetoric of equality among all citizens to reality. As a result, group identity draws some of its powerful magnetism from experiences of marginalization and unequal access to power and privilege. These historical and cultural experiences are complemented by the desire of individuals to maintain and transmit a distinct and unique set of values and traditions shared by the group. Amy Gutman (1994) expanding on Charles Taylor's (1994) argument suggests that full public recognition in a democracy requires two forms of respect: first, respect for the unique identity of each individual regardless of gender or group affiliation, and second, respect for ways of life and worldviews adhered to by or associated with members of disadvantaged groups, including women and racial, cultural, and ethnic minorities. In addressing the second requirement, she wonders whether public recognition of the characteristics and practices of cultural groups will take public precedence over a more universal identity based on a common humanity.

Gutman (1994) proposes that liberal democracy, in the United States model, supports cultural diversity drawing upon two universalistic, rather than particularistic, perspectives. The first perspective that supports multiculturalism is rooted in a politically neutral stance toward the diverse and conflicting definitions of a good life. In effect, liberal democracy recognizes the rights of individuals to pursue their own goals, which may differ significantly from those of others. This paradigm is best exemplified by the American approach to religious diversity. In the doctrine of separation of church and state, all citizens are free to pursue their own faith-based practices, while government institutions—particularly schools—avoid identifying with or endorsing any specific religion. It is not surprising, therefore, that religious diversity has not entered in any significant way into the multicultural discourse. Although differentiating between cultural and religious beliefs and traditions may create artificial dichotomies, multicultural theorists and advocates have sought to preserve the doctrine. Lacking the burden of religious persecution often observed in other countries, proponents of multiculturalism may be hesitant to disrupt a rather successful balance between faith communities and the state. Moreover, since the most significant social division in the United States emerged historically from racial oppression and racial prejudice, it is clear that multicultural education efforts must first deal with race and racism.

The second liberal democratic perspective is also grounded in universalism, but rather than expressing neutrality, it allows public institutions, including schools, to support minority group goals, provided the three conditions described below are met. Gutman (1994) states:

a) the basic rights of all individuals, including freedom of speech, thought, religion and association are protected, b) no one is manipulated (and of course not coerced) into accepting the cultural values that are represented in public institutions, and c) the public officials and institutions that make cultural choices are democratically accountable, not only in principle but in practice. The paradigm of this perspective is democratic subsidy for and control over, education. (pp. 10–11)

While the separation of church and state defines limits in American curricular content, the Constitution allows the states significant latitude in developing educational approaches and practices. Far from demanding neutrality, it encourages local communities to develop schools in their own "cultural image." Within the limits of educational freedom allowed by law, states must contend with the multiple voices of their constituents demanding recognition and respect.

Defense of multiculturalism encampasses a spectrum from those who see it as necessary because it is consistent with respect for individuals' rights and dignity (Gutman's first condition) to those who follow a social justice impulse to protect and preserve oppressed subcultures in order to reverse patterns of discrimination and marginalization (second condition). Yet the American educational establishment, emerging from the premise that all immigrant groups must be blended into a unified society, is generally wary and unsupportive of cultural agendas. While groups are free to assert their traditions and preserve their native languages, states are reluctant to lend active support to further those goals.

Bilingual education is a clear example of this tension; although supported by federal legislation and various court cases, it is often undermined at the local level by referenda, as is the case of California, or weak implementation of mandates, as happens in most states. Seen more as a political project than an educational one, bilingualism in the schools is often depicted by its detractors as un-American. It so inflames passion in some quarters that the English-Only organization has evolved into a powerful political force with an anti-immigrant agenda that seeks to ban the use of other languages in official documents, schools, and the workplace (Krashen, 1999). Bilingual advocates insist on the right of minority members in a democracy to preserve their language, traditions, and heritage. Occasionally, however, bilingual educators also resort to instrumental arguments to support their curriculum including : (1) instruction in the native language facilitates acquisition of content while the student is learning English, and (2) preservation of fluency in a foreign language has implications for competitiveness in the global marketplace.

Although never overtly stated, bilingual education may also reflect a wish that the teachers of minority language and the immigrant children be members of the same communities. Since nearly ninety percent of teachers in the US are members of the white, English-speaking, monolingual majority (National Center for Education Statistics, 1995), the odds in a given regular classroom are that the teacher will not be familiar with the language and values of the minority group. Since the courts opened the doors to bilingual education in the landmark *Lau vs. Nichols* decision in 1974, bilingual education has developed from a political agenda to an educational prescription. Although stopping short of mandating or even recommending bilingual education, the court in *Lau vs. Nichols* found that Chinese-speaking children taught in regular, English-language classrooms failed to learn because of limited ability in the language of instruction. In effect, the decision stated that equal treatment (i.e., instruction in English) resulted in inequity. The federal government addressed this court decision by instituting "Lau remedies," which laid the foundation for governmental support of bilingual education. Bilingual educators' high hopes have turned to guarded and defensive postures. Without unequivocal indications of superior results, bilingual education is implemented only reluctantly in many locales, where a pall is cast over its future. Neither special education's self-contained classes for the learning disabled nor bilingual classes—both of which separate students on the basis of a single trait in order to give them specialized treatment—has led to improved learning outcomes. We may tentatively conclude that, in public education, segregating students to work on their deficiencies is an approach that becomes tainted by low expectations and weak administrative support.

Bilingual education together with Afro-centric curriculum and even single sex schooling may be conceptualized as attempts to remedy the perceived inequities in American education. Advocates propose that the standard curriculum does not benefit all students in equal measure (Kincheloe & Steinberg, 1993) and, as some have argued, could be detrimental (Apple, 1993, Skrtic, 1995; Sleeter & McLaren, 1995; Tomlinson, 1988). Multicultural education has sought to carve a middle ground by proposing an inclusive curriculum that transforms regular education and avoids the segregation of students by salient group characteristics. The effort is based on appreciation and respect for all the communities represented in school and works to prevent the emergence of hegemonic narratives that can silence other voices (Campbell, 1996).

There are, however, unresolved questions in the multicultural approach. We may ask: Who defines group characteristics—society or group members, schools, families, or individuals? Do collective identities supersede and subsume individual identities? To what extent are members of groups free to identify themselves differently? Is there a role for education in opening options for individual identity outside assigned group affiliation? In this volume we have presented some of the complexities of multicultural work by focusing on how children and adults in schools negotiate personal and cultural constructions of identity and affiliation.

As a school psychologist working with high school students, I often encountered dilemmas of a cross-cultural nature that the literature on multiculturalism has largely failed to address. For example, Fia, a sixteen-year-old young woman explained to me that she was about to return to her native village in order to marry a forty-five-year-old cousin, already married and with children. The wedding was a family arrangement to which she objected but which she was powerless to overturn. We were not successful in persuading Fia's parents to listen and respect her wishes; they voiced fears that in America she would eventually dishonor the family by adopting local customs. She was legally signed out of school and sent to her native land.

Mae, another young immigrant woman I sought to help, was fourteen when her mother remarried and had a second child. The new husband, who followed a religious tradition from their native country, believed that evil spirits that could contaminate the baby possessed the older child. Under advisement of a "healer" and with her mother's consent, Mae was severely beaten in order to expel the evil spirits from her body. The story emerged when the family was invited to school to discuss Mae's increased social isolation. Unable to assure her safety at home and under guidance from a municipal agency, Mae was placed in a residential setting for at-risk youths while waiting for a foster care arrangement.

Although these examples may seem extreme, they serve to point to the uncomfortable tensions lived in schools when deferring to family culture and tradition fails to represent what we, as child advocates, believe is in the best interest of the child. The lines and distinctions between parental rights and the rights of the child have not been drawn beyond indications of physical danger. Thus, Mae could be removed from her home on legal grounds, but Fia was outside of our jurisdiction. Yet both cases deal with cultural constructions that are inconsistent with the protection of individual civil rights and freedom in a democracy. The multicultural discourse, reflecting fear of hegemonic positions, tends to abandon controversy about different definitions of personal freedom and supports, instead, a bland moral and cultural relativism. Uncritical celebration of culturally diverse practices and traditions, however, creates blind spots regarding the protection of individual rights, since different cultures have variable operational definitions of personal freedom.

Anthony Appiah (1994) addresses these provocative questions when he asks how group characteristics become socially defined and how individuals construct their own identities within, and at times in rebellion against, group affiliation. He expresses concern that if we are not permitted to be seen other than as members of an assigned group, we will establish a new form of tyranny of group affiliation. In responding to Taylor's (1994) defense of a French Canadian identity, Appiah proposes that each person's individual identity has two major dimensions: a collective dimension, which is the intersection of all collective identities (gender, ethnicity, religion, etc.), and a personal dimension, which encompasses other social or moral characteristics, such as wit, charm, and intelligence, that are not part of the individual's collective identities. This conception of identity, he argues, is "remarkably unsubtle in [its] understanding of the processes by which identities, both individual and collective, develop" (p. 156). Appiah clarifies that the distinction between these identities is sociological rather than logical. Collective identities, he states, provide scripts and narratives that people use in shaping their lives and in attaching meaning to their experiences. Thus individuals' life stories "should cohere in the way appropriate by the standards made available" within the culture to persons of that identity. But personal identity develops through concepts and practices made available to individuals by religion, society, school, and state and as mediated by family. The construction of identity occurs in dialogic context; dynamically formed, changes occur within parameters made available by our culture and society.

Understanding identity as a product of dialogue is a novel concept in multicultural education, which has so far overlooked the dynamic interplay that takes place as individuals negotiate group membership and personal aspirations. Basic ideas about the multicultural curriculum remain largely monologic and essentialized. By problematizing identity, Appiah (1994) challenges us to articulate a form of multiculturalism that allows latitude for individuals to form identities that may not simply cohere with the ascribed collective ones that are readily available. Supporting the essentialist model of identity, schools abdicate playing a role in shaping children's personal identities in favor of group and community priorities. While those priorities spring from parents' wishes to perpetuate their language, values, or traditions through their children and future generations, it is fair to ask how schools support children who prefer a different path. In cases of arranged marriages of minors or ritual genital mutilation, the silence of educators betrays a multicultural taboo—disapproval of others' cultural practices. Culturally diverse children, who are bicultural by virtue of their acculturation to American society, may experience greater tension and conflict than other children about preserving parental traditions. A school's reflexive support of native cultures may be interpreted as an abandonment of individual rights for the benefit of perpetuating traditional group practices.

While multiculturalism opens doors and demands respect for groups that have been historically oppressed, marginalized, or ignored, it may raise higher barriers for members of those diverse groups to access other domains of personal identity (Bursztyn, 1994). The social demand and expectation that one should organize one's identity around skin color, native language, gender, and sexual orientation are as confining as the ubiquitous small boxes on census forms and applications for admission to bureaucratic institutions. We cannot afford to support a form of multiculturalism that reifies culture and is indifferent to the wishes of individuals, for in doing so we risk weakening the democratic purpose of public education. Instead we should strive to address multicultural needs by drawing on the dialogic and dynamic nature of identity and fluid conception of culture(s).

Schools need not aspire to be culturally neutral or limit themselves to providing a stage for the display of constituent cultures. The role of school in a liberal democracy includes connecting human diversity with the opportunity for personal growth through exposure and experience with different cultural and intellectual perspectives. A multicultural school offers multiple opportunities for expanding children's cultural knowledge when knowledge of cultures is treated not as a static and bound entity, but as possibility or, as Gadamer suggests, as a "fusion of horizons" (Warnke, 1987). Strengthening democracy may well depend not on how we teach about the political system, but on how we transmit liberalism as moral faith and a way of life. As Dewey (1938/1963) believed, the moral meaning of democracy is found in the reconstruction of institutions so that they become instruments of human growth and liberation. Multiculturalism must embrace the moral commitment to democracy in order to avoid the pitfalls of monodimensional sectarianism.

REFERENCES

Appiah, K. A. (1994). Identity, authenticity, survival: Multicultural societies and social reproduction. In A. Gutman (Ed.), *Multiculturalism: Examining the politics of recognition* (pp. 149–163). Princeton, NJ: Princeton University Press.

Apple, M. W. (1993). *Official knowledge: Democratic education in a conservative age.* New York: Routledge.

Banks, J. (1996). *Multicultural education: Transformative knowledge and action, historical and contemporary perspectives.* New York: Teachers College Press.

Bursztyn, A. M. (1994). Gender, culture and psychotherapy. In R. T. Carter & S. D. Johnson (Eds.), *Race and gender: Teachers College winter roundtable on cross-cultural counseling and psychotherapy.* (pp. 40–44). New York: Teachers College, Columbia University.

Campbell, D. E. (1996). *Choosing democracy: A practical guide to multicultural education.* Englewood Cliffs, NJ.: Prentice Hall.

Dewey, J. (1963). *Experience and education.* New York: Collier Books. (Original work published in 1938.)

Gutman, A. (1994). *Multiculturalism: Examining the politics of recognition.* Princeton, NJ: Princeton University Press.

Kincheloe, J. L., & Steinberg, S. R. (1993). A tentative description of post-formal thinking: The critical confrontation with cognitive theory. *Harvard Educational Review, 63,* 296–320.

Krashen, S. (1999). *Condemned without a trial: Bogus arguments against bilingual education.* Westport, CT: Heineman.

National Center for Education Statistics (1995). *The educational progress of Hispanic students.* Washington, DC: U.S. Department of Education, Office of Educational Research and Improvement.

Nieto, S. (1999). *The light in their eyes: Creating multicultural learning communities.* New York: Teachers College Press.

Skrtic, T. M. (1995). *Disability and democracy: Reconstructing (special) education for postmodernity.* New York: Teachers College Press.

Sleeter, C. E., & McLaren, P. L. (1995). *Multicultural education, critical pedagogy, and the politics of difference.* Albany: State University of New York Press.

Taylor, C. (1994). The politics of recognition. In A. Gutman (Ed.), *Multiculturalism: Examining the politics of recognition* (pp. 25–73). Princeton, NJ: Princeton University Press.

Tomlinson, S. (1988). Why Johnny can't read: Critical theory and special educa-
    tion. *European Journal of Special Needs Education, 3* (1), 45–58.
Warnke, G. (1987). *Gadamer: Hermeneutics, tradition and reason*. Stanford: Stanford
    University Press.

Further Readings

Apple, M. (1990). *Ideology and curriculum* (2nd ed.). New York: Routledge.

Artiles, A., & Zamora-Duran, G. (1997). *Reducing the disproportionate representation of culturally diverse students in special and gifted education.* Reston, VA: The Council for Exceptional Children.

Banks, J. A. (1996). Multicultural education and curriculum transformation. *Journal of Negro Education, 64,* 390–399.

Banks, J. A., & Banks, C. M. (1995). *Handbook of research on multicultural education.* New York: Simon & Schuster, Macmillan.

Beckum, L. C., & Zimney, A. (1991). School culture in multicultural settings. In N. B. Wyner (Ed.), *Current perspectives on the culture of schools.* Brookline, MA: Brookline Books.

Bronfenbrenner, U. (1986). Ecology of the family as a context for human development: Research perspectives. *Developmental Psychology, 22,* 723–742.

Bursztyn, A. M. (1999). Psychological vistas on pre-referral interventions for CLD students. In M. Lupi & G. Rivera (Eds.), *A monograph on prereferral intervention strategies for linguistically and culturally diverse students* (pp. 36–58). New York: Hunter College–CUNY and NYS VESID.

Caplan, N., Choy, M. H., & Whitmore, J. K. (1992). Indochinese refugee families and academic achievement. *Scientific American, 266,* 36–42.

Cazden, C. (1994). What is sharing time for? In A. H. Dyson & C. Genishi (Eds.), *The need for story: Cultural diversity in classroom and community* (pp. 72–79). Urbana, IL: National Council of Teachers of English.

Cummins, J. (1986). Psychological assessment of minority students: Out of context, out of control? *Journal of Reading, Writing and Learning Disabilities International, 2,* 1–8.

Dambekalns, L. (1994). Challenging notions of curriculum development: Questions of multicultural context and content in how we encourage students to learn. *Visual Arts Research, 20*(1), 84–90.

Delpit, L. D. (1988). The silenced dialogue: Power and pedagogy in educating other people's children. *Harvard Educational Review, 58,* 280–298.

Dilger, S. (1994). Developing policy and programs for multicultural art education: Curriculum and instruction responsive to cultural diversity. *Art Education, 47*(4), 49–53.

Dyson, A. H. (1994). "I'm gonna express myself": The politics of story in the children's worlds. In A. H. Dyson & C. Genishsi (Eds.), *The need for story: Cultural diversity in classroom and community* (pp. 155–171). Urbana, IL: National Council of Teachers of English.

Egan, K. (1992). *Imagination in teaching and learning.* London: Routledge.

Eisner, E. (1992). The misunderstood role of the arts in human development. *Phi Delta Kappan, 73*(8), 591–595.

Freire, P., & Macedo, D. (1995). A dialogue: Culture, language and race. *Harvard Educational Review, 65,* 377–402.

Gadamer, H. (1967). On the scope and function of hermeneutical reflection. In D. E. Linge (Ed.), *Philosophical hermeneutics* (pp. 18–43). Berkeley: University of California Press.

Goodson, I. G. (1992). *Studying teachers' lives.* New York: Teachers College Press.

Grumet, M. (1995). Somewhere under the rainbow: The postmodern politics of art education. *Educational Theory, 45* (1), 35–42.

Harry, B. (1992). *Cultural diversity, families, and the special education system.* New York: Teachers College Press.

Heath, S. B. (1989). Oral and literate traditions among black Americans living in poverty. *American Psychologist, 44,* 367–373.

Hoffman, D. (1996). Culture and self in multicultural education: Reflections on discourse, text, and practice. *American Educational Research Journal, 33,* 545–569.

Jagla, V. M. (1994). *Teachers' everyday use of imagination and intuition: In pursuit of the elusive image.* Albany: State University of New York Press.

Johnson, H. L., Pflaum, S., Sherman, E., Taylor, P., & Poole, P. (1996). Focus on teenage parents: Using children's literature to strengthen teenage literacy. *Journal of Adolescent and Adult Literacy, 39,* 290–296.

Korn, C. (1997). Translating stories across cultures. *Education and Culture: The Journal of the John Dewey Society, 41* (1), 18–23.

Korn, C. (1997). "I used to be so smart": Children talk about immigration, *Education and Culture: The Journal of the John Dewey Society, 16* (2), 17–24.

Lincoln, Y. S. (1993). I and thou: Method, voice, and roles in research with the silenced. In D. McLaughlin & W. G. Tierney (Eds.), *Naming silenced lives.* New York: Routledge.

Lipman, P. (1997). Restructuring in context: A case study of teacher participation and the dynamics of ideology, race, and power. *American Educational Research Journal, 34,* 3–37.

Lyotard, J. F. (1984). *The postmodern condition: A report on knowledge.* Minneapolis. University of Minnesota Press. (Original work published 1979.)

Miramontes, O. B., Nadeau, A., Commins, N. L. (1996). *Restructuring schools for linguistic diversity: Linking decision making to effective programs.* New York: Teachers College Press.

Moll, L. C. (1998). Turning to the world: Bilingual schooling, literacy, and the cultural mediation of thinking. *National Reading Conference Yearbook, 47,* 59–75.

Nieto, S. (1999). *The light in their eyes: Creating multicultural learning communities.* New York: Teachers College Press.

Ogbu, J. U. (1995). Understanding cultural adversity and learning. In Banks, J. A., & C. A. McGee-Banks (Eds.). *Handbook of research on multicultural education* (pp. 582–595). New York: Simon & Schuster/Macmillan.

O'Loughlin, M. (1995). Daring the imagination: Unlocking the voices of dissent and possibility in teaching. *Theory into Practice, 34,* 107–116.

Pastor, J., McCormick, J., & Fine, M. (1996). Makin' homes: An urban girl thing. In B. J. Ross-Leadbeater & N. Way (Eds.), *Urban girls: Resisting stereotypes, creating identities* (pp. 15–34). New York: New York University Press.

Robinson-Zanartu, C. (1996). Serving Native American children and families: Considering cultural variables. *Language, Speech and Hearing Services in Schools, 27* (4), 373–84.

Rodriguez, N., & Villaverde, L. (2000). *Dismantling whiteness.* New York: Peter Lang.

Rotheram-Borus, M. J. (1993). Biculturalism among adolescents. In M. E. Bernal & G. P. Knight, (Eds.), *Ethnic identity: Formation and transmission among Hispanics and other minorities* (pp. 81–104). Albany: State University of New York Press.

Sass, L. A. (1988). Humanism, hermeneutics, and humanistic psychoanalysis: Differing conceptions of subjectivity. *Psychoanalysis and Contemporary Thought, 12,* 433–504.

Skrtic, T. M. (1995). *Disability and democracy: Reconstructing (special) education for postmodernity.* New York: Teachers College Press.

Sleeter, C. E., & McLaren, P. L. (1995). *Multicultural education, critical pedagogy, and the politics of difference.* Albany: State University of New York Press.

Suarez-Orozco, M. (1991). Immigrant adaptation to schooling: A Hispanic case. In M. A. Gibson & J. U. Ogbu (Eds.), *Minority status and schooling: A comparative study of immigrant and involuntary minorities* (pp. 37–62). New York: Garland Publishing.

Trueba, H. T. (1993) Cultural diversity and conflict: The role of educational anthropology in healing multicultural America. In P. Phelan and A. L. Davidson (Eds.), *Renegotiating cultural diversity in American schools* (pp. 195–215). New York: Teachers College Press.

Valdez, G. (1996). *Con respeto: Bridging the distances between culturally diverse families and schools: An ethnographic portrait.* New York: Teachers College Press.

Waters, M. C. (1996). The intersection of gender, race, and ethnicity in identity development of Caribbean American teens. In B. J. Ross-Leadbeater & Way, N. (Eds.), *Urban girls: Resisting stereotypes, creating identities* (pp. 65–81). New York: New York University Press.

Weil, D. (1998). *Towards a critical multi-cultural literacy: Theory and practice for education for liberation.* New York: Peter Lang.

Index

About the Editors and Contributors

ALBERTO BURSZTYN is Associate Professor of Special Education and School Psychology at Brooklyn College, City University of New York. His writing focuses on how schools and professionals address issues of disability, cultural diversity, and linguistic competence. In tandem with this line of study, he seeks to develop new paradigms of school and professional preparation that address the adjustment and learning experiences of children with varying abilities and from diverse backgrounds. He has worked as a teacher, school psychologist, and administrator in New York City public schools. He is the current Vice President for Education, Training and Scientific Affairs, Division 16, School Psychology, of the American Psychological Association.

BETH DOLL is Associate Professor of School Psychology at the University of Nebraska, Lincoln. In her writing and research she seeks to identify school mental health service models that use naturally occurring supports to enhance the well-being of students. As a secondary interest she conducts program evaluations that demonstrate the impact that school mental health services have on the success of all students. Dr. Doll has piloted a classroom-based curriculum for teaching self-advocacy skills to elementary school students, a recess-based intervention for fostering student friendships, and a whole-class assessment procedure for evaluating social support. She has worked extensively to create recess practices that minimize student isolation on the playground and has developed a curriculum for grades three through five titled *Feeding Friendships*. Her writings on issues of resilience, self-determination, the identification of emotional disabilities, and students' friendships appear in prominent national journals. Dr. Doll generally works within collaborative work groups that include school practitioners, university students and faculty, and other community members.

HOLLYCE C. (SHERRY) GILES is Assistant Professor in the School of Education at Brooklyn College, City University of New York. As Senior Research Fellow with the Institute for Education and Social Policy at New York University, the Public Education Association, and the Industrial Areas Foundation, Dr. Giles has investigated and written about parents' efforts to reform public schools. She worked in the New York City public schools for several years as a psychologist in the On-Site Mental Health Program of the Jewish Board of Family and Children's Services. Dr. Giles' current research interests center on the social, psychological, and political processes in family-school reform initiatives.

CHERYL C. HOLCOMB-MCCOY is Assistant Professor in the Department of Counseling and Personnel Services at the University of Maryland at College Park. She is a nationally certified counselor, and a certified school counselor and teacher in Maryland. Dr. Holcomb-McCoy's research interests are in the areas of multicultural counseling competence and training, counseling African American girls, and counseling in urban school settings. She is co-editor of the *Maryland Association of Counseling and Development Journal*, and serves on the editorial boards of the *Journal of Counseling and Development* and *Professional School Counseling*.

HELEN JOHNSON is a developmental psychologist who focuses on factors that enhance development in children facing adverse circumstances. Dr. Johnson has done extensive work on the early development of children born to substance abusing women and on the family contexts of language and literacy development for children and adolescents. Currently, Dr. Johnson is Chair of the Department of Elementary and Early Childhood Education at Queens College, City University of New York.

JOE KINCHELOE is Professor of Education at Brooklyn College and Professor of Urban Education at the Graduate Center of the City University of New York. He is the author of numerous books and articles involving the social, cultural, and political analysis of education. He brings these contextualizing lenses to the domains of curriculum studies; multicultural education; cultural analysis of childhood; issues of race, class, and gender justice; qualitative research; cognition; and social studies education. His most recent books include *American Standards: Quality Education in a Complex World—The Texas Case; The Encyclopedia of Educational Standards; The Sign of the Burger: McDonald's and the Culture of Power; Getting Beyond the Facts: Teaching Social Studies in the Twenty-First Century*.

CAROL KORN is a psychologist and Associate Professor of Early Childhood Education at Brooklyn College, City University of New York. She has worked as a school psychologist in New York City public schools and in clinical settings. Dr. Korn's research interests include the experience of cultural transitions, development of narrative in childhood, and the role of the arts in early education.

DEBORAH NELSON is a school psychologist for the Howard County, Maryland, public schools, a small suburban school district. She conducts training and provides resource support to collaborative problem-solving teams.

MARGARET R. ROGERS is a school psychologist who has worked as a practitioner and faculty member. Her professional and research interests involve multicultural training in psychology graduate preparation programs and cross-cultural school psychology competencies.

PETER TAUBMAN is Associate Professor of Education and the Head of Secondary Education in the School of Education at Brooklyn College, City University of New York. A former secondary school teacher and department chair, he is a co-author of *Understanding Curriculum* and the author of several essays on identity, autobiography, and teaching.

VERNITA ZUBIA is a bilingual school psychologist who works in diverse school settings to create culturally sensitive educational plans for individual students, classrooms, and schools. Her research and professional experiences focus on creating school cultures that support the academic success of Mexican American students, with a particular interest in the roles that schools can play in supporting smooth transitions between these students' social worlds of home, school, and community. Previously, Ms. Zubia taught middle school for ten years. With a team of colleagues, she created and taught in a dual-immersion bilingual program that addressed the instructional, linguistic and sociocultural needs of Mexican American students.